MILES across THIS TIGHTROPE

Simona M. **Ciarlo**

TATE PUBLISHING, LLC

Published in the United States of America
by Tate Publishing, LLC
127 East Trade Center Terrace
Mustang, OK 73064
(888) 361–9473

Scripture quotations marked "KJV" are taken from the *Holy Bible, King James Version,* Cambridge, 1769.

ISBN: 1-5988636-3-0

Table of Contents

Dedication

This book is dedicated in memory to my cousin,
Crystal Lynn (White) Davidson.

You are loved, missed, and will never be forgotten.
July 3, 1968–October 2, 2003

Acknowledgements

Loving thanks to my family, my brother Tony, my aunt Julie, and "dad" Chuck for allowing me to expand on our lives to show how much God has brought us through.

Mom, never think of yourself as a "bad mom"–you did everything to support us growing up and now with living back home. I love you and thank you for reminding me at times that the world doesn't revolve around *just* me when I have a hard time dealing with change.

Personal thanks to my grandma Mandy who helped edit my grammar in my earlier draft (and finding just how dyslexic I really am). I love you so much and thank you for being a constant shoulder to lean on and a strong, steadfast figure throughout my life.

Special thanks to all the members of Gospel Assembly for your love and support.

Thank you to all those who have taken an interest in Matthew–your kind thoughts and prayers have kept us strong.

Thanks to the hospitals for doing your best and for being patient with such a dramatic family. You are excellent hospitals; trying to do all that is medically possible for everyone in your care.

To Matthew, my brother–you have given us joy beyond our imagination. Your love, smile, and laughter has brightened this family and all those around you. God has used you to open our eyes how fragile life is and I believe He is not finished with you yet.

All our thanksgiving, praise, and glory go to our Lord and Savior, Jesus.

Foreword

God. Family. Heartbreak. Healing.

I admire Simona's mother for being so strong as she tried her best to provide for her children despite the numerous obstacles she encountered.

I admire Simona for being independent and because she has such an ambitious personality. She never once embellished on her own character—the Simona you read about here is the same woman I have known for sixteen years.

As you read this book, you will be able to experience Simona's anguish as she brings to reality how the senseless acts of others can affect an entire family. The story content is touching and real and the reader will surely admire how faith in God has brought this family closer together. When left with nowhere else to turn, Simona turns everything over to Him in order to achieve peace in her heart.

- Julie Palmateer
Registered Nurse

Introduction

It was very hard for me to start this book because it is so personal. I wrote this about my brother, Matthew, and his struggle with fitting in. This tender-hearted boy would try to fool everyone by putting on such a tough exterior, which one night nearly got him killed.

In addition, it will include events in my family's life that happened before and after Matthew's attack. I know I'm not any different from anybody else who has had tragedies in their lives, nor do I sanctify the pain that my family went through. This is just another story of coping and trying to put in perspective the reason *why* it happened.

In writing this, you will notice I will not be telling the story from a sister's point-of-view, it will be written as if someone else were speaking. The reason behind it is to not come across one-sided. Yet, certain memories unveiled and some of me emerged.

I don't want this to be a story of anger. I could easily write this book on how Matthew's attack was brushed off from the court as "just another kid who deserved what he got, by the company he kept." I could protest the injustice of our legal system or make statements that Matthew's disability is all in vain, because those who almost killed him never served the time they deserved.

I didn't want to write a book of revenge, but of forgiveness and faith in God. Odd as it may sound, what happened to Matthew was for the better than the path he was headed. I don't know if this was exactly God's plan for him. Whatever the case, you'll see how such an independent family stepped up to the plate, how even the best Christian can have their faith shaken, and how sometimes those we think we can trust can turn out to be the most selfish individuals that end up hurting a family already broken.

(Some names have been changed to protect their privacy).

Chapter 1

"For every man shall bear his own burden."
(Galatians 6:5)

Prelude

It was after midnight on May 11, 2002, on a little street of North Grand, that a gathering was taking place. A house was full of approximately 80 boys and girls, over 50 of them were under 21-years-old, with beers in their hands. Rustling of bodies swaying to loud music, laughing, and voices trying to have conversations over the tumult already pounding in their ears were there for one reason—to have a good time. They were only doing what they thought was cool. After all, every teen movie shows a keg party going on, with some making out, smoking, maybe even a joint or two, and even a fight. *This* was no movie, but it had all the makings of one.

The front door was open for easy access to come and go, no knocking to be invited in, which is sheer provocation for a mixed crowd and a recipe for someone to get hurt. Suddenly, a voice broke through the noise as though it were a sword piercing every ear, "Get out! The cops are coming!"

Soon everyone was in a panic. Beer bottles were being tripped over by the teenagers trying to escape what could get them arrested and doors were repeatedly swung against the walls from the many hands pushing them out of their way. Bodies were scattering across yards and between houses to avoid being seen; it was 2:30 in the morning and the majority was past curfew. During the commotion, there were a handful of party-goers circling the body of a boy, who lay bleeding in the middle of the street.

When the police arrived, an officer called out and asked, "Does anyone know the name of this young man?"

Joy through suffering . . . it sounds ironic, but is a lesson to be learned.

The Beginning

Matthew David Gioia (pronounced Joy-ya) was born September 26, 1981, a year later than his brother, Tony, who was born on September 3, 1980. They were close as brothers could be, always had each other's back, and what one didn't think of—the other would. Their personalities were night and day; they were so different, even in their appearance. Tony had blonde hair, blonde eyebrows, and bright blue eyes, while Matthew had dark brown hair, thick brown eyebrows, and deep, dark hazel eyes. Just by looking at them no one would think they were full-blooded brothers.

Their parents, Chuck and Cynthia, were married on August 12, 1979. Since it was the second marriage for both, the wedding was simple, just the exchanging of vows, and was performed at the pastor's home after the Sunday morning service.

Cynthia had a daughter, Simona, from a previous marriage. When Simona was six-years-old, her parents divorced, and she moved in with her maternal grandparents for three years until Cynthia came back for her. When Cynthia returned for her daughter, she was working full-time, and still brought Simona to her parents to care for her.

Cynthia met Chuck about a year and a half later, and Simona thought he was cool. He would sit and tell her stories about when he lived in California: how he got burned from a house fire as a boy; lost his pinkie by jumping railcars; and how he jumped a barbwire fence and got stuck, hanging and bleeding until help came. He told her of the celebrities, like Sally Field, who he went to high school with and how he knew Butch Patrick, who played Eddie Munster.

Unfortunately, Chuck had a terrible surprise when he was a late teenager. He found out that all his cousins, he had been growing up and hanging out with, were actually his brothers and sisters. Chuck was the 13th child to be born, and his mother didn't want him. She gave him to her brother, Charles, and his wife Myrtle. It was assumed that Charles and Myrtle couldn't have any children. When Chuck was brought to them, he was then re-named after Charles, to be Charles Anthony Jr.

Growing up with his "aunt and uncle," Chuck had seen how his father would beat Myrtle after being out all night getting drunk. Chuck had to learn how to cook, clean, sew, and practically do everything because his dad was always gone or drunk, and his mom used him to do her work. When Chuck found out who they really were, he rebelled—he felt used, unwanted, and that his life was meaningless. He began to drink, do drugs, and live a fast-paced life to make up for the time he believed he lost. He joined a rock-and-roll band and lived the lifestyle. When the band unfolded years later, he got married and had a daughter, Tina. After Chuck divorced, he moved around, and ended up in Illinois. He carried the anger within him, and for years and years, never contacting the parents who raised him.

Simona always hated when her mom would fight with Chuck and always seemed to make excuses for him, even when he came home drunk sometimes. She seemed to always stick up for him because he was this harmless, happy, I'll-do-anything-for-you, kind of guy.

They lived in a two-story apartment; front room and kitchen were on the first floor and two bedrooms and a bathroom on the second floor.

When Cynthia graduated from beauty school, her plans to be a beautician were put on the back burner; she was offered a better job–working in a Post Office. She was so happy and felt God had answered their prayers. Although she cut hair and did permanents on the side, the Post Office was better income. Now they would be advanced to middle-class status and hopefully someday invest in a house.

In January 1980, when Cynthia announced she was pregnant, Chuck came home drunk with the excuse he was celebrating. This started the beginning of a regular pattern.

On September 3, Cynthia went into labor. During delivery, a nurse leaned on the expectant mother to help her push and rocked up and down on her side, putting so much pressure that it ended up breaking Cynthia's rib. Now, Cynthia was in a different kind of pain. Finally, Cynthia gave birth to an eight pound son, Charles Anthony, named after his dad. Cynthia loved the name Anthony and expressed that every Italian family should have a "Tony," and everyone agreed that's what he would be called. He was born five minutes after midnight, with a full head of thick strawberry-blonde hair.

Cynthia's parents, Sam and Mandy, and sister, Julie, were waiting to see the newest addition to the family since Simona. Simona, being only 12 years old, was not allowed to go in to see her baby brother.

"I'm sorry; they don't allow children in here," the nurse exclaimed.

Cynthia thought it was unfair and felt bad for her daughter, but when Tony came home, Simona made up for it; she held him all the time and watched his every little expression.

Tony was born with jaundice, turning his skin a yellowish color, caused by Cynthia being O positive and Chuck being O negative, which the blood test showed at a ten. Later, two viruses showed up in his blood test which could cause blindness or death and the jaundice went up to an eleven. Cynthia was frightened as the doctors kept doing tests on him. She cried and prayed over her little boy everyday. Twenty days after his birth, another Biliruben test was done and the results came back showing Tony getting better.

The only thing Tony had to take was iron drops. He was anemic, but overall, he was healthy and doing well.

Simona would go to church with her grandma Mandy every weekend; Saturday night, Sunday morning, and Sunday night. One Sunday night, when her grandma dropped her off at home after the evening service, Simona's mom and step-dad had some friends over playing cards. The music was so loud; she couldn't believe Tony could sleep through it. She ran upstairs to check on him and found him fast asleep in his crib. She shut the door and leaned over the bedrail and vowed to her little brother, "I promise to be the *best* sister you could ever have and I will make sure no one *ever* hurts you. I can't believe you can sleep through all this noise. I love you so much!" then she mumbled to herself, "Gosh, if he was crying or something, they would *never* hear him!"

A Change in Dad

Cynthia told Chuck that he should call his parents and let them know they were grandparents. Chuck broke down and called, but it seemed to fuel the bad memories. Chuck never informed Cynthia of his past, so she thought she was helping a family reconnect.

Now that Cynthia was the bread-winner of the family, this was eating at her husband, who now had a hard time holding on to work due to his drinking habit.

Cynthia's hours at the Post Office were from 11 P.M. to 7:30 A.M. and this weighed heavily on the family, mostly Simona. Simona would come home from school, the family would have dinner together, and then her mom would have to go to bed.

Chuck would leave and head off to the bar, leaving Simona to baby-sit, do her homework, and then her chores.

One evening, Chuck came home drunk and saw the dinner dishes still in the sink. He started screaming at Simona, took her arm and pulled her to the kitchen, and ordered her to begin washing them. Unconsciously, Chuck seemed to have fell in the realm of treating Simona like he was treated growing up. His past began to haunt him, the anger fresh in his mind, the rejection still devastating, and the humiliation of being the last to know who he was, unleashed when he saw Simona through his drunken eyes and state of mind.

He walked over to Tony and noticed his diaper was wet. This really made Chuck agitated. He took Tony to go change him, staggering with the baby up the stairs. Simona was crying, fearing Chuck would drop him. She explained that she had just changed him an hour ago, but being the diapers were cloth it wasn't a surprise that he would be wet again. She pleaded with Chuck to let *her* change him. The crying and yelling woke up Cynthia and she came down to see what was going on. Chuck was trying to tell Cynthia, the best he could through his slurring, that Simona did not do her chores or change Tony's diaper.

Simona screamed out that she was doing her homework.

Cynthia took Tony out of Chuck's arms, "If you didn't spend all night at the bar, *you* could have changed him! Simona has schoolwork."

"You're always taking her side!" he screamed.

As Cynthia got ready and left for work, Simona waited until she heard Chuck snoring before she let herself fall asleep.

Chuck knew he had a drinking problem and hated how he felt when he drank. Unfortunately, the temptation was so strong; it physically hurt and wore away all rational thinking. The only way to make his demons stop screeching and ripping his soul was to just give in to the alcohol, even if it destroyed everything else in its wake.

Like anyone living with an alcoholic, Simona now hated when Chuck drank. He wasn't a bad guy all the time; matter of fact, the one thing she tried to keep alive was when he became a "dad" right when she needed one.

It was a Sunday morning and just Simona and Chuck went to church. Cynthia was not feeling well and stayed home with Tony. Just before church started, Simona was approached by her boyfriend, Clinton. Clinton told her that he wanted to break up because he was now seeing her cousin. Simona couldn't say anything to him, because she knew her cousin was a lot prettier than her and she couldn't compete. She did fairly well holding back the tears during the song service, but once the preacher got up, all she could do was stare at Clinton, already missing him, and the tears began to flow. Her heart was broke and Chuck could see the pain in her face. He motioned to Simona as to say, "Let's go home."

In the car, Simona poured out her feelings and Chuck let her know, "All guys are jerks, no matter how good they seem; inside is a pig." He touched her shoulder and said, "He doesn't know what he gave up. You're too good for him."

Simona felt his sincerity and that was the closest she ever felt to having a real father-and-daughter moment. That specifically always stuck out in her mind when his drinking began taking a turn for the worse. He wasn't funny anymore, he was transforming into a mean drunk, and his eyes began to look at her with hate, but she didn't fear him. She just knew when he fell asleep that he would be okay again when he woke up.

Simona's theory changed one February night and the pedestal she had put him on came crashing to the ground.

Cynthia was angry Chuck wasn't home yet before she left for work, but being that her daughter was almost thirteen, kissed Simona good-bye and said, "Don't be afraid, just shut your eyes and go to sleep."

Simona lay on her bed looking at her baby brother in his crib by the light of the moon gleaming through her large window. She tried closing her eyes, but with every sound they would flash open again. Suddenly, a familiar sound started her heart pounding; it was the slam of the front door and the mumbling of her drunken step dad. His voice would alternate from a low rumble to a loud clear cuss word. Something was different, he was banging things around. Simona began to trace her steps: the dishes were done, the front room was picked up, and Tony was dry and fast asleep.

Soon, she heard the thud of his foot against the stairs and she thought, "Shoot, why couldn't he fall asleep on the couch."

She sat up and peered through the crack of the bedroom door. She could see Chuck sway back and forth. Crashing against the stairway railing on the left, and then against the wall on the right, with the last few steps he fumbled up. She held her breath as she heard him walking down the hall. She lay back down, pretending she was asleep, but kept her eyes slit from curiosity. Soon her door opened and Chuck came in her room.

She felt his eyes looking at her what felt like an eternity. Fear crawled up and down her skin as she saw him move closer to her bedside. She closed her eyes dreading the closer he got that he could see her eyes looking at him. Millions of thoughts were crossing her mind as she tried to control her breathing from her heart pounding so hard in her chest.

He knelt beside her and sarcastically said, "Wake up—I know you're not sleeping."

She made sound effects as though he had woken her up and asked in a sleepy tone, "What's going on?"

"You think you're so slick, well let me tell you something, you're nothing but a punk." Then he began rambling, but all she could make out was, " . . . supposed to be seen and not heard."

Simona, still feeling uneasy, was trying to think ahead of Chuck's actions, by planning what to do, if she needed to escape and call for help.

Chuck continued, "When I was your age, I was cleaning, sewing, washing clothes, cooking . . . you are useless! You don't know how to do anything; you're a spoiled brat!"

Simona pleaded, "Please, I have to get up early to go to school . . . I'm tired."

"You're tired? Awww . . . Well, I'm not finished! If I want to, I'll sit here all night."

Simona's stomach became knotted by the feeling of being so uncomfortable; the urgency she felt for him to just *go away* was making it hard for her to control herself to stay still.

"What's the matter with you? Do you think I'm going to touch you . . . molest you? Well, if I wanted to I would," as he stroked his hand down her arm, "but I'm not . . . so relax!" and he began to sadistically laugh.

Simona didn't trust him, and felt he was giving off mixed signals. She looked at her brother's crib. She hoped Tony wouldn't wake up as she feared what Chuck might do.

"See, your mom is a woman, a woman who thinks she is perfect. I'm not perfect and she rubs my nose in it every chance she gets. She wants me to work . . . I work . . . I'm the man of the house. I am the king of this castle!"

Simona thought, "What nerve." Her mom was supporting this family and he walked around as though he was a gift from God.

After forty-five minutes of constant incoherent babbling, Chuck's words were getting thicker and his tongue and lips pasty as the saliva dried in and around his mouth. Simona couldn't take it anymore, she was tired, not only because it was the middle of the night, but being so tense and on-guard for such a long period, her body was starting to spasm and her mind was exhausted. She began moving and sighing loudly.

"What?" he blurted as if she had shook him awake, "What is wrong with you?"

"I'm tired," she said with a cry in her voice.

"Well, I guess I should let you sleep, right? After all, you're the princess, and the princess needs her sleep," Chuck said sarcastically.

He kept mumbling as he was getting up off the floor and headed toward the door. As he headed back downstairs, Simona was confident he was drained and would pass out.

The next morning, she placed a 6" switchblade on the window sill and concealed it with the blinds. She never slept with the blinds open again just in case he ever came in there for a repeat performance. She swore she would never endure that again and began building a wall between them.

Chuck's drunken episodes would result in calling Simona names and putting her down until she felt unworthy of anyone's love at all.

He shamed her and told her, "No one wants you! You will never get married, because no one can stand you. You're friends don't like you; they just put up with you. You're grandparents don't like you; they have to pretend because you're family."

She tried not to believe him, her eyes welled with tears, and Chuck could see he had hit a soft spot and dug a little deeper, "Awww, what's wrong . . . truth hurt?"

She became angry and something inside her lashed out, "I HATE YOU!"

Now, Chuck was mad; he was not going to put up with that, and started to chase her. As she tried to run up the stairs, he hit her–hard. It shook her whole body and the force threw her up against the wall. The wall had an edge to it for some reason, and her shoulder crashed into it; leaving a whelp there for over a week.

Chuck screamed at her, "See what you made me do!?"

Chuck had very little feeling in his hands from being burned as a child and could take a lot of pain; he felt the sting in his hand after he hit Simona. He knew if he felt it, she *really* did, and a fear crossed his mind that he could have really done some damage.

In her room, Simona wrote letters to all her friends and grandparents apologizing for being such a bad person and asked forgiveness. She thought maybe Chuck saw something she didn't and maybe her friends were actually being nice because they took pity on her.

After she passed out the letters, her friend Cher asked her, "What is this? You didn't do anything wrong."

"I'm not a very good friend and I'm just saying that you don't have to be my friend if you don't want to–I'll understand."

"What is going on? Why do you feel this way?"

"Well, Chuck . . ."

"Don't listen to him; he's a jerk. Don't let him upset you like this; you're a great friend."

Still, Simona thought Cher was only trying to be nice and began to withdraw in herself. However, deep down, she knew she was loved, but she was unable to control the dissociation she felt.

Cynthia had announced she was pregnant again, so Simona never told her what took place while her mother was working midnights. Simona didn't want to risk upsetting her mom and her new sibling.

Cynthia was torn about her feelings of having another child come into the world, but one thing was for sure, she was going to have it. She was just afraid for her children and the life they would have, because when Chuck was on his binges he became more violent. The fights between the couple had escalated and the family structure began to shift. He had already struck her several times; it didn't even matter that she was pregnant. He hit her while she was holding Tony, and even busted her eardrum once because she was defending Simona.

The uncertainty and turmoil was not what Cynthia wanted for her children. She thought if she decided to leave him, "How would I raise and support three children by myself?"

For a woman of thirty-one years old this was a difficult decision. She loved Chuck and didn't want to give up on him, because when he didn't drink he was the best guy in the world. He cleaned, cooked, and was very funny, loving and kind; but when he drank, he turned into someone else. Chuck's drinking was like Russian roulette. He would be free from the craving and be normal, but once it hit him, it hit him hard.

Cynthia finally sat Chuck down and told him, "I will leave if you don't stop drinking, we now have another child to think about and I can *not* deal with you acting like one, too."

Chuck cried because he knew she could make it on her own without him, and apologized. He worked at his sobriety keeping in mind all his blessings.

On March 1, 1981, Tony was having constant diarrhea, causing severe dehydration and a diaper rash. He was always crying and tugging at his ears, so Cynthia took him to the hospital and he was admitted. He had an I.V. inserted in his tiny foot to replenish his fluids and was diagnosed with an ear infection. For four months, this strong boy endured an abscess on his eardrum which was finally lanced and solid gold tubes put in both of his ears on July 6. In between those months, on April 12th—Simona's birthday—Tony began to crawl for the first time. She thought that was the best present ever!

Chuck and Cynthia bought a cage and a couple of parakeets. Chipper was the green male and Peaches was the white female. Tony loved those birds; he would climb the gold recliner and pull himself up to look at them. He tried talking to them, laughing at them when they would fly around the cage squawking, but most the time he would just sit and listen to them. He sat with them more than playing with his toys.

One evening, they sat around mulling over names for the expectant baby; it was suggested to keep the same initials as Chuck and Tony's, C.A.G.

Cynthia figured that she was having a boy because of the same symptoms she had with Tony. She liked the names Christopher Andrew for a boy and Christine Angela for a girl.

This did not set well with Simona, "No, I like the name Matthew David."

Even though Chuck was doing his best, he was three months without a drink, Simona still felt she had a right to have a say and insisted on the name she had chosen.

She was so adamant about it and her mom felt it; Chuck and Cynthia looked at each other and agreed, "Well, they are both good names . . . good Bible names, but it might be a girl."

"Well, Angela is fine, but not Christine," Simona demanded. She was trying to avoid the association of the "family" initials.

Toward the due date, Cynthia was having contractions. She would go to the hospital and they would send her home because of false labor. This happened more than once; so when she was actually in labor, she put it off as long as she could stand it. She lay on the couch doing her breathing exercises and watching some television. When the contractions started to become three minutes apart and the pain too much for her to handle, she finally decided to succumb and go to the hospital at 8:20 P.M., and at 9:35 P.M. she gave birth to a baby boy.

While still on the table, Cynthia considered having the doctors to sear her fallopian tubes; she didn't want to take anymore chances of getting pregnant again, but she changed her mind.

The baby was named Matthew David and it was ironic how he looked like Simona when she was born thirteen years earlier. This time, she was able to go in to see her new baby brother. Matthew was 7 pounds 15 ounces and also born a jaundiced baby, but that was to be expected. Thankfully, the Biliruben test marked that the jaundice was not at a dangerous level. No sooner than the family enjoyed the new limb on the family tree, the sleeping giant awoke and the old fears washed upon the surface when Daddy came home drunk.

Christmas that same year, Cynthia, Simona, Tony, and newborn Matthew were able to meet Chuck's parents, Charles and Myrtle. They came to Illinois to see their grandsons.

By the time the visitors were set to leave to go back home to California, Cynthia and Simona could relate to why Chuck kept his distance for so long. They were nice people, but Myrtle was one who was never satisfied about anything. They hugged and kissed them goodbye, while simultaneously thankful to be rid of them.

Chapter 2

"Wine is a mocker, strong drink is raging . . ."
(Proverbs 20:1)

Who's the Adult?

When Chuck would come home drunk, Simona would usually hold in the anxiety and wait until the alcohol would overpower him into a deep sleep. Now, Simona felt responsible for her brothers and began to intercede when Chuck was awake. Inside Simona knew Chuck would never change and that her mom couldn't always be there. She couldn't handle the insecurity of trying to protect them and keep things under control; it was tearing her up inside, but she tried to be strong. She knew the boys' dad loved them and was good to them when he didn't drink, but she was on edge every time he would play with them. She was beside herself to make sure that he wouldn't hurt the two innocent babies. She was now scared of him and uneasy. Her eyes would stay focused on Chuck as he picked up the boys, throw them into the air, and swing them around. She was so afraid that he would drop them, regardless if he was intoxicated or not. When he was drinking, Simona would speak up.

Once Simona mentioned, "Be careful," as anxiety began to turn in her stomach.

Chuck slowly turned his head and glared at her, "Do you *think* I would *hurt* my son?"

"No . . . not at all, but . . . it . . . it's just that . . . you been drinking and . . ."

"And . . . What? That I'll drop him?" and he began to laugh hideously and pretend he was going to drop Tony, "Whoa . . . oops . . . ahhh" then break out in laughter again.

He would pin Tony down and tickle him. Even though Tony would laugh, in between chuckles, his voice would crack in a cry. Tony may have been a little over a year-old, but he was still a baby and Chuck, being numb from drinking, couldn't feel how hard he was digging into the child's ribs. The playing would get out of hand and become abuse. Simona would hold her breath, her heart would skip a beat, and her stomach would churn as if it were doing laundry. She felt helpless and frightened, fearing Chuck would take it out on the boys if she said anything to him.

So, she ran to her mom. "He plays too rough with them."

When Cynthia confronted him, Chuck defended himself by saying, "I don't want my boys to grow up to be wimps. I'm teaching them to be tough," then looked at Tony and asked, "Right, my little man?"

"They're still babies, Chuck!" Cynthia responded.

Chuck sulked like a little boy who couldn't have his way. When Tony walked over to him, Chuck pushed him away, "NO, I can't play with you . . . Go away!"

"Oh, grow up!" as Cynthia stormed back up the stairs to finish getting ready for work.

When things get so bad, something always comes to a head; sure enough it had reached its peak. Simona came home from school, put her key in to unlock the door, and noticed the doorknob was loose. She had a strange feeling as she slowly opened the door to go inside. As she looked around, she didn't notice at first that the television was missing. She crept upstairs and noticed the bedrooms were ransacked; the drawers were open and clothes thrown everywhere. She called her grandma Mandy and told her the apartment had been broken into.

Mandy told her granddaughter that her mom and brothers just left her house and were on their way home, "She knows about the break-in, honey, don't worry . . . everything is alright."

When Cynthia arrived Simona was curious and trying to ask her what happened.

"It's nothing, don't worry about it."

"I do worry, Mom. Are you saying someone didn't break in?"

"I think it was Chuck, making it look like a break-in. He probably pawned stuff for money to drink."

Simona didn't say any more about it; she knew what kind of night it was going to be. Knowing her mom was off work for the weekend, she asked if she could spend the night with a friend. She prayed that God would protect her mom and brothers from Chuck while she was gone.

That night, sure enough, Chuck came home drunk. Cynthia didn't want him there and demanded for him to get out. It started out as yelling and cussing at each other, then a shoving match, but Chuck was so wasted that he couldn't even keep his balance. Cynthia began to shame him for stealing their things, just to sell them, and squander it away on booze. She picked up Matthew, who was crying from all the shouting.

"You are supposed to be the head of the household, but you go out and drink every night! You have children to think about, and yet you go out and indulge yourself while I'm at work supporting this family! When do I get to go out? When do I get a break?"

As Chuck was basking in his inebriated state and listening to his wife point out his faults that were tearing them apart, his demons unleashed to stop the truth from hurting him. He lunged at his angry spouse. He didn't see Cynthia as a human, but as his conscience that was standing in the way of his weakness. He didn't even notice she was holding their child in her arms. He swung and missed her; as he went to swing back, Cynthia took her free arm and pushed him away from her and Matthew.

The shove caused Chuck to fall backward and hit his head on the counter top in the kitchen. The backside of his ear had split open as it slammed against the edge; with his intoxicated state and amount of alcohol he consumed, he fell silent as the blood began to pour from his head onto the kitchen floor.

Cynthia looked at him, staring, wondering if he was dead. She grabbed her keys and her boys to escape and retreat to her mother's. Just before she walked out the door, she kicked her motionless husband to see if he would move. He lay lifeless, yet she still left.

Her imagination went wild as she and the boys showed up at her parent's house, she confessed, "He's dead! I think I killed him!"

"What?" Mandy exclaimed.

As Cynthia was pacing back and forth, Mandy told her daughter to calm down and explain what happened.

After Cynthia was telling her how Chuck lie bleeding in the kitchen, Mandy was stunned, "Cynthia, you have to go back . . . check on him, call an ambulance."

"I know, Mom, but I just had to get out of that apartment."

Cynthia went back home to face the possibility of what she might have done.

As she walked in, all she saw was a pool of blood on the floor, but no Chuck.

Many thoughts crossed her mind. Did someone hear the fight and call an ambulance? Did he get up and walk out? It turned out that Chuck wasn't that injured. The cut on Chuck had coagulated; it wasn't that deep, but the alcohol made his blood thin to pour as much as it did.

She walked up the stairs and found him in bed asleep. She felt relieved.

The next morning, remorse set in. Chuck agreed that he needed aid, "I'm sorry for the pain I've caused, I want to be the best husband and dad I can be. I know I need help; I promise, Cynt, that I will start going to AA meetings. I need your support. I need us all to go as a family."

Simona refused to attend, but during those meetings Cynthia found out Chuck's past. When she found out that she named Tony–Charles Anthony III; she was upset. If Chuck was drinking to escape a past and upset that he was renamed, then why name a child after the name of someone you were running from? She understood that *Gioia* was his real mother's maiden name, but . . .

"He didn't have to be a third!" Cynthia told Chuck.

New Start

Tony's hair turned to honey-blonde and was so thick and shiny that Cynthia never wanted to cut it. She let it get so long that people would tell her, "What a beautiful little girl."

This made Simona upset and she would beg her mom to cut it. Tony finally received his first haircut–3 inches off the back, still leaving hair over the neck.

Tony loved playing and teaching his little brother new things that the parakeets took second place. When he was 17 months, Tony would take Matthew's hands and play pat-a-cake and they would giggle and laugh. Tony always kissed him on the forehead, but sometimes get a bit jealous and bite him. They were boys and Matthew was pretty tough being only a year younger; he loved to wrestle with Tony and always looking around for him to be near. Their security was with each other. Tony also helped when it came to his brother; he would carry Matthew's diaper bag whenever they would go somewhere.

Just like Tony, Matthew also had an abscessed eardrum that needed to be lanced. Matthew didn't scream, but cried like his feelings were hurt as though those he trusted turned against him. He had gold tubes put in his ears, too. When both boys outgrew the solid gold tubes, Cynthia had them cleaned and added to a gold chain she wore around her neck.

Simona had to share the bedroom with her brothers. Yet, the two boys were getting too big to be sleeping together in the crib and there was no room to put another bed. The family knew it was time to move.

So, in April, 1982, Cynthia found a house four blocks away from her parents. The house had a basement, two bedrooms and a bathroom downstairs, and the upstairs was one whole room with a bathroom, which Simona was able to call her own. It was across the street from *Meadowview* shopping center, which included a movie theater and a restaurant called the *Little Corporal* where Barry Manilow had begun his singing career and just revisited a year earlier.

By moving, the family was hoping to have happier times. On Simona's birthday this year, Matthew cut his first tooth; Chuck was controlling his demons and was actually holding down a job. Cynthia wanted to show how pleased she was by embracing the family as a whole. So, she approached her daughter and appealed to her about having Chuck adopt her and carry his last name. Simona did not want to do it.

"We are trying to be a family now. You have two brothers who are going to wonder why your name is different from theirs. Can you at least try to really consider this? It would make me happy."

Simona contemplated it; she loved her mom and brothers, but was ashamed of Chuck. She decided to call her dad and tell him that she was being pressured to change her last name.

During the conversation, she was confused when she heard her dad say, "When I was given the name, *Koenig,* and passed it to you, I felt you were *really* my daughter."

"What do you mean . . . *given?*"

"I was adopted by *my* step-dad."

Simona felt deceived; she was 14 years old and this is the first she had ever heard of this.

When she tried to ask her dad what his real dad's last name was, he was vague and told her that he couldn't remember. Now, she felt the name she had was meaningless, it wasn't a history, it wasn't ancestry, and she felt she might as well change it; although she did reluctantly. She changed her last name to *Gioia,* only for her brothers, and no other reason. After all, it wasn't even Chuck's *real* last name, either.

As time passed, Simona practically lived in her room and tried to break away from her family downstairs. Now, she wanted to go away for two weeks to a church meeting in Belle Fourche, South Dakota for the youth. Chuck had started drinking again, but not where it got out of control, and Cynthia was worried he would; thus telling her that she couldn't go.

After much begging and pleading on Simona's part, and intense interceding from her grandma Mandy, her parents caved in.

Mandy put her foot down and stated, "She IS going!! And I'm paying her way."

Simona was pleased just to get away and not worry about anything back home.

Mishaps

On July 22, 1982 an incident happened with Tony; he was always sleeping or lying around. He didn't want to play or eat, and he had a fever. Cynthia thought that Tony must have ingested downers. He must have found Chuck's pills, and ate them like they were candy. Cynthia began to put everything up high, and put locks on all the lower cabinets. She couldn't believe that she never thought of doing that before and told her husband, "He's quick, Chuck! Don't turn your back for a minute."

Cynthia took her drowsy little boy into the emergency room and he crawled underneath the chair and went to sleep; when the nurse saw that, needless to say, Tony was admitted right away. The hospital began running every kind of test to figure out what was wrong, but had no answers. All they would say is that it was an ear infection. Tony's fever had been holding on strong for a week.

The family came into Tony's room to sit with him; it was the saddest sight to see a little child lay helpless in a big hospital bed. Cynthia, quietly choking back tears, snuggled up beside her son. Simona, looking at her baby brother, felt she had let him down. She walked over to the window, so no one could see the tears streaming down her face.

The next day, the doctors couldn't tell from the tests the night before, just what the cause was, and as the last resort performed a spinal tap on Tony. They told Cynthia that she had to make sure he didn't move, or be moved even some time after the test, or else there could be complications. Cynthia couldn't help it; she wanted to comfort her sick little boy and put her arm around him, ever so slowly, and pulled him to her. Not realizing she had done anything harmful, it caused Tony to have severe migraine headaches as he was growing up.

The results of the test read "*origin unknown.*"

On November 28, 1982, Tony said, "Matthew" for the first time, and Matthew smiled. Cynthia got tears in her eyes; her little boys were growing up and communicating with each other.

On December 16, there was an incident, this time with Matthew; he ended up at the hospital with a cracked collarbone. Chuck told Cynthia that he fell out of his crib. No one was home to witness what happened, but Cynthia had suspected Chuck was playing too rough with him. Matthew had to wear a shoulder harness until the bone healed.

Like any mother, Cynthia felt her boys were beautiful and wanted them to get into advertisement. She signed a contract with a Talent Agency and drove all three of her children to get their picture taken in Chicago on State Street.

The boys loved getting their picture taken and were very well behaved. Simona was excited too, she always dreamed of being an actress. Once Simona saw the finished pictures, she felt they were the worst she'd ever seen. Cynthia thought they were cute, but her daughter argued about the lighting and shadows.

"A department store could take better pictures than these; these are awful and far from professional!" Shaking her head, Simona groaned, "There's no way anyone would agree to put any of us in anything after seeing these pictures."

Cynthia didn't agree about the pictures, she still loved them, but she got to thinking that the whole thing probably was a hoax, and just treasured the pictures of her children.

- - - - - - - - - - -

One day, Chuck and Cynthia went to the fruit market and left the boys in the car. From the market, it was easy to keep an eye on them, but they were unaware that Tony tried to get out. He had pulled the lever, but was unable to push the door open with his little arms.

When the couple came back in the vehicle, Chuck got behind the wheel and drove out of the parking lot. As he turned to get on to Rt. 50, Tony's side of the door swung open and Tony went rolling out of the car on to the busy highway.

Cynthia didn't even have time to think about what she was doing, all she knew was her son flew out of the car, and she screamed at Chuck, "Stop!"

Before Chuck had a chance to brake, Cynthia had opened the door to go after Tony. She landed and bounced on the pavement, but got up and ran to her child. She grabbed him and scooped him in her arms, checking him out to make sure he had no broken bones, cuts, or bruises. Tony was fine, but it really shook up his parents, and from then on, Cynthia had to fight the boys to try and keep a seatbelt on them every time they went for a drive.

- - - - - - - - - - -

When Matthew was able to walk, caring for two kids running around was even more strenuous. When Simona was at school and Cynthia sleeping after working all night, Chuck was in charge.

Suddenly he heard the screen door slam and noticed the boys were gone; just that fast. He got up, ran to the door, and saw Tony go one way and Matthew in the other. Which one does he go after first? His head was swimming as his legs took him after Matthew, yet keeping his eyes on where Tony was going. His heart jumped as he saw Matthew head into the street. All of a sudden, he heard tires squealing and saw that a man had stopped his car and parked it sideways to make sure that no one could get around him and hit the young boy. Cars were honking and people sticking their heads out the window to see the desperate dad gather his boys from the four lane road. Chuck's body was buzzing from nerves as he brought the kids back inside.

"That's it, we have to move. This street here is too dangerous," he told his wife.

Cynthia agreed. Living right in the middle of town on a busy highway was no place to raise two rambunctious little boys.

A New House

March 1983, the family was moving again. Oh, how Simona hated to leave her big bedroom. She went into her bathroom, leaned outside the window, and wrote her name on the siding. She was going to miss the walking distance to the movie house and being so close to her grandparents.

The family moved into a big house the next town over on Evergreen. It had a wrap-around porch, a basement, front room, family room, dining room, kitchen, two bathrooms, and three bedrooms.

The boys' bedroom was the biggest. Their room looked like a forest; it was painted green and around the three large windows were sturdy, cardboard, cut-outs of trees and jungle animals. Simona had the smallest room this time; it wasn't even square, it was such an odd shape that barely fit her bed and two dressers.

Simona's friend, Cher, and the preacher's grandson, Colton, broke up. Cher then began to go out with a "bad boy"; he wasn't really *bad*, but he wasn't real into church either. Since Cher's parents didn't like him, they would meet over at Simona's house.

Simona was secretly in love with Colton. He was tall, thin, with strawberry-blonde hair, and beautiful blue eyes, and she was mush when she was around him. She thought she had a chance with him, now that her friend was going out with another guy. Oh, how she wanted to hold his hand. She loved his smile, and the fact that he was considerate and tender-hearted is what she loved the most. She thought about approaching him, (although she was told that the boys are supposed to ask girls out), she was going to try.

Well, before she had the chance she was told, "Colton's mother told him that he can date any girl in the church, but you; it's because you've *seen* too much."

Now, it was never confirmed if his mother told him that or not, but hearing it, if just a rumor, Simona believed it to be true. Simona became very upset at the church, her mom, and her grandma. Because the church was so small, everyone knew each other's business. Thoughts crossed Simona's mind that if only her grandma didn't ask the preacher's daughter-in-law to pray for her mom and explain the bad things taken place with Chuck's drunken, violent behavior. If only her mom would have just stayed in church and didn't marry this jerk, who kept causing a black eye on the family, then maybe, Colton would have been the one for her. Simona felt she didn't deserve this injustice; but then, she felt she didn't deserve the preacher's grandson, either.

Julie, Simona's aunt, planned a surprise birthday party for her. She asked Cher and Cher's boyfriend to take Simona somewhere while she set up the party at her sister Cynthia's house. Everyone hid their cars around the corner and Julie directed them to hide in the dining room, which was isolated from the main part of the house.

Simona was planning her night, after she escaped the two lovebirds; just to relax and watch some TV. When the three teenagers arrived, Simona saw her aunt's car at her house. Something wasn't right as she felt her face become hot; she was thinking something had happened to her grandparents. It was a fear that was as cold as ice and she was almost in a state of panic. As Simona opened the door, Julie grabbed her niece's arm and pulled her through the kitchen toward the dark dining room. Simona's eyes raced around at her mom and Chuck's faces; their expressions were solemn.

She wanted to cry and was about to when Julie whispered, "Come here, I have to tell you something."

She didn't want to hear the bad news and she was stricken in trepidation.

All of a sudden, Julie turned on the lights and everyone screamed, "SURPRISE!"

Simona couldn't catch up to what just happened and when she realized that it was a birthday party, there was more of a sense of relief than being happy. People asked her if she was surprised and of course she said "yes," because it was more out of shock than anything else. In the back of her mind, she still wished she could have just come home to relax and watch TV, instead of the party. She didn't like the feeling of being surprised although she enjoyed her friends being there; she began to realize just what a loner she actually was starting to become.

The family added a dog, Sparky, a female mutt. She had the roam of the neighborhood and ended up pregnant. When she gave birth they kept a boy puppy and gave the rest away. The new pup was named Reginald Van Snooper, "Reggie" for short.

Tony and Matthew loved playing with the dogs and no matter how rough the boys got, pulling their hair, trying to ride on their back, or even squeezing them with love, the dogs never bit or hurt them. The dogs were dedicated, loyal animals and Sparky knew she was loved.

One day, Simona saw Sparky lying on the porch, but she never bothered the sleeping canine. When Simona checked on her dog an hour later, Sparky hadn't moved. Although, she thought Sparky was just sleeping, she never opened the door. Later on, Chuck and his friend showed up as Simona watched the dog never acknowledge their presence. The two men walked up the porch, stepped over Sparky, and came into the house. Simona stared at them and knew the outcome before the words were even spoken; Sparky was dead. Chuck went back outside to prepare Sparky for burial after noticing the indentation on her side. He figured she had been struck by a vehicle and walked home to die; the bleeding was all internal. Chuck dug a deep hole in the unpaved driveway, placed Sparky in a garbage bag, and refilled the hole. He looked at Simona and knew the pain of losing a pet, so he said a few kind words over the grave for her to have closure. None the less, Simona felt guilty, thinking she could've prevented her dog's death with thoughts like . . ."Maybe I could have called for help; maybe she came home waiting for me to pet her so she didn't have to die alone. What if she was still alive the first time I had seen her on the porch?"

Sparky wasn't the first pet to die, (Simona's little dog, Taffy, was hit by a car when she was five), but this was the first time she felt she could have done something.

As for the parakeets, there were more eggs, plus a few babies had already hatched the week before. The ones that hatched didn't even have feathers yet. Chuck had planned to sell the baby birds once they were ready to leave their parents.

Oh, but the boys had a different idea. They pulled a chair beneath the cage, climbed on it, and saw some colorful eggs nested in the corner and picked them up to take a closer look. The adult parakeets flapped around and squawked loudly; trying to protect their young, but that didn't frighten the boys. Since the week-old newborn babies couldn't fly to escape, they were as helpless as the eggs.

When Chuck came into the kitchen, he saw the parakeet eggs broken on the floor and baby birds lying dead from the fall. Cynthia was sick over it and felt so bad for the baby birds. It was time to get rid of the parakeets. They decided to purchase an aquarium; at least fish would be quiet, less messy, and the boys wouldn't be able to catch them.

- - - - - - - - - - -

Matthew was the active one—always running, climbing, and expressing no fear. On November 8, 1983, curiosity got the best of him. He looked up and something caught his eye up high on the bookcase, so he began to scale it. As Matthew was trying to get his foot upon the next shelf, the piece of furniture began to rock;

shaking the items and vibrating them toward the edge. Hearing the ruckus, Cynthia headed toward the room. Suddenly, Chuck's pipe rack fell and hit Matthew in the face, splitting his mouth wide open. Cynthia had just missed pulling him out of the way; she grabbed him in her arms, saw the all the blood, and knew she had to rush him to the hospital. Matthew ended up getting three stitches; one inside and two outside of his mouth. It seemed like disaster was just waiting for him.

- - - - - - - - - - - -

In the meantime, there was a problem with the furnace. An inspector came out and told Chuck and Cynthia that it was a safety hazard and could blow. Since they were only renting the house, they were not spending the money to get a new one, and the owner refused to invest in one, too. Well, the couple was not going to stay in a house that was unsafe for them and their kids and started looking for another place to live. They moved out in the beginning of 1984.

Chapter 3

"The name of the Lord is a strong tower: the righteous runneth into it, and is safe."
(Proverbs 18:10)

Alarming Moments

The couple found a house a couple of blocks away on another street called Myrtle. This was the third house in three years, but Cynthia was pleased to see that the house included a fenced-in backyard. Now she could feel safe for her boys to play and not worry about Reggie running loose in the neighborhood.

The house was equipped with a basement, the first level had a little room off to the kitchen (which Cynthia made into a beauty shop area), and a front room with a fireplace, a dining room, and the front and back porch were both screened in. The upstairs consisted of three bedrooms and a bathroom.

In May, the boys were giving their mom a nervous breakdown. The fence wasn't a place of security, but of a challenge to the 2- and 3-year-old youngsters. They climbed over the fence and walked 2 1/2 blocks away. Cynthia was home alone when she discovered they were no longer in the backyard. She thought they may have come in, and began to call out for them, but in her heart she knew they were gone. She ran down the alleys screaming their names and praying.

Suddenly, she spotted them and darted so fast down the block to make sure they didn't get out of her view.

When she caught up to them she spanked their butts, reprimanded them, and then she hugged her babies close to her. She kept kissing them and repeating, "I love you."

Knowing they were unscathed gave her instant peace.

The next morning, Cynthia went to check on the boys. She couldn't believe they would still be sleeping, so she went upstairs and noticed their beds were empty.

All she could think was, "Now where are they hiding?"

She heard soft thudding and then saw a boy go past the window. They were on the roof! They had climbed onto the toilet and out the bathroom window. Cynthia crawled out the glass opening; as soon as the boys saw her they started running. She ordered them to stop and explained that they could fall. As soon as she grabbed them and walked them toward the window, she gave them each a swat on the butt and helped them back through the window. She couldn't believe they would think to do such a thing.

Later on that night, she took the boys to her parents. When she arrived, the only one there was her dad sitting on the front porch.

"Where is everyone?" Cynthia asked.

"Oh, your mom and Julie went for a walk to the park. Let the boys go down there and meet up with them." Sam said.

The park was on a hill that everyone in town came to go sledding when it snowed. It had a few swings, a slide, and a few other little rides, and about one block down the hill was the Kankakee River.

Cynthia sat and talked to her dad for about twenty minutes, and then decided to meet everyone at the park. When she stood at the top of the hill she didn't see anyone, and then her eyes caught Tony and Matthew way down by the river. She ran down the steep hill feeling she was going to fall flat on her face, but kept her eyes on her boys. Now Cynthia couldn't believe *she* allowed them do such a thing. When she came back to the house, Julie and Mandy were back.

"I'm sorry Cynt; I don't know what I was thinking." Sam felt so bad.

"It's my stupidity, too." Cynthia told her dad.

She thanked God that He kept His eye on her sons, "You're the only one who can keep them safe when I'm not thinking straight."

Her body quivered, thinking of what could have happened and painful memories emerged. She had lost two of her first cousins, who were brothers, (one who was also born the same day as she was), who drowned a year apart in the Kankakee River.

- - - - - - - - - - -

In June, the boys started J&J daycare. Tony loved going to "school" and was really excited learning how to write his name and numbers. On the 5th, Cynthia discovered Matthew had the mumps, and the next day, Tony did, too. She was glad they got them now, instead of when they started kindergarten.

- - - - - - - - - - -

Cynthia was having a hard time potty training three-year-old, Matthew. She couldn't understand why it was so easy for Tony, but Matthew was just not sticking with it. Matthew would go to the potty fine, but within a few minutes he was wet again. This concerned her and she asked some friends at work about it.

Her co-worker told her, "Watch him as he goes. If his stream is straight, then maybe he's just taking a little longer than usual to get trained, but if it's divided, then there is something blocking him and he's unable to completely empty his bladder and it leaks out later."

This made a lot sense and sure enough when Cynthia watched her youngest son try to use the potty, the stream was divided. So, she called the hospital and set up an appointment to get Matthew checked.

On November 26, after many blood, urine, bladder tests, and kidney ultrasound, the doctors had found that Matthew had a badly damaged kidney since birth, if not before. The local hospital knew it was out of their hands and suggested he go to Children's Memorial Hospital for more extensive testing.

On December 17, at Children's Memorial, the doctors found the blockage under Matthew's left kidney. Surgery was needed and they scheduled him for January 16th. Early on, Matthew could take a lot of physical pain, so it was hard for anyone to really know if he was hurting.

The new year came and the worried parents took their sick son up to Chicago.

Cynthia was beside herself as so many thoughts crossed her mind: "I should've had him checked earlier" and "Here he was suffering all this time and I never saw it."

She prayed over Matthew before surgery and they wheeled him away.

The surgeon had to cut Matthew from the back, around his side, and slightly on his stomach; leaving a long and profound scar. Matthew had tubes inserted to keep the urinary track open in case the scar tissue compressed over time, where it could block the urine flow again.

After the surgery, Matthew was different. He was so happy he didn't know what to do with himself. He was so used to pain because it was like second nature to him; he thought that was normal to feel like there was a thorn in his side - literally.

The operation was a success and Matthew only had to stay there for five days. Cynthia stayed at the Ronald McDonald House and couldn't say anything except great things about how wonderful they were. Her heart went out to all the other children there with so many other ailments like heart surgeries, cancer, and burns.

Matthew's hospital days were not done though. He was suffering with sore throats from the drainage and infection in his ears.

So, on April 17, he had to have his tonsils and adenoids out and tubes put back in his ears. He wouldn't swallow or talk for two days. He suffered more than when he had the kidney operation, but he was real brave and didn't even cry. He had pain for so long that his pain tolerance was high.

- - - - - - - - - - -

One morning, Simona came downstairs and noticed the fish tank was cloudy. The light was kept on all night for a bluish glow, and since the sun had a hard time shinning through the windows due to the enclosed porch, the glow from the aquarium was always very prominent. She knew Chuck always kept the tank clean and clear, so this strange white substance concerned her; she couldn't even see a fish. She went upstairs and told her step-dad that something was wrong with the tank. Once Chuck came downstairs, he was at a loss for words and couldn't understand what happened. Then it struck him, the boys. He called out to them and they came running to meet him.

"What happened?" Chuck asked.

"We gave them breakfast." Tony said.

Now it made sense, the boys had finished their cereal and poured the remainder of the milk into the tank.

"Grab me two buckets and fill one with water," Chuck commanded.

As he tried to seek out the fish, he put them in the clean water and suctioned out the milky-water in the other. He had thought there was no way the boys could hurt the fish; he stood corrected.

Moving Again

Chuck had been drinking on and off since that night he agreed to go to Alcoholics Anonymous, but it was getting worse every time that he fell off the wagon. He was getting drunk more and more and that violent temperament was coming back into full character. He was in and out of jail for stealing, because he needed money to buy alcohol. It never failed, it seemed every time the moon was full it pulled Chuck to drink. Every month Cynthia had to endure whether he could fight the urge, stop after he drank a few, drink enough to make him merry, or a lot to push him over the edge.

On this night, it was the breaking point for Cynthia. She wrestled in her mind of what kind of mother she was; she loved her children, she wanted to always be a stay-at-home mom, cook, clean, and make sure she was there for them, but she was always at work and felt pushed into having a career. She felt bad that she wasn't there for her daughter. She was young, too young, when she gave birth to Simona and felt a sense of guilt letting her parents raise her. She wanted to be there for her boys and now was the time to be a good mom. Cynthia began to resent her job and Chuck for taking her away from them.

Chuck came home drunk and little did he know how much Cynthia had enough; she put her foot down.

"Get Out! I don't want you here; I just can't do this anymore!"

He just laughed and said, "Yeah, yeah," as he walked back out the door, "I'll be back." He had heard her threaten so many times that this was just another fit, and when he sobered up, she'd let him come back. Then he disappeared, (like every other time she kicked him out), for about three days. This time, he was going to show her what it felt like to lose someone you love.

As the boys were playing outside in the backyard, Chuck pulled up and called to them. They saw their dad and happily ran to him; he hugged his sons, put them in the car, and took off.

Cynthia noticed that the boys were missing and was frantic. She couldn't find them anywhere and called the police. They came over right away, wrote down the boys' descriptions, and told Cynthia that they would be in touch. Thankfully, the police recovered the boys from their dad. Cynthia was never told by them, or even by Chuck, where the officers found Tony and Matthew, but Cynthia assumed it was at a bar.

The next day, Cynthia struggled with her weakness to forgive him (now more in fear of him doing such a stunt again). Chuck would call her on the phone, say beautiful words, and she really felt she "needed" him, but knew she couldn't let him manipulate her. She called her parents and they came over to help her be strong. This was the first time she ever saw her dad cry.

Sam was a tough Italian, not one to easily show emotion, but he was so angry and hurt from the pain Chuck had caused to his family that he wept for feeling so helpless.

He pleaded to his daughter to "leave the drunk" and as tears fell from his eyes he begged, "I can't take it anymore; your mother and I just can't take it anymore," meaning how much Chuck's abuse to her was hurting them. Their beautiful daughter was precious to them. Chuck's drinking had affected not only his daughter and grandchildren, but family functions and holiday dinners. Chuck's name was in the paper every time he was arrested, and he even went to church with alcohol on his breath; it was embarrassing and disgraceful.

Cynthia stuck to her guns for awhile, but she did take Chuck back after his promises to do better. She longed for the husband she married to sober up and come back in her life. Chuck hooked up with a generous man, Frank, who gave him a good job. Frank took a liking to Chuck and the family. It seemed Chuck was doing well and holding his own. Cynthia had hoped that Frank giving Chuck a chance to work would discourage him to drink.

- - - - - - - - - - -

In the summer of 1985, Simona was able to go see her friend, Lynn, in Virginia for a week. Simona met Lynn in church; Lynn was six years older and had taken Simona under her wing. She knew of all the madness going on in Simona's life with Chuck being an alcoholic. When Lynn got married and moved away, Simona felt more alone than ever. Since Simona was like a little sister to her, Lynn asked her to come for a visit. She was about to give birth to her first child, and wanted Simona there.

On the plane, Simona met a guy named John. As they talked, it was discovered that they were going to the same town in Virginia. The two agreed to meet sometime in the week to go fishing on his dad's boat. Simona had a wonderful time with Lynn, her newborn son Daniel, and fishing on the Atlantic Ocean. The week flew by, but it helped her come home refreshed.

- - - - - - - - - - - -

One Friday night, the family went to the drive-in and everyone fell asleep, but Simona. She had a hard time waking up Chuck, who was behind the wheel, and finally woke up her mom. By the time Cynthia got Chuck to move to the passenger side, so she could drive, the drive-in was deserted.

When they arrived home after midnight, the old man across the street told them, "Hey, some kids opened your porch door and stole a bike." The neighbor was too scared to do anything and Simona was furious the old man didn't stop him.

"He didn't yell? Say 'stop'? He didn't call the cops? They stole *my* bike!"

Simona had a yellow Huffy 10 speed, she had received for Christmas last year, and now it was gone.

Chuck and Cynthia discussed that the neighborhood was getting bad; more and more people were moving because of all the crime. People, who for generations lived in these lovely homes, now were selling them to avoid the danger. The more they heard from those who were vandalized–the less the newspapers reported it. Chuck talked to Frank, because he had some apartments. Frank told the family one was available and in a better part of town.

They were pleased and arranged for their dog, Reggie, to find a new home. It must have been God to cause them to move, because no sooner than they were out of the house it had caught on fire.

In November, they moved into an apartment on Stratford Drive. Things were not good between Simona and Chuck; someone had to leave. On Christmas morning, Simona got a handheld radio and went into her room, lay on her bed, and listened to Christmas music on it. She was getting into a funk and she couldn't bring herself to even look at Chuck. No matter what she said, wore, or did, she was insulted with a rude comment. She hated being cut down, so she moved in with her grandparents by the end of the month. Her grandparent's home was always open to her.

Being in a three-story apartment building, the boys played with their cars on the stairs. They were actually pretty good for being so enclosed, but the people living in the apartment complained of the noise and the family was evicted. Frank felt bad having to kick them out, but he said, "You need a house, especially with boys. I have one for rent if you're interested."

The family moved about a half-mile down the road, on February 1986, into a house on Marsile. It was smaller than the other houses they rented, but it still consisted of three bedrooms and a basement. Frank even bought the stove and refrigerator for them.

They were able to get another dog, Cujo. Cujo was a mutt, who looked just like the dog in the movie, Benji.

Cynthia talked to her daughter and asked her to come back home.

Simona Returns

Simona moved back home and was willing to forgive. Chuck saw Simona as a threat, because she would leave every time she was angry with him. Chuck seemed to feel resentment toward Simona, and felt she could influence Cynthia to kick him out again. So Chuck began treating her more like a child than ever before, to show Cynthia that Simona was immature. Although Simona was almost eighteen -years-old, she was sheltered and naïve. She became withdrawn and quiet, yet she developed a very keen awareness of her surroundings. She wasn't dumb, she just held everything inside. Being bullied by Chuck so long, she had never stuck up for herself; she was a classic introvert and overpowered by insecurity. She hated fearing Chuck, because she knew it was a barricade to her breaking out of her shell.

Simona was invited to a skating party and really looked forward to going. Chuck knew how much it meant to her and took advantage of it. He knew she didn't eat vegetables, and made her put a tablespoon full of peas on her plate. She detested peas!

He told her, "If you don't eat all of them, you can't go to the skating rink."

After the family was done eating, he was doing the dishes and watching her out of the corner of his eye, "Don't even think about giving it to the dog!" Chuck threatened.

She was stressed and trying to eat one pea made her gag; the smell, the texture. Her mind raced. How was she going to get out of this? She sat at the table alone and began to scheme. She was wearing tan culottes, and dark brown, knee-high socks. (Girls weren't supposed to wear pants according to the church she attended.) The culottes had no pockets, she thought about the napkin, but knew it would be too obvious for Chuck to check, and that would mean no skating party. No . . . it had to be on her person.

Simona had an idea!

She looked like she took a bite, made a face and winced, as she poured a few peas into her sock, smashed them against her leg, so as not to produce a bulge. She knew she couldn't do it all at once, because she had to act like she was really unhappy with eating them. Plus, she had to be careful to make sure not one pea fell to the floor, because she had to keep her head up, so Chuck couldn't see her bend down.

Finally, she said, "I'm done."

Chuck felt powerful and pleased he could *make* her eat all her peas. Cynthia was in shock. Simona waited until the coast was clear (just in case her leg looked slightly swollen), and went to the bathroom. She took off her sock, washed out the peas in the toilet, flushed them down, and put her socks in the dirty laundry basket. She felt a sense of accomplishment, pulling the wool over his eyes, and went proudly to the skating party. She had a great time as she told Cher all about her strategy; they had a good laugh over it.

In March, Simona noticed a red mark on her left arm. She thought it was some cut and put peroxide on it. Then, she put on triple antibiotic cream and a band-aid. During the week, she was wondering what was taking so long for it to heal and kept trying different ointments and alcohols.

She told her friends at school and Cher jokingly asked her, "Have you been shooting up?" and laughed. It did look like a jagged, bloody hole in her arm.

Simona laughed too, but in the back of her mind worried what it was exactly.

Five days later, she woke up to find her whole body covered with the chicken pox. She was so mad, "I'm seventeen-years-old! I already had the chicken pox! Didn't I?"

Then, Tony and Matthew woke up with them, too.

- - - - - - - - - - -

In June, Chuck and Cynthia wanted to have a family vacation and planned a trip to Orlando, Florida. Cynthia told Simona about it and she refused to go. She did not feel she "belonged" and that Chuck wanted his "family" vacation. She did not want to be stuck traveling by car with them. She did not want to be the "babysitter," and she did not want to be there if Chuck decided to get drunk and cause problems on the vacation. She gave up her chance to go to Disney World to avoid anymore resentment.

"Where are you going to stay at?" Cynthia asked.

"With Grandma Mandy and Pappy," she said, even though Simona was old enough to stay alone. Simona just felt secure at her grandparents and enjoyed being around them.

Chuck and Cynthia rented a van and took off. They stopped by Memphis, Tennessee and took the tour through Graceland. Cynthia loved Elvis, and had always wanted to visit, especially after he passed away if only to say "goodbye."

The boys loved looking at the *Lisa Marie* plane and Cynthia just loved the *Jungle Room.* She was thrilled to have the chance to go through what was once the dwelling place of the *King.*

Once they reached Florida, they stayed three days at Disney, and three days on the beach. This was Cynthia's first family vacation in another state since she was married to Simona's dad. The boys had a blast and the vacation was everything that the family wanted and needed.

When the family came back, Chuck felt like he was the head-of-the-household again. He was accepted as a good dad by taking his wife and sons on a vacation. Simona felt the vainglory he strutted, and she felt like an outcast. She stayed in her room–*all the time.* Cynthia was worried about her daughter and knew Simona was different; she was nothing like her when she was growing up.

"What is wrong with you? Go out! Get out and go have some fun," Cynthia told Simona.

"Where am I to go?"

"Anywhere; just leave."

Simona drove to Walgreens, got a magazine (Bop or Teenbeat) and parked her car in a store parking lot and read it. That killed about a couple of hours and she went back home.

Simona still never came out of her room and was becoming depressed; she didn't want to be around the "Gioia family." Cynthia was getting nervous and went to talk to her. As she went to open the door, it was locked. This made Cynthia upset, more out of fear than anger, and she screamed, "Open this door!"

"What?" Simona asked as she did what she was told.

"Don't you *ever* lock this door again! I don't want to have to break it down just to find you dead."

Simona was taken aback, "She actually thinks I'm suicidal?" Simona was down, but she never really thought of taking her life; but it did get so bad between her and Chuck that she ran away, again. Chuck assumed she ran to her grandparents like before, but she didn't—she went to Cher's. This really ticked off Chuck and told Cynthia to have her make a choice where to live–this running away thing was getting old. (Yeah, like his drinking wasn't getting old).

Simona decided to stay at her grandparents and Chuck quickly talked Cynthia into making Simona's room into an office. It wasn't long since Chuck got his way, he felt invincible, and went out and got drunk. Why not? Things were going his way and the step-child was gone. Cynthia knew the tide had come and was drowning Chuck again; he was unstoppable. She had kicked him out–again, and asked Simona to come back home to help watch the boys. Cynthia needed her daughter; she couldn't work, clean the house, and watch her sons by herself. Simona came back home willingly, with the confidence Chuck was gone for good, but he visited, and this made her uncomfortable. She knew that he would eventually sway Cynthia to let him move back. She was right.

Chapter 4

"The eyes of the Lord are in every place . . ."
(Proverbs 15:3)

Boys Will Be Boys

Matthew was now in kindergarten. He was a class clown, but he was a lover, too. Cynthia got a call from the school; it was the principal. Matthew was caught on the playground kissing a girl. Okay, you may think that's cute, but he was trying to french kiss her.

At first, it was funny and nobody thought anything of it, until Mandy asked, "Where would he learn something like that?"

Cynthia suddenly realized, "Yeah, where did he learn that?"

Chuck and Cynthia sat down with Matthew and asked in a calm way, so that he wouldn't feel cornered. They never expected to hear what would come out of his mouth.

"I know how to make babies. You get on top of a girl and do this . . ." and he moved his hips around and around.

If two parents ever dropped jaws, theirs hit the floor. Cynthia was furious, but held back until he answered where he had learned such a thing.

"Over at Brian's house, we watched a movie."

Cynthia called Brian's mother, and she couldn't apologize enough, "I don't know how the boys got my husband's VHS tape, but I'm so sorry."

What kind of parents keeps porn in a child's reach? Matthew was five-years-old and now the family thought, "His innocent little mind is ruined."

Chuck figured the boys needed skill, discipline, and registered them in soccer; he even ended up being a coach on Tony's team. Cynthia and Chuck felt sports was always a good thing for growing boys, sometimes it can help build character, but most of all, to focus their minds to more decent and healthy things.

Then, Chuck seemed to be losing the fight with his temptation, and being that a bar was right across the street from where they lived, did not make things much better. He would show up at Tony's soccer practice, drunk and stumbling around. Tony's little friends would laugh and point at him and scream out, "Your daddy is drunk!"

Tony was so embarrassed and for a little boy of six, he knew of humiliation.

Chuck walked in the door, cocky and arrogant, trying to talk to Tony as if he were a teenager. Cynthia was in the bathroom doing her hair and Simona was on the couch watching her brothers when Chuck came in. He was boisterous and grabbed Matthew, pinning him down, and commanded Tony to tickle him. Matthew couldn't break free and his little face looked as though he was being tortured; he couldn't catch his breath, and his face was turning a beet red.

Simona yelled in his defense, "He's not laughing - Stop being unfair!"

Chuck glared at her and then pushed Matthew away from him, "Go away."

Simona seemed to baby Matthew more when Chuck was around, because he tended to favor Tony. When Chuck's parents would come for a visit from 29 Palms, California, they favored Tony, too, because he carried the family name. They *never* called him Tony, he was *Sir Charles;* Matthew was nicknamed, *Bugaboo.*

Cynthia's side of the family didn't believe in holding any child in higher regard because of a name. They loved both boys equally and were disgusted by such behavior.

When Chuck pushed Matthew away, he grabbed Tony just when the boy had taken a bite of his peanut butter sandwich. Chuck threw Tony on the ground and tickled him; with Tony's mouth being full, he was trying to chew and keep the bite from being caught in his throat while laughing.

Simona saw this and screamed in horror, "Stop! He's going to choke! He has food in his mouth!"

Chuck was sick of her telling him what to do and started yelling back, "What? I can't play with any of my sons? He's fine!"

"He has a peanut butter sandwich in his mouth, let him swallow first."

Cynthia heard what was being said and came out to defend all her children. When she began telling Chuck to "knock it off," he got angry and started acting like a child.

Cynthia went into her room, grabbed her purse, and told everyone to get into the car. Meanwhile, Chuck is still ranting and throwing pillows and such, as the family piled into the vehicle.

Cynthia drove around and asked her daughter what was going on, to open up and tell her the truth, to tell her *everything*. Simona let a few things out into the open, mainly how Chuck had been drinking every night lately, and how he treated the boys. She never went into what he was doing to her, because she felt as long as it wasn't physical, she could handle what he dished out.

Cynthia knew she had to let him go and stand her ground. This wasn't about her anymore and what she wanted; her children were being exposed to the drunkenness and violence for too long. Working so much overtime and odd hours, Cynthia was in the dark when it came to Chuck's behavior. Now realizing the effect it was having on her children, Chuck had to leave.

When she came back home, she overheard him making a cocaine deal over the phone. "Cocaine - when did he start doing drugs?" Cynthia's couldn't believe she was so unaware of how deep Chuck had spiraled. She grabbed him by the back of his head, pulled his hair, and forced him out. She knew this was it, if she didn't stand her ground now, she never would.

After she kicked him out, Chuck ended up in jail for theft to feed his habit.

Months later, after Chuck was released, Cynthia refused to take him back, so he headed to California.

It was 1987; Simona graduated and quit church. Although, she still believed in God, she felt that she didn't belong there anymore. She was losing her faith.

She was dating a guy she could see herself marrying. He was a Jewish boy named Bruce.

Simona was now in charge of the house and her brothers.

By this time, Tony was feeling like the big brother; he didn't act like a child anymore. The last words his dad told him before he left were, "You're the man of the house now," and Tony took that literally. This made everyone worry about him; Tony was too young to have that much burden.

Matthew was still having trouble with wetting the bed. No one could tell if it was because he was a heavy sleeper, the tubes that were put in this urethra weren't helping him "feel" the need to go, or if psychologically he was having this problem.

Cynthia invested in an expensive system which included an alarm going off to wake up Matthew to go to the bathroom. Instead, the alarm woke up everyone *except* Matthew. Tony would get down from the top bunk and try to wake up his slumberous brother, and Cynthia would come in the bedroom, pick up Matthew, and try to make him walk to the bathroom. The system was useless.

- - - - - - - - - - -

The boys gave Simona a difficult time over the summer. Her brothers would take off to play with friends and always be out of earshot. So, she would have to get in the car and look for them.

Cynthia gave her daughter a smaller version of a station wagon to drive that was given to her by a friend at the Post Office. The vehicle was an automatic and ran beautifully, but had a little problem when putting it in park, (she would have to shift it back and forth until it could catch and fasten in that gear).

One day, Simona went to "find" her brothers. She got into the car, and drove about a quarter mile when she spotted them. She pulled up to the curb, threw it in park, and as she was getting out to retrieve them, they hopped on their bikes and tried peddling away from her. In the mist of a few seconds, the car popped out of park and rolled up over the curb, across the grass, and headed for a house. Simona ran after it, trying to jump in to hit the break, and instead hit her head on the frame of the door. All attempts were in vain as the car hit the porch of an elderly lady. When the front door opened, Simona was panting so heavy; she couldn't say anything at first.

The old woman stated, "If you wanted to come for a visit all you had to do was knock."

Simona began apologizing and promised, "If there is any damage, I will pay, I promise."

"Oh, don't worry about this old house. You just better get that car fixed."

Simona thanked the lady profusely, and when Simona turned around, her brothers were out of sight. She drove back to the house and the boys were already inside.

Another incident was when Simona was trying to clean the house, Bruce and their friend Wheels came over to visit. Tony and Matthew wouldn't play in their room and wanted to go to the park. It was actually their grade school's playground which was right up the street from their house.

Simona told them, "I'll be watching you. *Don't* leave the park; I don't want to have to go after you again!"

Cynthia was sleeping after working all night, and had already been on her case about cleaning, so Simona told the guys to keep it down. "I just don't need her getting up and yelling."

Every so often, Simona would peer out the front door and check on her brothers. As she dusted, Bruce would sit and talk to her. Wheels (who carried around a boom box) slipped in his favorite group, *Styx*. Simona's mind was preoccupied; for some reason, she just kept looking out the door. As her eyes were focused on the playground watching the kids, she heard sirens. When she turned around, there were police cars, fire trucks, and an ambulance rushing toward the back of the house.

Wheels got up and asked, "Hey, what's going on?"

"I don't know. Was there some kind of a parade happening today?" Simona asked.

"They're probably on their way to the station," Bruce said.

The station was located a half mile behind the house. When she looked back toward the park; she still saw the kids playing. Wheels, curious by nature, went toward the kitchen to look out back and said, "Hey, Look! They stopped. Let's go check it out!"

The three walked out the backdoor and across the yard. The police cars, ambulance, and fire trucks no longer had sirens blaring, but the lights were still flashing.

Suddenly, Simona saw two little boys in white t-shirts, covered with black soot. As she met up with them and the police officers, her head was spinning . . . it was Tony and Matthew–she was in BIG trouble! Panic set in.

When an officer approached her, with his hand on the boys shoulders, Simona felt her heart pounding, "What . . . How did . . . When did . . ." She wondered who the kids were that she was watching at the park and what happened to both her brothers' blue shirts.

Bruce put his arm around Simona and whispered, "You better get your mom."

The officer asked, "Do these boys belong to you?"

"They're my brothers . . . what happened?"

"They must have been playing with matches, because they set your neighbors barn on fire."

Simona walked back to the house, with her heart pounding, and entered into her mom's bedroom, "Mom . . . you need to get up. The boys were . . . uh . . . they had matches . . ."

"What? Weren't you watching them?"

"Yeah, but I thought they were at the park . . . and well . . . the police need to talk to you."

"Police? Oh, no!"

When Cynthia saw the boys and heard from the officer what they had done, she smacked Simona right across the face. The guys and the police were startled; then Cynthia asked about damages and what she would have to pay. Fortunately, the neighbor didn't press charges; he knew the barn was old and needed to come down eventually. He was just glad the boys didn't get burned. She thanked God, because the consequences could have been horrible.

Come to find out, the boys were quite the little pyromaniacs. When Simona cleaned their room, she found under their bed several burned papers and matches. They must have seen their mom take out the matches from the kitchen drawer when she had to light the pilot for the stove.

The boys also vandalized the front of their white brick home by trying to sign their names with blue spray paint. Cynthia was at a loss. She tried to just pass it off that boys will be boys, but deep down she couldn't help but worry about them and how they were going to be when they got older. She hoped they would outgrow all the mischievousness.

A week before Christmas, Simona went into the boy's room and found a particular toy on the floor that she had never seen before. It was a silver ball, but when you pulled the pieces out, it became another object.

"Wow, this is cool! Where did you get this?"

"It's a transformer," Tony said.

"Hey, mom, where did they get this? It's neat."

When Cynthia saw the toy in Simona's hand, she started screaming, "Did they open their Christmas presents?!"

The boys knew Mom was upset with them and tried to get out of trouble by lying, "We found them buried in the backyard."

Simona scanned around the boy's room; sure enough there were about four more of these toys. When Simona bent down to look under the bed, stuffed under it was the Christmas wrapping paper. Busted! Simona had to laugh, but Cynthia was both hurt and outraged at the same time.

- - - - - - - - - - -

Bruce and Simona had been disagreeing over his car. Bruce loved his Chevy Impala and insisted on spending every dime on it. He put on dual exhausts, painted it from gray to black, changed everything under the hood to chrome, and installed tachometers, lights, a horn used on semi-trucks, and numerous other little expensive "toys." Simona didn't care about that; but when it came to dates, they consisted of just driving around in his car–no movies, dinners, or dances. Simona thoughts were, "How boring." She tried to give Bruce ideas of new places to go, like maybe a concert, instead of just driving around the town square, but Bruce took it personally.

When Tony had one of his bad migraine headaches caused from the spinal tap, he went into his mom's bed to lay down in the dark. Since Chuck was no longer around, Simona treated each boy with the same love; her heart went out to Tony suffering with such pain. She turned down the television, and made sure that Matthew stayed quiet too. Suddenly, Bruce drove by and revved his engine, so loud that it shook the house. Tony cried out in pain, rocking back and forth on the bed, and trying to shut out the noise. Bruce's exhaust rumbled and clacked in a stuttering ricochet sound that bounced off the building across the street, shaking the windows of the Gioia's home.

Simona felt her face get red; when she caught up with Bruce, she made sure he knew exactly how she felt, "I don't care if you're mad at *me*, but *think* before you do something *stupid* like that again! Tony had one of his bad headaches and you crackling your *dual* exhaust hurt him more than you *trying* to hurt me. Don't take your ego out on a helpless little boy or the neighbors–*tell* me how you feel, instead of trying to get my attention by laying on the gas."

Bruce's mouth fell open and his face flushed, "I'm sorry, I feel so bad . . . I would never have hurt Tony on purpose. I . . . I don't know what I was thinking . . . I'm sorry–tell your mom and Tony I'm sorry, too. Okay?"

Simona forgave Bruce. After all, she loved him.

Wind of Change

Wheels' girlfriend, Tasha, was visiting him. Oblivious to everyone, she actually ran away from home and was hiding out at his house. Tasha was abused and wanted to get away from her step dad; she was only sixteen-years-old, but she could pass as twenty-three. Wheels, afraid his mother would find Tasha there, asked Simona if Tasha could stay with her. Simona asked her mom. After much deliberating between Cynthia and Tasha's mom, Tasha was able to live at Cynthia's–on the condition Tasha contributed to paying her own way.

Simona and Tasha converted the basement into an apartment and painted the walls black and white checkered on the masonry blocks. Simona's old room was made into an extra room for guests or when the boys become older could each have their own room.

No sooner than Tasha was established with her things, Chuck decided to return from California; he missed his boys. Cynthia let him stay in Simona's old room. In just over a month with Chuck back in the house, he was sliding back into his old ways.

One day, Tasha went to visit her mom. Packing her things, she noticed some of her music compact discs were missing. Right away, Simona thought about Chuck. She began taking inventory. She stood on the bed, pushed the drop ceiling to the side, and pulled out a tin box. This was where the girls kept their money for rent to Cynthia, insurance, and savings. Sure enough, Simona's money for her vehicle insurance was gone. Simona was working two jobs and providing her own way; money became very important to her. Seeing the money missing, something inside Simona snapped.

After Tasha left for her visit, Simona told her mom that Chuck had stolen from them. Cynthia didn't know Chuck was still drinking and since she didn't know Tasha very well, asked if maybe she had taken it.

"Tasha didn't steal her own cd's, Mom. I know it's Chuck. He's not working, so he has to be getting money somewhere."

Later that night, Bruce stopped by to see Simona. She was still screaming about her money being gone and Bruce tried to comfort her, but she couldn't stop pacing the floor.

Suddenly, they heard pounding upstairs and then yelling. Simona knew that it was Chuck; he had come home drunk. She ran up the stairs so fast, Bruce didn't know what she might do and was a little afraid to follow her. When Simona approached the dining area, she saw Cynthia yelling at Chuck for having the nerve to come back in the house drunk after everything that happened nearly a year before.

Chuck became very cocky and began yelling back; just then Simona broke in and screamed, "Get out of this house!"

Chuck turned and walked toward her until he was an inch from her frame, smiling as if to say, "And what are you going to do about it?"

Simona scolded, "How *dare* you come back in this house *drunk* from stealing my insurance money! I worked hard for that, and you just go in my room, snooping around to find something to pawn and drink on . . . you even stole my friend's cd!"

"Yeah . . . and . . ." he said as he smiled caustically.

Before Simona could control herself, she felt a ball of fire and energy rise from the sole of her foot, travel down her arm, and she smacked Chuck across the face so hard his head was thrown sideways. She was shocked by her actions, but before she could react, Chuck smiled and smacked her right back. Simona bent forward and charged at him like a football player; her shoulder rammed into his gut. Chuck picked her up and threw her across the room, luckily onto the couch, but she got right back up and headed for him again.

As this was going on, Cynthia's feet were heavy like bricks cemented to the floor. Her mind was racing about what she should do; break up the fight? Call the police? Scream?

She looked down and saw her little boys standing in the hallway, watching their dad and sister violently attack each other - this vision pulled Cynthia out of her dismay and tried to break up the fighting.

Bruce saw Cynthia try to get Chuck off Simona. Bruce found himself grabbing Chuck in a head and arm lock and helped Cynthia push Chuck out the front door.

Simona's adrenaline was still pumping and she couldn't break her grasp, Cynthia pried her daughter's fingers and screamed, "Let go!"

Once he was out, Chuck stood cursing at the house, Cynthia called the police, and Bruce sat Simona down to console her.

"Wow! You're pretty tough. I didn't think you had that in you." Bruce said admiringly.

"I can't believe I did that . . . it was as though every thing he's ever done to me just broke free. I feel terrible that Tony and Matthew saw that! I hope that they never, ever, become violent . . . I just hope this didn't trigger anything in their heads."

"Shhh, I'm sure they see you as a big sister that would stand up to protect them . . . even from their dad."

"I saw their faces, watching, but I couldn't stop . . . I just couldn't stop going back after him."

"It's okay. They're young enough; they'll never remember what happened."

"I don't know. I remember things when I was younger than them; like it was yesterday."

Needless to say, Chuck and Cynthia became legally separated and were divorced by 1989. A feeling of peace came over the whole family.

Meanwhile, Chuck was jobless and would sleep in bins that were attached to the sidewalk for people to donate clothes and things for those in need. Chuck was getting desperate and got caught stealing; he was put in jail. Once released, he went back to California.

One night, Bruce and Simona sat in his car and talked about marriage. Bruce didn't know how it would be possible since his mother didn't like *any* girl he went out with (she was definitely a protective mother), but his dad liked Simona.

Simona stated, "It shouldn't matter if you're mother approves of me or not, it's what you want . . . it's your life Bruce. It's you, who is going to marry me–not your mother."

"She is difficult and it wouldn't matter who I brought home; she would not approve," Bruce said unhopefully.

Simona made a suggestion, "Okay, let's do this . . . You bring home some tramp, you know, dresses *punk* and looks easy. You're mom would be *begging* you to go back out with me."

"That's sounds good," Bruce said, "She would freak if I did something like that."

Sure enough, a few months later, Bruce did just that, but Simona was unaware about it. Soon, Bruce was not coming over very much and ignoring her, so she called him.

"Where have you been?"

"Oh, working a lot of overtime. I've been tired . . . look, do you want to go out for dinner?"

"Sure."

When Bruce took Simona out–he had in mind to break up with her, but he didn't *say* anything. He asked her a lot of weird, sexual questions, and she felt something was wrong, but she didn't *say* anything, either.

Then Simona found out a week later that Bruce was seeing the "tramp" - it all made sense. She wanted to wait to make love until they got married, but Bruce couldn't wait.

It broke her heart and she felt responsible that the scheme backfired; however, part of the plan did work . . . six months later when she ran into Bruce's mom.

She told Simona, "Oh, how I wish my Bruce would have stayed with you. He is so different and that woman he's with is tearing apart my family."

"I wish we were together, too, because I still love him."

Bruce's mom continued telling Simona about the new couple, "She's pregnant and they're not even considering getting married."

Simona's heart sunk, this wasn't Bruce. She knew he didn't love that girl, but now he was going to be a dad, and she knew that meant a lot to him.

Simona started to receive letters from John, the guy she met on the plane to Virginia. He wanted to come see her with the intention of dating. Once he arrived, he came across as very aggressive; something Simona didn't notice about him before. It had been four years since she seen him and his actions just blew her away. He carried on as if he had been part of the family all this time; he teased her brothers, cut down her mom's elephant collection, and even made the comment, "Your mom wears too much make-up."

Simona felt her blood begin to boil and thought, "What nerve! Who was this guy anyway coming in here making such crass remarks?"

He insisted on going for a drive so they could talk in private. Simona was nervous and all she could picture were red flags popping up and waving uncontrollably, but she wanted to be friendly and make sure she didn't tick this guy off.

Tasha tried to talk her out of being alone with him, but Simona had a plan. She agreed to go on the drive. She directed John to the hill she used to go sledding as a form of conversation. She suggested they park there, after all, he didn't know her grandparents were right up the street. This way, if she had to make a run for it, she knew she would be safe.

It all turned out okay, they just talked, but Simona longed for him to leave. John only stayed three days, but that was enough for Simona, and to see him leave was a relief. He did write her after his visit, but she never wrote him back.

Those familiar words of Chuck's rang through her head, "You'll never get married . . ."

It seemed that the guys she wanted didn't want her; the guys she didn't want pursued her endlessly. She was not about to settle with just any guy.

Tasha was trying to get Simona to move out and get an apartment together.

Simona felt trapped. "I can't leave . . . my mom needs me here; my brothers need me."

Tasha asked, "What are you going to do . . . live here forever? You're almost twenty-one years old!"

Simona felt bad, but still she looked at apartments and when one was found, she broke the news to her mom. This did not make Cynthia very happy; she felt the ground sink beneath her—who would watch her boys while she worked? Out of fear and frustration, she attacked Simona with threatening words, "If you leave, you leave for good! You can never come back!" Simona believed her, but decided to move out anyway - a month before her 21st birthday.

Chapter 5

"God is our refuge and strength . . . in trouble."
(Psalms 46:1)

Just Mom and the Boys

After Simona left home, Cynthia had to find a babysitter. She hired an Indian girl, Hammah, who was going to college across the street at Olivet, to live in her home and watch her boys. But Tony was a "Bart Simpson" and Hammah couldn't handle him. Tony and Matthew never listened and always teased her. She told Cynthia that they were just too much for her and she couldn't watch them anymore. Hammah ended up moving out and Cynthia worried about who could watch her boys. To make matter worse, Cynthia was hit by another stint of bad news. She was told by Frank that he was going to sell the house, so Cynthia attempted to get a loan to buy it. Unfortunately, she just didn't have the financial means and had to find another place to live. She was disappointed, because she loved that house and it upset everyone that their dog, Cujo, had to be given away.

For the summer, she let the boys go see Chuck's parents in California for two weeks; Chuck was still serving time in jail. As the boys went to board the plane, Cynthia cried. She loved her boys and feared for them; she was scared about how dangerous it was having her two little ones traveling across the country alone.

While in California, Tony, Matthew, and their grandpa would go to the donut shop every morning. They had a good time in 29 Palms, but when it was time to come home, they were ready.

Cynthia found a house on Bel Air and she and the boys moved in August.

Two days before Christmas, Cynthia smelled smoke and called the fire department. When the firemen arrived, they found a small fire in the attic which was caused by faulty wiring.

The firemen brought in their hoses; soaking everything in the house. The couch, carpet, and furniture were so drenched that the family had to stay in a hotel. Cynthia gathered the presents and her boys, and booked into the Holiday Inn. Cynthia, at first, was down because Christmas was being spent in a hotel with no tree, but soon it unfolded into a little vacation. She and her sons went swimming and enjoyed their time spent gathered together in a small room. They talked, laughed, and played; it was their favorite Christmas memory ever!

When they were able to go back into the house, Cynthia was confronted by the landlord. He scolded her as if the fire were her fault. He was so tight with his money that he didn't want to fix the house right away; leaving Cynthia to look for another place to live where it would be safe for her children.

No sooner than the New Year hit 1990, Cynthia moved her family into a duplex on Hemlock. She was dating a really nice guy from the Post Office who had a son and two daughters. He was being transferred to another Post Office down in southern Illinois. Since Cynthia wasn't sure just how she felt about him, she ended their relationship.

The boys made all new friends. They were still able to go to school in Bourbonnais, but in the neighborhood they met quite a few kids from Bradley. This is where they gained a reputation as the "Gioia Brothers"—already well-known by the time they reached High School.

The boys started going to the YMCA after school and playing basketball. The YMCA was a few blocks from their grandparents and the boys would walk over to see them after practice. Sam was very protective and felt the need to pick them up sometimes; he didn't trust anyone and was not going to have anyone hurt his grandsons. He would watch them until Mandy came home from *Secrets* (a clothing boutique where she worked), and she would gladly make them dinner and talk with them until Cynthia came to pick them up.

During this time, Tony was trying to break free from having Matthew always following him around; he wanted to be independent. This hurt Matthew a lot, but at the time, Tony didn't care. Tony just wanted his own friends.

Matthew wasn't very good at picking the right friends and he hung around who would let him. He wanted to fit in and was still doing zany things to get others to notice him; to think he was cool, and to make them laugh. He fell into the wrong kind of crowd and began experimenting in adult activities. Matthew was not afraid to take a dare and would do whatever the others asked of him just to gain their approval.

The Guy Next Door

Tony met up with a kid, who knew the man that lived in the next duplex over, and thought about hooking him up with his mom. The guy next door was named William, and he was a construction worker and a part-time photographer. He had a full head of hair and a thick fumanchu mustache. He had two boys from a previous marriage, who were both around Tony and Matthew's age, Junior and Aaron. William agreed to meet Tony's mom; he saw Cynthia and stated, "She's hot," and asked her out.

It wasn't until the end of summer that Cynthia agreed to go out with William. After dating a few months, William asked Cynthia to marry him, but she wanted to wait until she knew him better. The one thing that stuck out in Cynthia's mind was that William mentioned, more than once, that he kept having dreams he was going to die by age of forty..

The beginning of 1991, Cynthia and William got along great and their relationship was wonderful.

William proposed and Cynthia said, "Yes."

In June, the same month they were to marry, Cynthia began moving her and her boys' things into William's duplex and put the rest in storage. She asked Simona to come and help her. Cynthia and Simona spent a lot of time apart, especially with both working full-time now. Simona noticed that William spent all day working on his white Lincoln instead of helping his soon-to-be wife, and she mentioned it to her mom.

"He only has two days off and wants to get done what he can, before going back to work. Besides, we can handle it, right?"

Simona couldn't help but be skeptical now and was just looking out for her mom. Since she knew her mom was getting remarried, Simona wanted to change her last name from *Gioia.* She didn't want to go back to her previous last name and she wasn't near getting married any time soon to look forward to a name change. Simona considered taking her maternal grandparents name, but because she respected them so much, she was afraid if she did something stupid it would shame their name and she did not want to disgrace it. Instead, she called her paternal grandma to ask about the last name of her dad's real dad. She was told the name was '*Ciarlo*' (pronounced, see-r-low) and she believed that to be a "cool" name, so she ran to a lawyer and made *Ciarlo* her legal last name.

June 29, 1991, William and Cynthia exchanged their vows. Cynthia's sister, Julie, was the matron of honor. Simona was one of her mom's bridesmaids, along with Julie's daughters, Diana and Candice (who was the flower girl). Tony and Junior were ushers and Matthew and Aaron were groomsmen along with William's best friend, Denny, and a cute little boy named Logan was the ring bearer.

At the reception, Cynthia's father was in his glory; his two brothers were there. Remo played the piano, Albert sang, while Sam whistled. Simona met up with a boy she used to play with when she was younger, Rick. He was tall, lanky, and had blonde hair and blue eyes; he resembled Colton. Since Simona and Rick were once close friends, she was hoping they might develop into something more. Rick gave Simona his phone number on a piece of paper. Simona was so excited that she ran to her friend, Michelle, who was helping the disc jockey, Wesley. Wes was a friend of Simona's and had a crush on her for a long time, but she didn't feel anything for him.

Simona did not have anything to put the paper in to, so she told Michelle to hold on to it for her. Wes believed that he still had a chance with Simona, and out of jealousy destroyed Rick's phone number.

At the end of the evening, Michelle told her Wesley threw it away; Simona was furious, "Why did you let him see it?"

"He asked to see it."

Simona had no way of knowing how to get a hold of Rick after that night. She accepted that she may never get married, so she married her job and lived only for herself.

A year after her mom's wedding, Simona bought a trailer for the sole purpose to build credit, sell it, and put the money down for a house; which she was able to do a couple of years later.

The guy next door, Patrick, was "stalking" her and nobody could help, not even the police. (This was with written and signed statements from other neighbors that saw Patrick enter Simona's trailer, but prior to their statements had assumed she gave him a key). Simona signed a statement on August 13, 1993, but it was regarded as only a precaution in case she ended up a casualty. The reason was because the stalking law could not protect her due to the fact they lived within the legislative limitations.

The trailers were only separated by a maximum of maybe 15 feet apart, the police nor the park couldn't do anything unless something happened to Simona and *proven* that Patrick did it. Simona worked midnights and already knowing Patrick had broke into her trailer, began memorizing things exactly where they were before heading off to work. One night in particular, she took note of the surroundings, petted her cat, Tori, and locked her door. As she turned around, she saw Patrick standing in front of his picture window staring at her. His lights were off and he was standing very close to the window, but Simona pretended that she didn't see him. She had to walk between her truck and Patrick's trailer to get to the driver's side door. Just as she unlocked the door, Patrick pounded on his window. Inside Simona's heart jumped, but she turned around, trying to show no fear, and saw him waving goodbye to her. She waved back, jumped in her truck, and took off.

That morning when Simona arrived back home, she knew something was not right. She looked around, but because she was frantic, her mind couldn't remember what was different. Suddenly, she looked down the hall and had seen her bedroom door was closed. She never closes her door, but she couldn't remember if this one time she had. She knew Patrick had been there, probably stealing more of her underwear, but this time closed the door, as though to taunt her. When she opened the bedroom door, Tori ran out! Simona's skin turned cold, she remembered petting Tori at the front door before she left. Since the cat couldn't close the door behind her, she knew Patrick came in again.

Simona called her mom and explained the fear she was living in, "He's probably tapped my phone too!"

Cynthia told William and he became upset. He had every intention to go and kick this guy's butt, but Patrick never came out of his trailer. William checked her trailer inside, out, and under for any signs of tapping or snares.

Simona explained to William that when she first moved in the trailer, Patrick was just a friendly neighbor, but then began getting obsessed and coming over uninvited. When she would tell him she was busy, Patrick would shock her with some information on her.

"Soon, he began telling me things about *me* and saying he was Satan. I was afraid. Then he told me how trailers are the easiest things to break into, and that I should be glad he's my friend, because I wouldn't want him as my enemy."

William assured her that Patrick was not Satan, and that he was probably standing outside listening to her talk to friends or even on the phone. "It's true about trailers and the fact you can hear right through the walls. I'll prove it to you."

William sent Simona outside and he talked to Cynthia in a normal tone of voice, Simona could hear every word.

"If he gives you any more problems–call me–then I'll show him who Satan really is." William said.

What Simona didn't know was that William was pretty close to being just that to her mom and her brothers; she was kept in the dark on his behavior.

When the wedding was over and the new family was all settled down; William began showing his true colors. Seems he didn't like "sharing" his place and became very demanding. He wanted a four-course dinner on the table when he came home and a wife who obeyed his every word. This was something that Cynthia was not used to; she worked just as long and hard as William did, and to come home and make a big dinner was tiring for her. (Besides, Chuck used to do the cooking).

Soon William started taking his hostility out on Tony and Matthew; but when his boys were there, he was a lot more tolerant. Even Cynthia felt that her daughter wasn't allowed over to visit; William didn't like company and wanted his own little family, not everyone else who was related.

Since Cynthia felt she "knew" William well enough to marry him, she didn't want anyone to know that she felt she made a mistake. She was keeping her hell to herself and she knew if she said anything, all the backlash she would hear, especially from her father who made a comment at the nuptials, "When is the fourth wedding?"

William was getting more violent and he didn't even drink. He was just a natural savage. He had already hit her twice on two separate occasions. Cynthia thought she could deal with his evil ways, but when it came to her boys, well that is when she put her foot down. William would have the boys put their hands behind their backs and kick them in the butt to where they would land on their head.

When Tony would see William scream at his mom, he tried to be the "man" and stick up for her. One day, William and Cynthia were arguing outside when Tony tried to break it up. William got angry at Tony for trying to interfere and pushed him to the ground. William then pulled Tony by his leg all the way up to the house, into the door, across the floor, and into the boy's bedroom. Tony's shirt had inched up around his neck which left cement scrapes and rug burns on his back and sides as he was struggling to break free. Tony was tough though, and tried to show his "new dad" no fear.

Cynthia was devastated, "*Nobody* will treat my boys like *that . . . especially you!*"

William's pride was on the line. He wasn't going down by a ten-year-old and some woman. So, he hit her! Not just once, but over and over, not with an open hand, but with a fist. This was the worst that Cynthia had ever endured in her life.

This time, she went to the police station and had them take pictures of what William had done, just in case he finished the job, but she couldn't bring herself to press charges. She went to her mom's to tell her what was going on and ask what she should do, even though she already knew the answer.

Mandy held her daughter and said, "I just don't know how much harder I can pray."

Mandy chaperoned her daughter back home and noticed that William was watching a dirty movie on the television. He must have seen Mandy, because the coward hid in the bathroom. He knew his mother-in-law knew what he did and would not come out. Mandy scolded him from the other side of the door and didn't mince her words.

About less than a week later, Simona came by her grandparents for a visit. She walked by the dining room table and seen pictures of her mother's beaten face and blackened eyes. Before Simona could utter a word, Mandy exclaimed, "You weren't supposed to see those!"

"What? Not supposed to see them? Why would this be kept from me?"

"You're mom didn't want to worry you."

"I'll kill him!"

"Now Simona, between you and your grandfather, I can't take any more *killing* talk."

Simona was named after her grandpa, Simon, whom she called "pappy." She was the clone of him: walked, talked, and thought like him. He was her hero and the only father figure she cared to acknowledge.

When Simona was at work, she called Tasha. Tasha was only Simona's roommate for a year and went back up north, but they talked once every few months.

"I've got a favor to ask . . . I know you have to know somebody who could take someone out."

"Are you talking about murder? Have you lost your mind Simona? You're talking on a phone . . . at work . . . Think!" Tasha scolded.

Tasha knew Simona was all "talk" and didn't mean what she was asking, besides she didn't know anyone who could or would do such a thing. Simona told her what William had been doing to her mom. Sure Tasha was upset, even mad; she loved Cynthia very much. Still, there was no way she would have Simona get in trouble by doing something stupid. She agreed to feeling angry, furthermore trying to talk Simona down.

"Look, I know you're upset . . . you feel helpless, it's understandable what you're going through right now, but there's nothing you can do about it. Take it easy. Things will work out, you'll see. Just promise me that you will stay cool, okay? Don't let yourself be swallowed up."

Simona took in a deep breath, she did feel better getting these heavy feelings off her chest, and promised Tasha she would *stay cool.*

After dealing with William during the first year of marriage, Cynthia knew she couldn't continue her life with him. She would take the boys for a drive and ride past an empty house off Rt. 45 on

Hanson and say, "That's where we are going to live . . . I don't know when, but we will."

Tony and Matthew had got on the football team at school, but since they were still scrawny, the coach never let them play. This upset Tony because he wanted to be big, not just to play football, but to stick up for his mom, and to really have the strength to knock William out. The coach didn't let Tony play in the games, which made him feel even more weak and useless.

One desperate night, Cynthia remembered seeing a gun on top of the refrigerator.

When she saw William was getting increasingly more enraged, she grabbed the gun, and pointed it at him, screaming, "I'm not afraid to use this!"

She called the police and told them to come quick, because she was going to kill him. She didn't know it was a BB gun; William sat there with a smirk.

When the police arrived, they told her it was a BB gun and there was nothing they could do; but she ensured them that William had a *real* gun. When they searched his Lincoln, the police found and retrieved his gun. William only received a warning.

William had a feeling Cynthia was looking for places to live, by the little ways she was acting, and he wasn't going to have her leave him. When Cynthia headed to the bank to withdraw some money to get that place for her and the boys, William had already emptied out their account. She went into her car and cried. Most of the money in there was hers and now she had to make a new plan. She went back home and struggled through the next several months trying to save some money to move out. She hid her money in the credit union at work.

When Cynthia had enough money, she ran to the landlord of the house on Hanson and put down the security deposit and first months rent. Now, it was just a matter of time to get the chance to escape. It was January 1993 and Cynthia couldn't celebrate until she knew her and her boys were safe.

As expected, William became mean again. Cynthia told the boys to grab a few things, (especially their pillows and blanket); she was taking them out of this house for good. In the car, the boys were so happy they kept laughing; you couldn't even wipe the smiles off their faces. Cynthia was overjoyed to see her boys smile and laugh again. Cynthia picked up a gallon of milk and some bread at a gas station and headed to their new house. It had a garage, so she parked inside and closed the door. There was no furniture in the house; they slept on the floor, but didn't mind. This was their new home; a place away from William.

Meanwhile, William drove around looking for them. He assumed they were hiding out at Sam and Mandy's, but they didn't even know where their daughter and grandsons were at this point. William searched everywhere, but had no luck.

The next day, Cynthia started her New Year by bringing three guys from work to help her move: Sammy, Dale, and Harry. William was home when they arrived. Sammy, a big, black man (who was the gentlest guy you'd ever meet) told William, "We have no problem with you; we're just here to move the lady out. Just don't get in our way."

William cried like a baby; he was not only scared of Sammy, but his pride was wounded. Unfortunately, Cynthia's belongings in storage were ruined. The storage leaked and her furniture was growing mold. She had to throw out a majority of her things.

Cynthia, Tony, and Matthew were happy and secure in their new place, and she filed for divorce. When the divorce was final, Cynthia tried to put those bad feelings toward William to the side. After all, hating him would only destroy her.

A year and a half later, Cynthia went to Knights of Columbus for an over 40s singles meet. When she arrived, William was there. She sat down next him and they talked for awhile. The gathering was at a lull and Cynthia suggested to William to pretend that they didn't know each other and get up and dance to help break the ice for everyone.

William refused and wouldn't dance with her; he was still bandaging his pride almost two years later.

Cynthia said, "Fine then, I'll just find someone else who wants to have fun."

She approached the table of a man named Dick and he was thrilled to dance with her. William got mad and left. After the evening was over, Dick asked Cynthia if he could see her again; she said "Yes."

On their dates, he took Cynthia to country line dances. He bought her cowboy boots, hat, buckle, and a shirt. She enjoyed the dates and dancing, but he was getting on her nerves. He talked in triplicates. His famous saying was, "good, good, good."

This drove Cynthia nuts; she thought that maybe she was getting too set in her ways. She knew that this relationship wasn't going to be long-term and had to figure out a way to end it. She finally had a good enough excuse, come Christmas.

Chapter 6

"For we walk by faith, not by sight . . ."
(II Corinthians 5:7)

Blown Away

On Christmas Eve 1994, Cynthia was at work when she saw the police at 3:00 A.M. and talking to her boss. She didn't know they were questioning her boss about her being at work all night. After work, she went out with her co-workers to the bar to celebrate Christmas. Cynthia was one who hardly frequented the bars anymore, but her friends asked her to come and that they would enjoy her company.

Meanwhile, Matthew had received a phone call around 4:00 A.M. and pretty much had a hard time going back to sleep; he waited for his mom to come home. When Cynthia drove into the garage and walked into the house, Matthew was waiting to talk to her.

"Mom, William's dead."

"What?" and she began making phone calls to find out what happened.

William was forty years old; his premonition had come to pass. William was at a bar earlier that evening and was spying on a couple of kids who he believed were selling drugs. Now, William was campaigning to become a Treasurer for the city and felt his clout in this town made him invincible. He circled around the block in his white Lincoln several times and ticking off the underage boys.

It is believed that one of them waited for him the next time he came around the block. As his car was stopped at the red light off Court Street, one of the boys approached William's vehicle and knocked on the window. William rolled down the window about two-thirds of the way, when suddenly the youngster pulled out a semi-automatic and shot William assassination style. William was found slumped over the steering wheel, with a bullet to his temple, a bullet in each lung, and a bullet in his heart. He died around 2:00 A.M. There were several casings of shells found through the car door, back window, and on the ground.

When Simona found out about the shooting, she was shocked and scared. She automatically called Tasha and asked if she had fulfilled her request (which now she felt she wish she hadn't asked). Tasha laughed at first, because she had no intention of doing it, but she quickly became shocked when she realized that William was dead by such a heinous act.

The police had a difficult time in finding the source, since William had so many enemies, and they weren't afraid to admit it. William had ticked off a lot of people and maybe those peculiar and particular feelings were just warning him to straighten up, but he never learned his lesson and he was never afraid to die.

After what William had put Cynthia through for years; his passing was a little too much for her to handle. She mourned and felt sorry for him that his life touched a lot of people in the wrong way. Cynthia and Simona went to the wake and it was quite eerie how he resembled Chuck in that casket. William's hair was cut and slicked back (a hair-style he would have never approved of) and his mustache was trimmed up to the corners of his mouth. William seemed to have a smirk on his face as if to welcome his death.

29 Palms Visit

It was years since Chuck had seen his sons and was missing them very much, so he called Cynthia to send them to California. She didn't want to, her fear was that he might *keep* them there. Then thought that they wouldn't *want* to come home or worse yet that he would be mean to them, but she knew she couldn't keep them from their father. She didn't want her sons to grow up and be angry at her for keeping them from him.

She told Chuck that she couldn't afford the airline tickets, but he assured her that he would send her money for them to come back home.

Once the boys arrived, Chuck greeted them with hugs and they were happy to see him. Unfortunately, Matthew's time there was full of pain, anger, and hurt. Tony was the favorite and Chuck's mother Myrtle made it obvious. Tony's name was *Charles* there and Matthew's was "*retard.*" Matthew couldn't understand the change they had toward *him.* He was confused, because the last time he was there they all had a nice time.

One day, Chuck took the boys to the beach. Cynthia had bought the boys new outfits and shoes for their vacation. Matthew loved his new pair of shoes and was very careful not to get sand in them. He even watched the way he walked so he wouldn't scuff them. Chuck noticed this and while Matthew was swimming decided to play a joke on him and filled Matthew's shoes with sand. When Matthew came back on to shore and ran toward his towel, he saw his shoes full of sand and his eyes filled up with tears. Matthew was so hurt that he ran away to cry in private. The feeling of being an outcast weighed on him and he began to fill up with anger; this anger would carry over in his adult life.

When Chuck took the boys back to the house, Matthew called his mom crying to come home. Cynthia was mad that Matthew's own dad and grandparents could treat him differently; as though he was no relation to them at all. She paid to get him home as soon as possible; Tony stayed a little longer.

Drugs

Tony and Matthew had made friends with some kids who knew a drug dealer. The first time Tony had encountered a joint; he didn't know what it was, how it worked, or what it did. He was scared, but to prove he wasn't chicken, Tony took a hit and at first felt nothing. He didn't know how to inhale, but with the smoke billowing around the room, Tony ended up getting a contact high. It made him feel light and laugh, (although he had no idea what he was laughing about), and his body felt tingling like a light tickle.

Soon this turned out to be a job for Tony. He notice how his friends would fork out money for a little bag of pot and he decided to begin selling it to buy things for himself, like music cd's, clothes, and just pocket money to eat and go to movies. Tony was like a conscious business man and he knew how to walk-the-walk and talk-the-talk.

Matthew, on the other hand, wasn't that conscious. He too, had his own friends and they began doing something more than just pot; they were dabbling into cocaine. Matthew felt alone in so many ways that he just did whatever it took to not feel isolated. He smoked pot, did coke, and began drinking alcohol. He was hanging around an older crowd and he liked that they thought he was funny. Matthew went over to a friend's house and his friend's mother made a move on him and is thought to have molested him. Matthew was in way over his head and was getting to the point that he no longer had control. His wanting to fit in became a *need.* He would have bouts of guilt overcome him that he started to get depressed and cry.

Since Tony came across as very responsible, he could convince his mom that he and Matthew were good kids while she was at work. She felt she could trust them alone. Many times while the boys had the house to themselves they would have their friends over to party. They would get drunk, do drugs, and after the fun was over, Tony would shoo them out of the house, clean it up, and go off to bed. Matthew would crash, before the party was even over, and therefore never helped Tony hide the evidence. When Cynthia came home she had no idea what had just taken place a few hours earlier.

Tony was missing his dad and wanted to spend a year in California. This was Cynthia's worst fear: her son leaving. Tony was fourteen-years-old and it was closing in on the last semester at school. He wanted to spend the summer in California and start his sophomore year of school in 29 Palms. Cynthia knew she couldn't stop him and fretted not seeing him during the age of 15. She was going to miss his birthday, Christmas, the summer, and the following summer. It seemed like a lifetime.

Simona felt bad Tony was leaving; she felt she was a bad sister not to be there for him more. She came over, sat with him in his bedroom, and talked to him and apologized for being absent in his life.

"I'm not leaving because of you; I just miss Dad."

Simona still felt it was because of her, because if she gave him the attention and love he needed and deserved, he wouldn't be missing his dad. Simona rode with her mom to take Tony to the airport; it was harder on them to see him leave more than Tony would ever know. Matthew didn't want to go to California; he wanted to stay at home. There was no way he was going to endure what he dealt with last time; he was still angry. It killed Matthew to see his brother leave; he felt like an only child. This only pushed him even more to embrace his friends tighter, but he wasn't as responsible as Tony and he wasn't as cautious.

One night, Matthew threw a party (just like he and Tony always had), but this time (as usual) he passed out and his friends were still there getting drunk and high. When he awoke, nobody was there, the door was wide open, and his mom's room was ransacked. They had stolen Cynthia's jewelry—her baby ring, her diamond and emerald ring, a watch with a gold face and beautician scissors as the hands (Simona had bought her for Christmas), and many other valuables. Cynthia came home to a mess and when she noticed what was gone; she sat down and cried as though her heart was ripped out. She didn't have much and those things meant a lot to her; she felt raped and full of anger that Matthew could have allowed such access into their home.

When Matthew was at school, Cynthia snooped around his room and in his drawers. She found a mirror and a razor blade; she knew what that meant and she couldn't believe that she had been so blind. Had Matthew resorted to snorting cocaine?

She couldn't handle it and called Simona, "You have to come here, and you have to talk to Matthew. I just can't do it . . . I'm at a loss . . . I don't know what to do."

Simona came over and inspected Matthew's room, too. She was also at a loss; she had been so out of touch with her brothers that she didn't know where to begin.

If she scolded Matthew; she figured he'd just laugh in her face as if to say, "You're going to be a big sister, *now?*" Or if she tried to talk to him; would he even listen?

Finally, she just swallowed her fear and drove to his school. She went into the office to have someone page him out of class. When Matthew walked in the office and seen his sister waiting for him, he was speechless and his mouth agape.

Simona was going to tell him, "This is it, you're caught; it's over." But instead she lovingly said, "Mom called me and I went through your room. Matt, what are you doing?"

Matthew's head went down. He didn't argue with his sister, he knew what she was talking about, and he knew what they had found. Still, as teenagers do, Matthew made it sound more innocent than it was and promised that it was a one-time thing and would never happen again. Crossing his fingers to ease his guilt, he didn't know if he could hold to that promise.

Matthew hardly left the house and would sit on the porch and watch the traffic go by. He kept seeing a guy walk by everyday, and one day while Matthew sat on the front porch, the man walk by again, and this time said, "Wuz Up?"

Matthew found out the guy's name was Stan and was known as *Wildman.* He was from Alabama and had a big afro for a southern white guy and an unkempt beard. His speech was broken, but he was very respectable to the ladies (as he called them).

Matthew had a great idea to match him up with his mom, and when Cynthia took one look at him, screamed, "NO WAY!"

Stan was a charmer and soon his looks didn't matter to those who really got to know him; soon Cynthia was under his spell. Cynthia knew Stan drank, but he wasn't a drunk like Chuck; Stan was still just Stan. It didn't take long for Cynthia to see Stan for who he was, sure she felt sorry for him and they ended up to be good friends, but their romantic relationship was very short-lived. What Cynthia didn't know was that Stan was into rock cocaine, but Matthew knew.

When Tony left for California, he ended up getting into some trouble of his own.

Chuck was still into his old, bad habits and Tony was right along with him. It was the same as being home and partying, but this time with adults. Since Tony was planning on staying there for a year; he made sure he had a savings account set up, so he could take care of himself. He didn't realize the trust he put in his dad was going to come back and bite him. Chuck had remarried and this woman was just as bad as he was–when Tony went to pull some money out of his account it was all gone. He believed she had stolen from him. He was upset, but knew he should have known better. He chalked it up that he learned a lesson . . . to trust no one, not even family, when it came to money.

Matthew did go visit Tony for a week and while he was there, Chuck and his new wife wanted to get "family" pictures taken; Chuck, his wife, her kids, Tony and Matthew headed off for the portrait studio. Matthew couldn't wait to come back home. He just felt he didn't belong and didn't care if he was a mama's boy; he missed his mom.

Once school started, Tony wanted to do well in his new classes. Unfortunately, there was so much partying at his dad's that there was no time for him to study. The party life had caught up with them and soon the police came to raid the house. Tony had a marijuana pipe down his pants. An officer searched him and found the pipe; laying it right beside Tony. Tony liked this pipe; it was different than any other pipe he had seen and decided to hide it somewhere next to him hoping the cops would forget about it.

About twenty minutes later, the officer happened to search around Tony again and found the hidden pipe. Tony was trying to be cool and got a little over confident in the confrontation. Chuck lowered and shook his head; he feared Tony was going to be hauled off to jail. Instead, the officer wrote Tony out a ticket for possession of drug paraphernalia. He was issued a court date and sent to the neighbors that night. Tony moved in with his grandma Myrtle and knew he had to call his mom and explain what happened.

Cynthia was not surprised, yet upset that Chuck hadn't even begun to grow up after all this time, "Give me the phone number where you are staying and the address, so I can send you money to come home. I'll call you with the time of the flight you will be taking."

Tony was willing and ready to come back home; Cynthia was happy to have her son *willing* to come home.

When Tony got back, he and Matthew were closer than ever. Tony had gone through his "own time" and really realized he missed his little brother. He felt bad how he treated him the last six years and brought Matthew into his circle of friends. Sadly, now, Tony's friends weren't much better than Matthew's. Instead of being separate, the brothers now kept up on parties, drinking, and drugs together. Since Tony was home, he was able to be more discrete in what they were doing, without having Mom know; Cynthia trusted Tony, but Tony conformed to a good façade.

Meanwhile Stan just couldn't stay away from Cynthia; he loved her and in a way she was the one he couldn't have. He was always there for her though: he helped her when she needed it, fixed things for her, and gave her money to help her from going under. With two teenage boys in the house, they ate like men and grew out of their clothes faster than Cynthia could buy them. Stan wanted to act like a "dad" and in his way helped support them. The sad thing, Stan was just as much of a kid as they were, and being a single "wild" man, he tended to pass on the wrong kind of morals and values.

One night in June, 1996, Stan and Tony got into an argument. Stan slapped Tony in the face. Tony was not going to cower, especially to Stan. Tony called 911.

When the police arrived, Tony wanted him arrested for abuse; so Stan snitched Tony out about the little baggies of pot he had stashed away. An officer handcuffed both Stan and Tony and took them to jail. This was the first time Tony had been arrested for drugs. He was put on probation for one year.

Cynthia's landlord didn't want a bad reputation and told her that she would have to leave the property if the boys continued their bad behavior. Cynthia was devastated; after dealing with Matthew's parties and his thieving friends, now Tony ended up arrested. Being Tony was in trouble with the law; the family would now have to move out. How could her boys do this to her? How could they do this to themselves?

She screamed and scolded, but the boys were so independent that they felt powerful over their mother by thinking, 'What is she going to do about it?'

Cynthia questioned, "Why ruin your lives like this? Do you want to end up like your dad?"

Both boys just patronized their mother and made their pie-crust promises that they wouldn't do anything like this again. What they were *really* thinking was that they were promising to never getting *caught* like this again. Tony kept good on his probation; he didn't smoke any pot for the whole year.

Tony's Love

September, Tony registered back into BBCHS and met a girl, Shannan, who was also new to the school; she transferred from Herscher High School. When the class called for students to team up, Tony and Shannan were partners and they hit it off. Shannan was seeing someone else at the time, but Tony was persistent and kept asking her out. When Shannan felt the guy she was recently seeing wasn't measuring up to what she'd like in their relationship, she ended it. Once word got out that Shannan was available it seemed guys were making their move. Tony asked her to escort him to Homecoming in October and she had already had other offers. She was going to make sure Tony was serious, because she wasn't going to waste her time at a formal dance and not have benefiting memories to carry with her.

"Does this mean we're dating?" she asked.

Tony replied, "Yes, if that's alright with you."

Tony was happy to have a girlfriend and he even got hired for his first job—working in the produce isle at Kmart. There was a reason for that job, and that was to get a car to take Shannan out.

Chapter 7

"Let not your heart be troubled . . . believe in God . . ."
(St. John 14:1)

Inglesh Avenue

Cynthia was driving to her mom's to visit. When she turned the corner, she noticed a *For Sale* sign in a yard a half-block from her parent's house. She knew the people moving, because she used to play with their boys in that house when she was young. She felt a sense of nostalgia and felt it would be wonderful to live again in her old neighborhood where she grew up. She told her mom and dad that she was going to buy it.

Right away, Sam was like, "No, you can't afford it. Just forget about it, Cynt."

"Why? This way I can be close when you get old and take care of you." Cynthia believed she was meant to be there, close to her parents, and she wasn't taking "no" for an answer. She applied for a loan and she was accepted; she now had a home again. It was a nice, big corner house with a basement and an attached garage. It had three bedrooms, a bathroom, front room, family room with a fireplace, and a sun room. The basement also looked like it could be an apartment with a bedroom and bathroom. The doors at the top of the stairs led in to the kitchen or out into the sunroom which led to the outside. Tony made sure he took the basement for himself and Matthew took the bedroom right across from his mom's room.

The family moved their stuff in October of 1996 and soon realized how much was really wrong with their new home.

What Cynthia didn't expect was the people moved out for a reason, they wanted a *better* house. Since Cynthia knew the sellers, she trusted them, but she was taken. The sellers didn't warn her of any faultiness. It was infested with termites and the basement had leaks around the perimeter of the walls. The family room was an add-on and was obviously never inspected by code, because it was too close to the next door neighbors. The room was not insulated; it was always cold and hard to keep it warm. The fireplace had to constantly burn. The sunroom was an add-on too. It was added from the house to the garage; the job was so poorly done that the roof leaked every time it rained or snow would melt.

Tony's Situations

After Tony's one year probation was over, he got together with a couple of his friends and went out to the state park to celebrate. Tony was rolling a joint when the conservation police rode up on his bike. Tony's friends warned him a cop was coming, so he swatted the pot he was rolling onto the ground.

When the officer approached, Tony looked at him like he was doing nothing wrong.

The officer ordered Tony, "Take your weed out of your left pocket."

He knew where Tony had the pot (among other drug paraphernalia), because he had been watching them through binoculars. So, Tony reached in his pocket, pulled out the marijuana, and threw it out into the water. This made the officer mad at Tony, so he threw him up against the railing of the handicap spot by where they were parked. (Not thinking, Tony forgot to grab his pipe and pack of papers in the other pocket, so the officer ended up having something to bust him with after all). He cuffed Tony and was going to take him to jail, but instead wrote him a ticket. Since Tony had $100 in his pocket it was like posting bail for himself. Tony shook his head in agreement to what he was feeling; it was time to grow up. That was the last time Tony smoked pot—June 1998.

Meanwhile, Tony was seeing the affects the drugs were having on his friends. He was so blinded by the money and had convinced himself if he sold the drugs to his friends that they wouldn't get a bad batch that could kill them. Regardless, Tony's friends were addicted and began stealing, pawning, and even going to lengths to do favors for Tony, like repairing his car, just to score to get high. Tony had been expanding his goods from pot to cocaine to acid, and whatever else he could come across to make more money, but now he was feeling bad. His guilt was constricting him as he watched his friends squirm for another fix. He watched as they went to jail for stealing, just to get money for him, but he woke up. He knew he had to grow up, he quit doing drugs, and now he was going to help his friends. He painfully held back tears, thinking what he had been doing to them for so long that he wanted to wake them up, too.

He tried talking to them about quitting, "It's time to grow up. I'm not . . . I can't . . . give in to your habit anymore."

As hard as he tried, his friends liked the way the drugs made them feel. When Tony gave up selling, they still managed a way to get what they wanted through someone else.

As for the charges against Tony, they were dropped because the officer didn't show up for court. Tony had a new outlook and was becoming a responsible young man. In September, he was hired on at a steel plant and is still a dedicated worker.

Matthew's Love

Matthew was being pried on by his best friend's girl. Her name was Alayna and she would flirt with Matthew behind her boyfriend Todd's back. Todd would hug her in the hallway at school and she would look at Matthew and lick her lips at him. Best friend or not, a girl acts like she's interested in you, all common sense is lost and hormones start to fly. The flirting would continue when Alayna would accompany Todd to Matthew's house. She lost her virginity to Todd in Matthew's room; when it was Matthew she was really thinking about. She really wanted Matthew and finally broke it off with Todd. Todd was broke up losing Alayna, but Matthew was *still* his friend.

Matthew and Alayna's memories began the summer of 1997 when their first date was at the Bourbonnais Friendship Festival. They would talk about how much they had in common and how they felt they were soul-mates; Alayna was taken by Matthew and was so happy that they were finally together.

Alayna loved the fact Matthew was funny as well as caring. They would go to Blockbuster to rent videos and she observed how Matthew approached a little handicap boy. Matthew bent down, talked to him, and played a game with him while the boy's mother looked for a movie. Matthew never treated him like he was different, because in Matthew's mind that little boy was just like him. Matthew knew what it felt like to be made fun of, picked on, and treated differently, and he just wanted to let the boy know how it felt to be included.

Boys and Sex

By Christmas, Tony and Matthew invited both their girlfriends, Shannan and Alayna for the family holiday festivities. Christmas Eve was spent over at Julie's house. Julie had divorced her daughters' father in October 1996 and was now seeing a chiropractor named David. He was a soft-spoken man, who had a daughter between the ages of both Julie's girls. This was an opportunity for the family to really spend time with David and get to know him.

Everyone had dinner over Christmas music with the fireplace burning and opened gifts. The family even bought Shannan and Alayna Christmas gifts to let them know they were part of the family, too.

It *seemed* Shannan and Alayna weren't too close to their family, because they spent all the holidays with their boyfriends. It was so bad between Shannan and her mom that Shannan ended up moving in with Tony down the basement. The only good thing about

Shannan moving in was that Tony and Matthew's friends didn't come over quite as often; and when they did, they left by curfew.

Yet, this living situation did not set well with Mandy, who believed they were too young to be "shacking up" and doing "God-knows-what" when they're both barely out of high school and not even married. Mandy loved her grandson and didn't want him to shame himself, or the family, and insisted her daughter start setting some boundaries.

Cynthia had been going back to church on a regular basis and knew her mother was right. She had started to really feel convicted about the paths she walked and didn't want her boys to grow up with the same regret.

By the time Tony graduated high school, Cynthia told him and Shannan that as long as they were holding down a job, they should start looking for a place of their own.

"If you love each other; get married, but you can't live here if you're living in sin."

Tony and Shannan were upset, but agreed to find a place to call "home" and moved out.

Matthew's Circumstances

When the unwed couple moved out on their own, Matthew was still wanting to party. He asked friends to come over and they would go into the basement. Cynthia's work schedule changed from 9:00 A.M. to 5:30 P.M. She hoped the new shift would help her have a better control of her boys and limit their parties; she was mistaken. Unfortunately, Matthew hadn't learned his lesson from other times before; since Tony wasn't there anymore, the parties would get out of control. Music would be blaring to the sounds of The Doors, Phish, and Pink Floyd. Cigarette smoke would be billowing along with a few who were smoking pot; beer cans and beer bottles were hid under chairs and behind doors.

Cynthia would go downstairs and yell at Matthew to turn down the stereo. When it got past curfew, she would go back and yell at the friends to get out. To her surprise, they didn't budge, and might as well have told her to *make* them leave. She was appalled by the crude behavior and had a wave of fear come over her. She remembered these boys (and girls) growing up, and to see them disrespect her, it made her wonder what happened to get them to this point. She felt her work had kept her away from being able to raise her boys' right. Then, she became angry at Chuck for ruining their family, because if he were here they would not have spun out of control. She was ticked off that time passed so quickly. She always thought she would be able to fix the problems when the warning signs presented themselves, but she just didn't have the tools. Now, she feared her son's friends. Her mind was running away with her: Would they come after her for trying to throw them out? Would they beat her or try to kill her? It wasn't impossible; she read about teenagers killing their parents or grandparents over things like this. She ran to her room and shut the door. She began to pray and started crying. She was a prisoner in her own home and she had to figure out a way to restore the situation.

The next morning, she called her mother and told her what was going on and Mandy replied, "Call the police! It's that simple."

Cynthia knew it went beyond just calling the police, and of course, she didn't want Matthew getting in trouble with the law again; she just wanted the kids to listen to her.

Cynthia confronted Matthew about it, "I don't like having to feel fearful in my own house. When I tell them to leave; I want them to leave right then and there!"

Alayna was proving herself to be good for Matthew, because their relationship kind of put a stop to the parties. Alayna didn't like Matthew getting together with his friends to drink. It may have helped Cynthia had voiced her concerns of Matthew's partying in passing to Alayna. Alayna ended up becoming a strong figure in Matthew's life.

Matthew had to tell his mom some news and feared the outcome; Alayna was pregnant. Cynthia was not surprised, yet being a mother, she was saddened that he and Alayna were so careless; after all, they weren't even out of high school. Mandy was equally upset;

here she went on and on about Tony and Shannan, because they were living together, that she didn't even think about Matthew and Alayna.

Matthew had plans to go into the Air Force (so had Alayna) once they graduated, but now that was put on hold. Matthew got a job at Burger King. He liked the fact he made some cool friends. He really liked making money and saved up to buy a car.

After a few weeks of announcing the news, Matthew had to announce that Alayna had miscarried. Matthew was devastated. Going through that kind of pain, he did not want any more children (or at least until he was much older). Alayna, on the other hand, had already been so excited about the birth of a child that she told Matthew, "Let's try again." Matthew was afraid and told her that they should wait until they were married. Alayna was very persistent and she ended up pregnant again a few months later.

Stan

Stan still kept in contact with the boys and found out Tony had moved out. So, he called and asked Cynthia if he could rent out the basement. He promised Cynthia he'd pay rent for his space and then some. Cynthia caved in and told Stan the littlest screw up he would be kicked out. She had an ulterior motive - she knew Stan would have his things stored in the basement and that he would have to sleep at night; therefore, Matthew would be unable to have his friends down there to party.

Stan was a welder and worked daily with getting his hands dirty. He could wash all he wanted, but his skin was charred and filthy looking. When Stan moved in and took over the basement, the neighbors didn't like the way he looked with his afro hair, dirty overalls, unkempt beard, and his black tarnished pickup truck. They seemed to enjoy gossiping, while watching him drink his beer and smoking outside. Soon, they let their imagination run, until they became so paranoid that they began calling the police. Now, there wasn't anything the cops could do to arrest a man for drinking a beer in the driveway, but the neighbors didn't like being told they were wrong. They began elaborating that the guy was selling drugs and guns out of the house - which wasn't true. They didn't have a clue how their false accusations were about to destroy an innocent family.

Odd as it was, Stan was helping in some situations; he helped Matthew to get a better job and told him to " . . . cool it with the party life, because you don't want to end up like me."

Matthew knew he had to pick up some responsibilities; he had a child on the way and he wanted to be a good dad. Matthew even quit doing drugs and just had a beer once in a while, but unfortunately, his attempt to be good would have a reverse outcome.

Jett

A very pregnant Alayna had got into an accident; she rear-ended an elderly couple. During the impact, she hit her head. She was brought into the emergency room and fully examined. Thankfully, she and the unborn baby were fine.

On March 13, 1999, Matthew and Alayna became the parents of a baby boy, Jett. Matthew borrowed Simona's video camera to record Alayna in labor, but the closer the contractions, the closer she was about to knock the camera out of his hands.

Alayna had to be induced, because she was swollen and her body was suffering from toxicity. When Jett was born, he came out chalky and Alayna was freaking out, but Jett was healthy and very alert. Matthew was proud and told Alayna, "I want to be the best dad I can be," meaning it with all his heart and falling in love with Alayna all over again.

Six days after Jett's birth, Alayna suffered a seizure. Everyone grew concerned. Was it from hitting her head during the accident, the toxicity, or from her being induced?

Her doctor prescribed her some medication and Alayna didn't have anymore seizures. Eventually, she just weaned herself off the pills.

During this time, Matthew was working at the steel plant and putting in so many hours; he would come home and fall asleep.

Matthew was finally in the process of growing up and he was proud of himself. He bought a beautiful, white Cougar and loved that car. He would drive it just to drive it with no destination in mind. On the weekends, he was off and would hang out with a friend or two when he wasn't over at Alayna's visiting his son.

The Sign of a Bad Change

Meanwhile, the police wanted the neighbors to basically *shut up*, so they sent a kid named Dirk over, who was an informant for them. They wanted him to try and make a "sale" to show their concern for the neighborhood. Stan and Cynthia were at work; Matthew was the only one home. Dirk went to see Matthew (the two knew each other in acquaintance). Matthew was clueless and never picked up what was going on. Dirk asked Matthew for some cocaine, but Matthew told him he no longer did drugs. A few minutes later, Dirk asked for an aspirin and Matthew gave him two; then Dirk handed Matthew $20.00. Matthew spent a half-hour with him, talking about Jett, and figured Dirk was just being nice by offering to pay him for the aspirins. Plus, Matthew wasn't going to turn down money; he could use it for gas.

After Dirk left, he took the aspirins and ground them up, put them in a baggie to look like cocaine, and gave it to his parole officer.

That night, Stan was in bed asleep, Cynthia had just got home from church and was watching television in the family room, and Matthew was in his room with a friend listening to music. The police and D.E.A. arrived and probably knocked on the front door, but since Matthew couldn't hear over the stereo and Cynthia didn't hear over the T.V. in the other room, the cops busted down the door. Matthew and Cynthia heard a boom, but had no idea what it was until officers were spreading themselves throughout the house like cockroaches. They pulled Matthew and his friend out of the bedroom and made them go into the family room where Cynthia was sitting in her pajamas. She almost had a heart attack when the police approached her and demanded she "stay on the couch and don't move."

They made their way to every square inch of the house and Cynthia looked over at Matthew and asked, "What is going on?"

Matthew was speechless, he had no idea. He had been good. Soon, there came Stan being pulled up the stairs, barely awake and in his boxers, and was also made to sit on the couch with the rest of them in the family room. The D.E.A. ransacked the basement, pulled down pieces of ceiling, and ripped down doors. Cynthia began to cry. Why was this happening; things were finally quiet and now this? Matthew knew they were looking for drugs and wanted his mom to stop crying, so he called to the officer "watching" them and asked if he could give them what they were looking for. The officer followed Matthew into the bedroom and Matthew pulled out a one-hitter pipe that was sitting in his closet, from months ago, when he stopped smoking pot. The officer took the pipe and put hand cuffs on Matthew while reading him his rights. There was barely enough resin in that pipe to scrape under a baby fingernail, but the cops were patting themselves on the back for doing their job.

Another officer found Stan's gun among his things. Stan never used it, he just brought it with him from Alabama, but since it was registered and concealed, they couldn't arrest him, but they did tell him that he had to move out. After it got quiet, Cynthia sat and cried. What possibly gave them the power to come in and destroy her home? How could the police make someone move out if they weren't doing anything wrong? She couldn't even lock the doors, because they had broken them and her basement looked like a tornado crashed through it. She began having pains down her arm and in her chest, she felt like her body was on fire, and her skin crawled like bugs were tearing through it. She prayed and prayed all night and tried to think of a way to bail Matthew out. She knew the police had no right to arrest him; there was no pot in the pipe, it had been smoked, and the officers could tell it was old. Everyone thought that the reason Matthew was arrested was because of the one-hitter; it was considered drug paraphernalia. Matthew thought, "If the one-hitter is considered such an offense, why do they sell them at the record store across the street?"

Matthew felt all the good he was doing was all for nothing and he began to rebel harder than ever. He began to hate the police; after all, they tore up his home, made Stan move out, and hurt his mother by putting up a huge sign in the front yard, telling the whole town that his home was a drug house. What a black mark on the whole family! How embarrassing! The whole family was devastated! Cynthia wanted to crawl in a hole and die. Her parents were sick and outraged that the community they lived in could turn and play judge and jury, by placing a metal sign in the front lawn, as if they were conducting a crucifixion. Then the newspaper took a picture of it and put it on the front page for everyone to see, even those extended from the city limits. When Matthew went out to read the sign; he saw the neighbors watching him. The sign stated that if it were taken down, by someone other than authorities, that they would be persecuted. The neighbors were eagerly waiting to call the police, if he merely touched the monumental expression of their concern for their neighborhood.

The newspaper never let it die! The police raided another house, the same night as they raided Cynthia's; the people in that house were caught in the middle of smoking a joint when the cops came through the door. The newspaper got the two homes mixed up and printed that the woman of the house was smoking pot when the D.E.A. arrived. Well, that woman was not Cynthia, but the journal put Cynthia's address.

The anger that poured over the whole family was indigestible. Along with Cynthia, her dad, Sam was so stressed that it began to affect his health. He was the type of guy who would get mad if you talked louder than a whisper outside, so that the neighbors didn't hear. Even if voices escalated in the house, he felt the neighbors could hear through the walls and windows, and would reprimand them with a low-key "shut up."

To now consciously know that everybody knows his family's business, and to know it was extremely exaggerated in the papers, was literally making him ill. He couldn't handle what he thought people might be saying about him or his family. It was a shame to his name and the humiliation was taking a toll physically on his body.

Sam told Simona what happened and she was outraged. She came by to see the sign in the front yard. All this drama was eating her up inside, too, as she heard people at work discussing the portrayal of her family as "drug addicts," "low-life," and "scum."

She knew she had to come to their defense and tried explaining to them what really was going on, but people will believe what they want and just snickered behind her back. She hated the town she lived in and wanted to move away. Mandy was equally upset, but she leaned on the Lord and tried explaining to Simona and Cynthia that their faith was just being tested. Cynthia agreed and knew she had to be steadfast and trust in God, but Simona hadn't been in church for years and she didn't agree. Simona's mind was reeling on how to take control of the situation, and both her mother and grandmother told her, "By Praying."

Simona's indignation was too great for her to hear such simple words.

That sign stayed up on that corner lot for five whole days and even had the street light to keep it visible for five whole nights.

Matthew was never charged, his name was put in the newspaper though, but he couldn't be charged in court. The police knew they overreacted, because when they got the results from the baggie, it was discovered that it was not cocaine, but aspirins. Cynthia thought that she had a solid law suit against the police, D.E.A., the city of Kankakee, and the Mayor who was conducting such action to be brought upon people without getting the facts.

"What happened to innocent until proven guilty?" Cynthia cried and she reached a state of depression that everyone was afraid she was going to take her own life.

Before Cynthia had a chance to go up against and fight the system, the Mayor died of a heart attack. Prior to the death of the Mayor, political power had gone to his head and done more harm than good. He was at his height of glory by putting "slum lord" signs in front of condemned apartments and houses, and put up signs in neighborhood parks to be used *only* by those residents; it was like he was playing a game of *war.* Now, to falsely mark a family by placing a sign in their yard as a drug house had turned a boy who was finally getting his life together to throw it all away. Matthew was angry and figured that it didn't matter if he was good or not, so he quit his job and went out on drinking binges. He even fought with Alayna and accused her that Jett was not his child, saying, "He doesn't even look like me!" Matthew became depressed and violent; Cynthia didn't know how to control him.

One night, Cynthia called up Alayna and thought maybe she could come over and talk some sense into him. When Alayna arrived, Matthew was so drunk and unruly that he began screaming, as though demons were ripping his soul. He put his fist through his bedroom door and tore it off the hinges. Alayna came into Matthew's bedroom to try and calm him down, but he wanted nothing to do with her. He was so convinced she was cheating, that Jett was someone else's child, he warned her, "Get out of my face! You don't want me to lose it on you!"

As Matthew ran out of the bedroom, through the front room and into the kitchen, Cynthia was standing by the sliding glass doors trying to stop him from leaving. Matthew felt trapped and ran back to his bedroom. This time, Cynthia was right behind him and pushed him on the bed (breaking her little finger on her right hand). She jumped on her son, trying to hold him down; she placed her hand on his head to rebuke out demons.

Matthew knew what she was doing and sarcastically screamed, "I am the Devil!"

He took all the strength he had, pushed both women away from him, ran back to the kitchen, and fled out the sunroom door. During which Cynthia grabbed the phone to call the police on her own son, for his own safety.

The police didn't arrest Matthew that night, he hid from them; when he came home he apologized to his mom and cried. He was just so hurt by all that had happened, how nobody believed in him, and how he blamed himself for what he was doing to the family. He was tender-hearted, cared deeply, kind to strangers, and respectful of his elders. He couldn't understand why bad things always happened to him and why the cops hated him so much. He knew of other kids who were worse than him, but he knew he could be better, too. He just wanted to stop hurting. He wanted to be happy, he wanted to be good, but every time he tried to start another day, the memories of how every one just seemed to *pick* on him would fill his mind and break his heart that he would drink to drown them.

Chapter 8

" . . . the Father of mercies, and the God of all comfort . . ."
(II Corinthians 1:3)

The Last Grandchild

Julie married David in May 1998. David, besides being a chiropractor, was also great when it came to construction. He built and added-on two more bedrooms to the house they lived in so each girl could have her own bedroom, he built a deck from their backdoor to the swimming pool, and he built a two-story shed so Julie could do her pottery.

Julie and David announced a baby was on the way. Cynthia was finished with bearing children and this would be Julie's last child as well, and the last of the grandchildren. When Julie became pregnant it was a surprise—a very welcome one, but it came with a toll. The effect of being pregnant at her age, Julie's resistance went down. The cells not willing to make the necessary change in her body had caused cancer to set in her thyroid. It was very stressful for the family, because Mandy's niece developed breast cancer after she gave birth, which spread, and she passed away. The thought of this baby growing up without a mother became a concern among everyone.

August 17, 2000, Julie gave birth to her first son, Jonathan. He was 10 pounds. Julie's doctor wanted her to get treatments started as soon as she gave birth. Julie began her treatments and did them faithfully; thank God, the cancer became controllable.

A Large Loss

One day, Sam went to see his friends at the junk yard. No one knows what exactly happened, but Sam got lost on his way home. He was too proud to ask for directions or to call home for help; the later it became, the more his wife paced the floor.

When Sam finally arrived home, Mandy (out of relief he was back) screamed, "Where were you?"

After Sam explained, Mandy decided to take away his keys which really upset him; this was taking away a man's independence. The fear that he could have really became lost or endangering someone else was overwhelming. For Sam, that was tough to swallow.

Soon his body wasn't allowing him go anywhere. Even if the family was getting together for dinner at Julie's, Sam refused to leave. He never let his wife and kids know that he was *that* sick. He hated doctors and blamed them for killing off his family (Sam was the last one left out of his father, mother, two sisters, and three brothers). He made the excuse that someone had to be home with the dog, their Bichon Frise, Benjamin.

In October and November, Sam had been in and out of the hospital. He had lost a vast amount of weight, his feet were always swollen, and he couldn't stay out of the bathroom. Sam was a bad patient because he had no patience.

One occurrence, the hospital had him hooked up to an I.V. to replenish his fluids and he had to use the restroom. The nurse, nor the assistants, answered his call light. After it was on for awhile, Sam became upset, pulled the I.V. out of his arm, and went to the bathroom by himself. His blood squirted everywhere from the needle being pulled out and there was a trail from the bed to the bathroom. When the nursing assistant came in the room to turn off the call-light, she began to panic and sent housekeeping in to clean up the mess. What Sam did, made its way around the *whole* hospital.

The hospital wasn't much of a wake-up call for Sam's family. They were unaware of the seriousness of his condition; except Simona was leery. She would call to show him she cared or go see him to keep him company - if just to listen to him rant, rave, or complain. Simona was afraid of losing her grandfather, and it was so disturbing that she would have nightmares of him dying. She was the closest of all the grandchildren, since she lived with her grandparents for almost five years. Plus spending the night on the weekends and visiting; their love was her *home.*

Sam was turning a gray color and complained more than usual. He was going through "shell-shock" from his war days (a condition that hadn't bothered him for over forty-five years), and he was forgetting little things caused by dementia. The family figured he was either trying to get attention or that age was catching up with him; nobody wanted to come to the realization that the man was actually really sick. The last few years of his life, Sam was irritable with himself and his surroundings that he would often lash out at his wife. Mandy had a hard time dealing with the way Sam had changed—putting up with his sarcastic remarks, put-downs, and cussing at her. Sam's behavior was hurtful to Mandy - not only emotionally and mentally, but being a Christian, spiritually as well.

After Sam was released from the hospital in the beginning of November, he still was not feeling well. He noticed how Mandy waited on him. His eyes looked at her, not physically, but through his heart and told her in the most sweetest and sincere way, "You are a good woman."

That was his way of apologizing for the way he had been acting toward her, and sure enough those few words stripped Mandy of all the hurt and anger she was harboring over Sam's actions. Sam knew how special he was to have Mandy for a wife, and knew he hadn't treated her in the best way.

On November 13, Simona came by for dinner. She and Sam sat at the table, while Mandy was preparing the food. Sam looked at her and in a plea, replied "I can't die."

By the look on Sam's face, Simona couldn't tell if he was asking her or telling her. It was now evident he was in pain, real pain, pain that he hid shown through his eyes, and she felt powerless. Was she his link on this earth? Was he asking permission or how to go?

After that comment, Mandy put the food on the table, prayed over the meal, and fixed Sam's plate, but Simona sat speechless and afraid. She couldn't bring herself to look back at him; he was a picture of dread and she couldn't bear the thought of thinking the inevitable.

Sam looked at the food and stated, "Here I go again" and headed back off to the bathroom. He stayed in there the whole dinner, and as Simona went to leave, she yelled to him "goodbye," but either he didn't hear her or he couldn't respond.

Those words "I can't die" sat with her the rest of the night; they were talking to her.

In the meantime, Mandy sat on the couch to watch some television, when Sam called to her. He had lost his bowels as though they had exploded. The toilet, floor, and walls were covered with feces. Mandy was horrified; the sight was unimaginable and she just couldn't figure out how it could possibly end up everywhere. She calmly gave him a towel to clean up around him, as he sat on the toilet, and she began to clean up the rest. She then ran a bath and helped clean up her husband, but she had no idea what was happening. He sat on his knees in the tub, and cried out as though the touch of the water was painful. Mandy wrapped him in a towel and brought him in the back bedroom to put him in bed, but even the bed was painful. He popped right up, bent over, and crouched down on to the floor and got into a fetal position. Mandy felt helpless and called Cynthia and an ambulance.

When Cynthia came down, the paramedics arrived; they helped put Sam on a gurney. Cynthia and Mandy tried to help him be relaxed, because lying flat was an excruciating position for Sam. Sam kept repeating, "I'm dying; I'm dying."

Cynthia had a feeling that her dad knew something was serious, because she saw the fear in his eyes as though he was searching for solace. She knelt down beside him, tried to comfort him, and said, "Dad, if you think you're dying, you need to ask Jesus for forgiveness and believe that He is your Savior."

Sam nodded his head, yes, and began moving his mouth, saying his prayer.

Mandy patted his hand and said, "Its okay, Dad, you're going to be fine."

Still, both Cynthia and Mandy weren't aware that Sam's body was shutting down; they thought once he went to the hospital, he would get better. So, Cynthia headed back home. Mandy grabbed a book to read (thinking that she would be sitting in the waiting room) and didn't ride in the ambulance. Instead Mandy drove her car thinking that she'd be bringing Sam back home.

Once Mandy arrived to the emergency room, she asked what room her husband was in, so she could continue to help him be calm, since he hated the hospital so much. As she proceeded to his side, she had no idea what she was about to encounter. Sam was already in a coma and was almost gone from this world. Mandy looked upon him as he lay there on the bed, still—his mouth open, and his eyes slit. She felt a wave of grief wash over her and realized that she was losing her husband that night. She was ashamed of herself for not getting in the ambulance with him. She couldn't understand what happened between home and the hospital. The last words she heard him utter was "I'm dying."

She went to call Cynthia, but just as she was about to walk out of the room, her daughter was there. Something had told Cynthia to keep her mother company, and when she saw her mom, she knew that she was losing her dad. Mandy had to call Julie, Simona, and her church; while Cynthia called her boys.

"I can't die" hit Simona on her way to work at 10:30 P.M. and she finally broke down and prayed, crying, "Lord, I know he's in pain. I know it's not going to go away and I can't stand to see him that way, so please just take him; if that's *your* will."

Those were the hardest words she ever had to say and a feeling of ease came over her; she didn't think anything of it. When she was at work, she was slacking off talking to a co-worker, when she heard her name over the loud speaker. She thought the supervisor was going to have her change tasks, so she wasn't rushing. Then she heard "come to the office or call" the extension. This was new and she figured she better go see what he wanted.

As she walked in the office, her supervisor told her, "Phone call."

"Hello?" Simona asked curiously.

It was her grandma's voice. "It's time," she whispered.

Simona felt the air get thin and she knew . . . she began to scream, "NO!" and pounded her fists on the table. Her supervisor looked at her; he already knew and he had compassion in his eyes. A supervisor, from another department, was sent down to escort Simona to the exit and to make sure she was capable of driving.

Simona's head hung low as her grandma said, "Please, take your time getting here. Don't get in an accident, please!"

Simona hung up and her co-workers gathered around her to offer a ride. Simona was not having it; she had to get out of there and be alone. She needed to clear her head, without someone trying to console her during the half-hour drive. She just shook her head and repeated, "No . . . Thanks, I'm fine . . . I can drive myself."

As she drove, it began to snow; it was the first snowfall of the year. All she could think was how fast God had answered her prayer, but she wasn't ready for it to be so soon. She knew she caused this and so she had to face up to it. When she entered her grandpa's room, it was real . . . *his* prayer was about to be answered soon.

Her family hugged her as she walked to his side. She bent down and said, "I love you," and began to talk into his ear.

When Cynthia went to talk to her dad, she noticed a tear falling down his face. She announced, "He's crying."

Sam was a tough guy on the outside, but he was tender-hearted and had a heart of gold. He fought in WWII and hid in fox holes until his feet turned black from frostbite. He saw his friends get cut in half by bullets, who were sitting by his side, and he survived. Now to finally die was upon him and it was wonderful to see his whole family around him. Yet, Sam was still holding on.

The family kept talking about how their pastor was out of town, but that one of the elders would be showing up soon. The family felt bad that it was going on one o'clock in the morning, and they wanted Sam to be prayed for before he died.

Brother Clyde, one of the elders, showed up to the hospital to pray. During this time, Simona held on to Sam's right hand, while her aunt Julie held on to his left hand. No sooner than the elder and family were in midst of prayer, Sam passed away. His waiting was over and he could finally let go; he held on for them to bless his soul before leaving this earth.

Simona opened her eyes, looked at her grand "dad," as she held his hand; as her eyes looked upon the heart monitor, it flat lined. She bent down and softly said in his ear, "I love you, Pappy."

The nurse waited until the "Amen" before she made her way in to turn off the machine and note the time of death. No one picked up what was happening at first. When they saw the nurse turn off the monitor, Julie exclaimed, "He's dead?" and began to cry as her hand gripped her dad's hand tighter.

The family cried and said their goodbyes; it happened so fast, but at least they surrounded him for a few hours doting over him with love and praise. Sam was a man who was never a drunk (he just drank his cup of wine with dinner) and he never cheated on his wife. While in the Army, he wrote to many women and he had his choices, but he married Mandy and was proud to say they both wed as virgins. He loved his daughters and grandkids and his trust only went as far as them; his hard-headed Italian nature was suspicious, but he was not a mean man and never physically fought with anyone. He could whistle sounds of the war he heard, as he hid beneath the earth, from the different noises of bombs, bullets, and grenades. He could also throw his voice like a ventriloquist. He was a lover of music and could whistle songs in perfect pitch. He couldn't stand the new "alternative" music and he couldn't stand beards on men; to be a real man was to be clean-cut in his mind. Sam was unique and he was a tough mold to follow; his daughters tried finding their "dad" in the guys they dated, but it was far-fetched. They only made men like that once in a blue moon.

The family hated to leave Sam's side, but most of all, the girls worried about Mandy. Simona knew already she was going to stay with her. She wasn't about to leave her grandma to go home and be alone, too.

The next day, Cynthia and Julie came over to take their mother to the funeral parlor to make arrangements, but it was Simona who contributed to the casket. Simona, her grandma, mom, and aunt looked around at the different coffins, but only one stood out and Simona said, "This one!"

It was a black onyx casket. She always associated her grandfather around the color *black:* He talked proud of being an Italian (from the "boot" of Italy) and how he seemed to be the only one in his family with dark, Italian skin. He had a love for black panthers. He loved the black in his hair when he slicked it back with grease. She also remembered a black and grey Ford that he drove when she lived with her grandparents and how Sam loved the look of that car. When Simona pointed out the black onyx casket, the family had agreed it was *Sam.* The casket was engraved with his name on it and Simona could feel her pappy's approval.

As the wake took place, Simona stood there feeling alone. Her grandfather hated things like this, and normally she would be sitting and talking to him, instead of mingling with the guests. The thought of him not being there to talk to or hear him was beginning to fall on her hard; their connection was severed. She didn't want this to be real.

Tony and Matthew loved their grandpa and they took after him by trying not to cry in front of everyone. Julie was beside herself and couldn't take being alone; she held tightly to David and Jonathan and was happy that her dad was able to see and hold her son after he was born.

Cynthia held little Jett in her arms to look at his grandpa one last time; Jett leaned over and touched him, saying, "Papa, wake up, wake up, Papa."

Cynthia cried for the loss of a great-grandpa for Jett. She knew how much her own boys adored him and how her dad would have been a great male influence on him, too. Sam taught Tony and Matthew how to be gentlemen toward women; be respectful, truthful, and cherish family.

Simona, Tony, and Matthew were pallbearers and carried their grandfathers' casket to his resting place. Sam had a 21-gun salute and the American Flag covered his coffin; he loved the military although he wanted nothing to do with getting his Purple Heart medal. He believed death was eminent. He fought for his country proudly and saw his friends die; he didn't want a bunch of pomp and circumstance or rewards for being wounded. He talked of his fight on Anzio Beachhead in Italy and how he barely escaped death from setting a bomb; and being wounded, had to crawl on his belly to safety before it blew up. After his death, Mandy was given Sam's Bronze Star from the service and his flag, which was draped across his casket, was put in a flag holder.

Later on, the family had realized that with Sam's feet being so swollen after he came home from the hospital that his doctor had forgotten to give him his water pill during his eight day admission. Plus, as he laid there in the hospital bed, he never had inflatable boots on his legs for his poor blood circulation. All the kids told Mandy she should sue the hospital and doctor for killing him.

Mandy didn't believe in suing and reminded them, "Dad was suffering; even if he had the water pill, the boots, or the best care, he was suffering and was getting worse. I don't know if I would've been able to care for him like that and would've felt guilty to put him in a nursing home."

It was true what she said - Sam didn't want to live like that either; his liver was mush, his lungs were bad from smoking for years, and he had defeated prostate cancer a few years earlier, but developed cancer in his bowels. Although his absence left a huge, empty space in their lives, he was no longer miserable in his body.

Chapter 9

"He that hath no rule over his own spirit is like a city that is broken down, and without walls."
(Proverbs 25:28)

Calm before the Storm

After the death of Sam, and Julie's cancer scare, things in the family were settling down. Easter 2002, Cynthia asked Matthew if he would like to accompany her to see a play, called *The Passion* where members of the church reenacted the crucifixion of Jesus. To Cynthia's surprise, Matthew wanted to go with her. During the play, Matthew watched intensely and seemed to be moved, and when it came time for the son of God to be beaten and nailed to the cross, Matthew had tears rolling down his face. After the play was over, the pastor asked if anyone would like to come up to the front and give their life over to Jesus. Cynthia could tell that Matthew was battling himself from taking that step down the aisle; Matthew's "self" won.

Cynthia warned Matthew, "When Jesus knocks you should open the door, because the next time, when you expect him to knock, He may just pass you by."

Easter had past and the next get-together for the family was for Simona's birthday. The family sat outside on Mandy's deck; it was a beautiful April day. The family was surprised to see Alayna show up with Matthew since they heard they broke up, but Matthew told them they were still friends for Jett's sake.

Jett and Jonathan played in the backyard as Simona opened her gifts. When everyone started to leave, they hugged and kissed goodbye, but no one could ever prepare them for their next get together–the day before Mother's Day.

Bad Love

Alayna loved Matthew, but their relationship was rocky; she was busy going to college to become a nurse and was not giving in to Matthew's propositions. One day, Matthew was babysitting Jett and after he put his son to bed, Matthew lit some candles above the bed and waited for Alayna. When Alayna came home, she complained how tired and hungry she was and that she just wanted to go to bed. Matthew was disappointed, but he understood, and they went to sleep. Matthew was feeling what he put in the relationship was not satisfying and he just got tired of being put on hold. Matthew's friends convinced him that she didn't love him and that they weren't married, so he should break it off and find someone else. Matthew did just that; even though he truly loved Alayna, he just wanted her to let him know that she loved him, too.

On one occasion when the couple decided to call it quits, Alayna had a guy over and Matthew watched as they left together. Matthew then crawled into Alayna's window to wait for her to come home. When she walked into the house, she saw Matthew asleep on the couch. She woke him up and they had words. Alayna told him it was *his* idea to break off the relationship, while Matthew tried to make her realize how strong of a bond they had; he believed they were soul mates.

Matthew's heart was broken and he went home and cried. Cynthia tried to console him. He knew Alayna was his only love and for her to turn him away was killing him. They would break-up and make-up over and over; it was wearing thin on both of them.

Soon, Matthew was getting serious with a girl named Junie and he even introduced her to his mom. Seemed everyone liked her;

Cynthia, Tony, and Shannan, but Alayna was not happy. When Matthew hooked up with Junie, she happened to live right across the street from Alayna, and this just continued the game between them.

One day, Matthew came over to Alayna's, his shirt was off, but tried to avoid her seeing his back. She knew something was up and demanded Matthew show her what he was hiding. It was a tattoo that took up the whole upper part of his back, just below his last name, *Gioia,* that was tattooed a couple of months earlier. This new tattoo was a scene of a castle, a wizard holding a head with a sword through it.

It was repelling and Alayna asked, "What's that supposed to mean?"

Matthew was going to great lengths to try and find who he was, and for some reason thought the tattoo would make him look cool. After all, Junie liked it, but knowing Alayna didn't approve, he felt again insufficient.

Junie wasn't who Matthew wanted, sure she gave him what he physically needed, but she was not who he loved. No matter who he tried to convince, it was Alayna who was always in his heart. Junie was someone Matthew was trying to make Alayna jealous with, but still Junie was not playing the "girlfriend" role very well. She was a drug user and a partier, and a girl who would sleep with anyone, at anytime, for a high.

Matthew knew this and when Junie announced that she was going out with her girlfriends, he knew what that meant. He tried to talk her into staying home, watch a movie, and make some popcorn, but to a girl like Junie that sounded so *Mayberry* that she just had to laugh at him. She went out anyway and this left Matthew angry, hurt, and desperate. He went to play basketball with some buddies. Alayna came to mind and he called her on his cell phone to tell her what he was doing. She was his heart, she was the one that held that lifeline, and Matthew knew he could never live without her; Alayna *was* his soul mate.

A Tragic Decision

Matthew ran into a friend, Nate, who told him about a party and asked him to go.

Matthew declined.

Todd was married and had two boys and another on the way—he asked Matthew to come over for dinner, "Hey, I'm cooking some steaks on the grill; why don't you come over?"

Matthew declined.

Matthew called his brother, Tony. "Hey, Bro, what are you doing tonight?"

"Me and Shannan are going out of town to see a concert."

"Oh, okay, I was just wondering. There's a party tonight and I didn't know if you wanted to go."

Even though Matthew didn't really want to go, he ended up driving over to the party later on that night. Everyone he seemed to run into that day had no desire to go to the party. Matthew was never good at "signs" and never read in to any warnings, but still, he knew Junie was out having fun and he was going to do the same. He kicked back, talked with friends, and began to drink; Matthew was angry inside and couldn't control it. He began smart-mouthing, being cocky, and hateful; he was irritated and wanted to run from it all. It was almost 1:00 A.M. and he decided to leave. His intensions were to go home to his mom's, not back to Junie's.

Some reason Nate got a phone call on his cell about that time. When he hung up from that phone call, he made a call to a friend and asked him for back-up because, "Gioia is gonna get his butt kicked." No one knows if what was about to happen was a set-up or coincidental.

Matthew was just out the door when he noticed a kid, surrounded by at least five or six others, was getting picked on the next yard over. Matthew walked over to the "gang" and demanded, "Leave the kid alone."

Although Matthew felt his own anger burning on the inside, there was a piece of him that never wanted to see anyone get hurt or cornered. He didn't know this was some initiation, he didn't see the danger that was before him, all he could see is a kid outnumbered and he wanted to help.

The gang consisted of four males: "Doughboy," who was twenty-years-old; "Li'Mex," a nineteen year old; and two teenage brothers known as the Bolton Boys, Randy and Ronny, (whose grandfather was a police officer); then there was a girl involved, Darcy, who was Li'Mex's pregnant girlfriend.

Matthew approached the group and asked, "What's going on?"

Doughboy warned Matthew, "Stay out of this."

"Why don't you guys go pick on someone else?" Matthew spit out, along with some other choice words.

Doughboy seemed shaken at first; the others listened to Matthew and headed back to their van.

Matthew should have left well enough alone, but he was drunk and became cocky, "Yeah, that's right! Leave!" Matthew seemed to yell at the van, walking toward it, and pointing his finger.

The gang even proceeded to drive away, but then put the van in reverse and got back out. This time, Darcy was carrying something in her hand and the others seemed to have their "battle-faces" on and headed right toward Matthew. Matthew stood his ground. He wanted to find out what the whole situation was about to begin with, but the others seemed to be adamant on their original plans–they wanted a fight. Doughboy and Matthew soon were exchanging words when the two became physical: a push, a shove, a few hits. Then Doughboy made a fist, and with all he had, threw a punch busting Matthew in the left eye. Matthew went down on his knees when Darcy, who was apparently holding a shock absorber to a hatchback (similar to a crowbar), struck him on the back of the head. Matthew fell to the ground and as he lay there, the others repeatedly kicked him in the head. As Matthew's brain crashed and bounced off the walls of his skull; he laid there lifeless. The horror of watching such an act had a few screaming and running away from the melee. One boy tried helping Matthew, but Li'Mex felt compelled to go after him. Once Li'Mex reached the kid, the gang member ripped out the boys' eyebrow ring and roughed him up.

Meanwhile, Matthew's friends didn't even try to stop the beating; they were scared and unwilling to get hurt themselves. Matthew was the one to always help out anyone in need and was always considered *cool* by his friends. Obviously, it was because his friends were weak and never had a softened heart; they let their friend get plummeted in front of their eyes. Matthew knew he wasn't perfect, but he tried to be the perfect friend.

When the gang finally stopped stepping on Matthew's head and took off in their van, fear was hanging heavy in the air. The images were bloodcurdling. Matthew lay on the street with blood surrounding his head, beer bottles scattered throughout the yard, and kids standing around in disbelief from what they had witnessed as fear filled their heads. Fear if Matthew would die, fear of going to jail for drinking and/or doing drugs, fear of telling on the gang that they might come after *them,* and fear of guilt that they could watch and not reach out to help. The mixture of fears made them more stupid then not sticking up for Matthew and that was trying to pick him up.

Nate and some other boys gathered around Matthew and grabbed his arms and legs. They proceeded to move him when they (being drunk, scared, and awkwardly carrying a dead-weight body) stumbled and dropped Matthew less than fifteen feet where they had lifted him. Nate, finally in defeat (and finally using his head), grabbed his cell phone to call the police. He laughed at Matthew because he was snoring; in his mind he felt that Matthew was just passed out from drinking. Nate didn't know that Matthew was taking his last breaths—he was dying.

The police arrived and saw the destruction of the yard, a boy lying in a pool of blood, and noticed the other pool of blood a few feet away. Every time an officer tried to ask a question to one of the boys, they each gave a different answer. The cops knew they weren't getting a confession; they weren't even getting a fact to work with, until one officer asked, "Does anyone know the name of this young man?"

Nate spoke up and said, "Matthew, Matthew Gioia."

The whole time the police were trying to figure out what happened and get some answers, Officer Dennis was holding Matthew's head together. Dennis was mortified by the feel of it—the boy's head was soft and squishy. The only thoughts that were running through his mind were, "This boy has to get to the hospital *now* or else he will die in my arms."

Finally, the ambulance arrived on the scene. Once inside the ambulance, the paramedics had to intabate Matthew because he was no longer breathing. After precious minutes flew by, finally Matthew was on the way to the hospital.

Meanwhile, Nate called Cynthia to tell her about Matthew, but the police were so frustrated with him by now that they wanted him off the cell phone. He refused to get off it. While Nate was trying to explain to Cynthia that Matthew was on his way to the hospital, she could hear the cop in the background yelling to Nate, "Get off the phone."

Soon, the cop just threatened to arrest him for not cooperating. Nate managed to get out, "Kankakee Medical," before he hung up. Nate didn't know that he was one of the reasons Matthew was barely hanging on to life. He should have helped his friend, he should have called the police a lot sooner (like when the beating was happening), he should have never tried to move Matthew, and he should have just told the truth in the first place, so that the police and ambulance could understand just how to treat him.

At the hospital, Matthew was in and out of consciousness and angry. He was still fighting, flailing his arms and kicking his feet, and trying to cover his face. He kept reliving what happened to him over and over every time he would become conscious again.

Cynthia arrived at the hospital around 2:00 A.M. and waited to see her son. Time was ticking by and she asked a nurse when she could see him; the nurse told her that it still would be awhile. She decided to go home, to change for the day, and grabbed a book to keep her busy. Before heading back, Cynthia called her mom and Alayna to tell them about Matthew. Although she knew Matthew and Alyana were broke up, she saw Alyana as family and thought she should know.

When Cynthia went back to Kankakee Medical, she was able to go in and see her son; she knew she would not be reading. Her heart sank in her chest, her son Matthew was lying lifeless with dried blood scaled on his skin among fresh blood still seeping from his head. Cynthia thought he was dead and began frantically crying; she couldn't handle this alone and called her mom to come there immediately.

Mandy arrived and walked in to see Matthew; all she saw was blood: bloody towels, bloody gauze and bandages, and the blood of her grandson all over the floor.

Her first thought was "How can anyone survive the loss of this much blood?"

One glance and she began praying, grabbed her daughter and wept. Mandy's heart was shattering and she could not find any words to console her daughter or herself; all she could do was call on God.

When Alayna arrived at the hospital, it was around 4:00 A.M. and she had brought two-year-old, Jett, with her. When the nurses saw the boy, one stopped Alayna and told her that she would watch him as she went in the room. Alayna thought the same thing as Cynthia, that Matthew was hurt, just some cuts, roughed up, maybe a broken arm or leg, but nothing prepared her for what she was about to see.

The first thing Alayna noticed was the blood, blood was everywhere, and Matthews' clothes, his shoes, and jacket were full of blood. She ran to him and saw his hair, slicked back with gel and his well-kept goatee and she gathered herself to whisper in his ear, "I'm here, Matt, you're going to be okay."

He looked so good, but he was white—pale white—from the amount of blood he lost. She couldn't believe her eyes as he lay there; she had just talked to him and he sounded so alive. She thought Matthew was just hurt, not critical!

The hospital informed Cynthia and Alayna that he would need to be taken by helicopter to Chicago Medical Hospital, because they didn't have the doctors capable to do brain surgery. As Cynthia and Alayna walked out of Kankakee Medical, they discussed driving together to Chicago Medical.

"I'll meet you back at your house after I drop Jett off at my mom's."

Cynthia agreed, "Fine, but I want to pick up Matt's truck first before we head up."

Cynthia knew Matthew would have a fit having his white pick-up truck sitting somewhere other than home. Besides, she didn't want anyone vandalizing it either.

When Cynthia and Alayna headed to the 500 block of North Grand, where the attack took place, many emotions weaved in and out of them. As they turned on to the street, they feared this would be the last place Matthew would remember.

Alayna wanted to walk the small half block to find any sign of blood on the gravel, concrete, or street. After all, there was so much on his clothing, hair, and body. She needed to know the exact place to try and get a picture in her mind, to make sense of questions, which already were haunting her. When she finally climbed into Matthew's truck, she could smell the mixture of his cigarette smoke and cologne hanging in the air. Alayna felt her eyes fill with tears. A feeling of loneliness blanketed her from the thought if she could never be with him again. A desperate ache came over her and she knew she had to be with him. The fighting, the games, the time slipping away from them was senseless; it dawned on her that he was reaching out so many times and she ignored him. She needed him. She wasn't giving up on him this time; she was going to be the girlfriend he so much wanted and asked for without saying it in words directly to her.

Surgery

Cynthia and Alayna arrived at Chicago Medical around 6:00 in the morning and waited for Matthew to come out of surgery. When the doctors came out, they informed the two women that they had to put Matthew into a drug-induced coma. He kept fighting and it was causing his brain to swell.

Matthew's head was shaved on the left side where they had operated. He had a gathering of fourteen inches of staples, from when they peeled back his scalp to remove the excess blood that was clotting in the brain. Dried blood was between each staple and there was a screw in the top of his head that was draining the spinal fluid. Matthew's left eye was black and swollen shut and a brace was around his neck. He was hooked up to a machine that read his blood pressure, heartbeat, pulse, and pressure in his head. He also had an I.V. in his arm to put back the blood he had lost over the last four hours. Cynthia and Alayna sat by Matthew's side, as in their hearts and minds they began to pray for him to recover.

Chapter 10

"They that sow in tears shall reap in joy."
(Psalms 126:5)

The first sign of joy is . . . Comfort.

Walls Closing In

Cynthia called Chuck to let him know that his son was in the hospital. There wasn't much Chuck could do at that point, but he did fall off the wagon in hearing the news; it had been almost a year since he had a drink.

Cynthia didn't know Tony had gone out of town that Friday night, so she left a message on his answering machine that Matthew was in the hospital at Kankakee Medical. Tony also had messages from friends, who had heard about Matthew getting hurt and left messages for Tony to call them back to see how Matthew was doing.

When Tony and Shannan arrived home, Tony noticed the caller ID displayed Kankakee Medical Hospital and when he heard the messages, he became shaken and called the hospital right away. When he asked for Matthew Gioia's room, the operator on the line had told him that Matthew had been released. Tony took in a deep sigh of relief when all of a sudden the phone rang–it was his aunt Julie.

"Where were you, Tony? We've been trying to get a hold of you. Matthew is at Chicago Medical Hospital."

It seemed the walls in the spacious front room of his house began closing in around him; he knew it was serious and Tony lost it. He felt his chest cave under him from the heaviness of his heart and began to sob. After several minutes of being unable to control his heart from breaking, he knew he had to collect himself. He had to gather enough strength to drive almost two hours up north to see his brother. Shannan tried to console Tony, but there were no words that could be said until they saw Matthew for themselves.

Although Simona was around for family get-togethers, holidays, and called often, she had moved about an hour away to be closer to work. Mandy missed her granddaughter being "home" and was the one to tell Simona about Matthew.

Simona arrived at Chicago Medical. As the elevator doors opened to Matthew's floor, she saw her family and members of the church grouped together quietly speaking. She noticed her mom, Grandma Mandy, Brother Clyde and his wife, Colton and his wife, and Alayna's mom, Linda.

Before Simona's foot stepped onto the floor, Mandy was walking toward her with her arms spread out to embrace her. They only hugged for a few seconds, because Simona was antsy to see Matthew. Mandy kept her arm around Simona and led her to his room. Simona held in her sorrow very well as she looked upon her youngest brother hooked up to several devices. She noticed the main machine which consisted of Matthew's heartbeat, blood pressure, temperature, and a gauge that monitored the pressure in Matthew's brain. While Mandy and Simona were in there, Alayna came in. Simona noticed the numbers getting higher on the pressure in Matthew's head and asked Alayna about how much pressure is acceptable until it's considered dangerous. Alayna started to blurt out a number, the same time she looked at the machine, and ran out of the room to get a doctor. Simona's heart skipped a beat, "Hold on, Matt!" as she squeezed his hand.

A doctor came into the room and casually said, "His brain is filling up with fluid . . . we're going to have to relieve the pressure by going in."

"He's going back in surgery?" Alayna asked.

"I'm afraid so."

Simona's head was spinning, trying to sort out what had just happened. She asked one question and it sparked her brother going back in for a second brain surgery. She only saw him a matter of a few minutes. When the three women made it back to the waiting room to tell everyone that Matthew had to go back into the operating room, Simona was already breathing heavy and felt she was going to hyperventilate.

The doctor came out and warned the family, "Matthew having the second surgery could be detrimental."

Everyone began asking him questions that he just didn't have the answers to, until he finally had to plainly say, "We cannot guarantee that he will make it."

Cynthia, engulfed by guilt, thought she had caused Matthew to end up there. When Matthew was letting his life go to waste after the raid, and began drinking and doing drugs again, Cynthia knew that she couldn't deal with another incident with the police again. She knew if Matthew kept it up that the raid would be legitimate the next time. She feared she would lose her home, as well as her son, who would be sentenced to jail; if not prison. Cynthia would pray and ask God to do "whatever it takes" for Matthew to stop his destructive behavior. Now, she wanted to take those three words back so bad. Matthew was going back to have his head cut open, again, with no promise he would live through it.

The church members gathered around to comfort the family and began to pray for Matthew. Simona didn't want to pray, she needed air, and felt the room getting smaller by the millisecond. She broke from the group and repeatedly pushed the elevator button, she ran her fingers through her hair, and felt nauseous. When the door opened, she ran inside. All she could see was everyone staring at her as the elevator doors closed. They didn't look at her out of shock, disbelief, or anger; they looked at her with the thought of "if it were me in this situation." Simona could feel their consolation.

During surgery, a portion of Matthew's skull had to be cut out and removed, so that if the brain should swell again, it had room to expand. If they attached the bone, this would cause pressure, and Matthew could suffer more brain damage from a stroke, blood clot, or aneurysm.

When Matthew came out of surgery, the only ones left at the hospital were just the family, except for Junie, Nate, and Todd, who drove up together. Alayna was upset that Cynthia even called Junie, but Cynthia was just going by what she thought Matthew wanted; the last thing she heard from Matthew about Junie was that he loved her. Alayna acted like a cat thrown in water. Everyone knew she was in a jealous rage. Alayna's mom tried to calm her down, but it didn't matter what she said, Alayna wanted Junie banned from the hospital.

"He's *my* son's father and she is *not* a part of this family!" Alayna screamed.

Everyone in Matthew's family seemed to side with Junie, because they all knew Matthew was broke up with Alayna. Simona, on the other hand, didn't like the new girlfriend from the start. Simona and Alayna decided to go see Matthew in his room. They were on each side of him when Junie entered. Alayna tried to control herself from going off on her, while Simona was trying to figure out what it was that she didn't like about this new girl in her brother's life.

Junie put out her hand to shake Simona's and told her, "I love your brother very much. I will never give up on him; you have my promise."

Simona responded with an "okay," but she thought that Junie sounded too rehearsed. Silence seemed to fill the room. Simona stood touching Matthew's shoulder, praying for him under her breath.

Junie broke Simona's moment with God by pointing to the clip on Matthew's finger that displayed a red light, "What's that?"

"It measures Matthew's oxygen." Simona said in monotone.

"He looks like E.T. - phone home." Junie laughed.

Simona and Alayna looked at each other in utter disgust and Simona knew what she didn't like about Junie–her immaturity. Matthew needed a woman with a good head on her shoulders and someone to lovingly guide him to be a good man.

Simona knew that Matthew fluctuated with his actions; one day he would be responsible and the next day he wanted to have a good time and party. He needed a woman in his life to give him that "*want*" to be responsible and having a good time would to be with her.

Alayna did not want Junie in the same room as Matthew and suggested, "We should leave so someone else can come in and see him."

When Alayna, Junie, and Simona walked in to the waiting area, Mandy stood up and asked Nate and Todd if they would like to see Matthew. The guys had no idea what to expect, and were quite unsure if they should even enter his room as they slowly walked down the hall behind Mandy.

Mandy stood beside the bed and reached down to hold Matthew's hand. Nate and Todd stood motionless as they looked upon their friend. Tubes emerging from out of Matthew's head, nose, mouth, chest, and arms; the boys could not take their eyes off him. They stared at him; waiting for him to acknowledge that they were there. Soon Nate's eyes began to shift from Matthew, to the floor, and back again. Todd's eyes, on the other hand, began to fill with tears. He felt his body give way to the sorrow as he fell back into the empty chair behind him. Unspeakable grief overcame him as he inhaled deeply, lunged forward with his head in his hands, and cried his eyes out. His heart was breaking. Todd wept, and he wept, and he wept, as the realization set in depth to the condition of his best friend. Todd was so sad that he just sat there, with his elbows on his knees, unable to stop crying.

Mandy could see the young man unable to handle such sadness. Although *she* still needed consoling, she went to Todd, put her arms around him, and said, "All we can do is pray. Only God can bring him through this; we have to trust Him."

Later on, Junie's parents showed up at Chicago Medical to bring her back home. She began crying hysterically, throwing herself up against a wall, falling to the floor, and wailing as if Matthew had just died. After nearly fifteen minutes of this, she finally stood up. Junie began hugging Nate and Todd, crying on their shoulders for at least a whole five minutes each. Mandy, feeling sorry for the distraught girl, stood shaking her head. Alayna was just about to strangle Junie and Simona was trying hard not to bite through her lip from the irritation of such a dramatic performance.

Simona whispered in her grandma's ear, "She should win an Oscar."

Mandy kindly disagreed and stated, "She's hurting."

"So am I, but I'm not flopping on the floor like a fish."

Her grandma knew it was a bit over the top, but she was trying to be kind.

Meanwhile, the doctor had told the family that Matthew had a good chance if he survived the night. That was so stressful to hear, because they were unable to stay at the hospital with him. Cynthia was not about to drive home because she wanted to be at the hospital as early as possible. She decided to get a motel room, and Simona, Alayna, and Tony agreed to stay with her.

The room consisted of two double beds; Cynthia and Alayna shared one bed and Simona and Tony on the other. Time seemed to stop. The atmosphere was heavy as the four lay in the dark room. Lights from passing vehicles tried to break through the closed curtain, along with muffled sounds of people walking and talking outside the door. Cynthia and Alayna didn't move, but the sounds as though they were asleep could be heard. Tony tossed and turned, played with his cell phone, finally made a call to Shannan to say "goodnight," and still continued to toss and turn. Simona felt like an elephant was sitting on her chest and sucking the air out from around her with his trunk. She thought of her pappy and thought if he weren't already dead that this would have killed him. She focused on Matthew lying up there in the room all alone, by himself, and was wondering if he even knew what happened to him. She wondered if her grandpa was sitting with him keeping him company. She thought of Jett and she thought of when Matthew was that age. Her mind wouldn't turn off and that elephant was crushing her when it was actually her heart breaking into pieces.

She nervously got up and went into the bathroom and shut the door. Before she could make it to sit on the edge of the bathtub, tears were running down her face and she felt her body start to buzz. She cried out loud as her hands forcibly rubbed together, uncontrollably from left to right, as though she was about to wring out blood. She was afraid to be heard, but she would hear herself blurt out one cry after another. Now, she didn't feel she was any better than Junie. She looked up as if she was looking God right in the eye, and as her tears burned out of her ducts, she begged and pleaded for Matthew's life. She didn't ask out of selfishness, but for her mom and Jett and for Matthew to be able to see his son grow up. She knew tragedies happen to families' everyday and there was no guarantee that God would treat her family any different, and it was *that* fear that made it unbearable to get through the night. Simona knew that people make promises to God all the time, especially in situations like these. She knew that she had to make a promise, if He would allow it, that she could keep; she promised that she would go back to church if God spared his life.

When the sun rose, it was Sunday, Mother's Day, and every one was expecting a miracle. Alayna figured Matthew was awake and wanted to hurry and get to the hospital. She assumed everything would be fine, but she was wrong. They headed to his room and found Matthew was still holding his own, but he wasn't awake yet.

The doctors couldn't understand why Matthew wasn't "up" yet, because the drug-induced coma they put him into should have been worn off by now. They began to run more tests and found that Matthew suffered an aneurism, behind the left eye where "Doughboy" had punched him, but still he should have awakened.

The doctor approached Cynthia to have her sign a release to insert a feeding tube into Matthew's stomach, since it was questionable when he should awaken.

The day was long as they had to take turns sitting with Matthew; only two at a time. By the afternoon, Matthew had even more visitors. While in the waiting room, Cynthia would read a book, Mandy would work a cross-word puzzle, others would talk among each other, but Simona couldn't seem to do anything like read or even talk; she felt she was in a dream. She sat on the window sill and looked outside and up at the sky. Shannan walked up and tried to talk to her, but eventually went back to sit by Tony. Mandy would try to console her granddaughter too, but she knew that Simona was drawn inward. Once in a while, Simona would glance around the room and observe everyone. All she could think of was how could anything ever be the same again. She looked up at the sky and noticed how gray, cloudy, and cold it was for being May. The smoky, low-hanging, billowed clouds seemed to set her mood. She grabbed a sheet of paper and a pencil and wrote to try and release some of her pent up feelings -

To Truly Love

To truly love is pain . . . if you didn't love - you wouldn't care.
To see someone hurt - you hurt.
You learn to stop thinking of yourself.
Suddenly your worries, agony, and complaints don't matter anymore.
To truly love is tears . . . tears of heartbreak - tears of joy.
To love . . . you will cry.
Physical pain cannot compare to the tears of love
Those tears are hot and hard to hold.
To truly love is hope . . . to pray . . . to believe.
Only God gives true meaning to love.

Junie arrived just in time to hear the doctor's theory on Matthew's condition.

When the doctor returned from putting in Matthew's feeding tube, one of the test results came in, he said, "It doesn't look good."

He tried to break it to the family that Matthew was in for a long recovery, but hinted to never fully recover. Junie was as shallow as Simona and Alayna thought. After she heard Matthew might never be the same again; Junie was never heard from again. She had someone else by the end of the week.

To make the day even more dismal were the stories flooding the streets of Kankakee about what happened to Matthew. Alayna's cell phone was ringing nonstop with one version after another. There was gossip he was the victim of a gang initiation and rumored that he was kicked in the head by at least twenty guys. One witness said Matthew was whacked in the head with a crow bar. All kinds of several other gruesome details of exaggerated theories became too much to take.

Alayna was mad and becoming enraged with every speculation. She tried to talk with Tony, Shannan, and Cynthia to decipher what might be real or fictitious. Cynthia stood up as though she was going to be sick, put her hand over her mouth, and began to shake violently as tears and wailing emerged from the depth of her being.

Simona ran up to her mom, and hugged her, as Cynthia exclaimed, "I don't know how much more of this I can take! I'm not going to make it through this . . . it hurts so much!" Cynthia began to shake and cry and stated, "Happy Mother's Day."

Later on, everyone sat down to figure out days and times to be with Matthew. Since everyone was needed back at work, Simona and Alayna still planned to be there everyday.

A Sister's Devotion

Simona tried to go back to work for that Monday and couldn't make it through the first hour. Her heart was heavy and she couldn't bear to think of her baby brother up at the hospital all by himself. The thoughts crossed her mind of "what if he 'woke up' from the coma," "what if some kind of complication happens," and "what if the doctors have questions about him." She tried to do her daily job and realized she couldn't hold back the tears filling her eyes.

Her friend Connie approached her and told her, "Go to him; don't feel this place will fall apart if you're not here. Don't sacrifice yourself for *this* place. Go to your brother."

She needed to hear that; it made the uncertainty whether she should stay at work leave her. She wanted to be with Matthew and that is where she was going.

A doctor came in no sooner than Simona got there. He was glad a family member was there regarding Matthew. She was thankful that Connie gave her that "push" she needed to leave work; she believed it was God working through her friend.

Later on, Alayna arrived and they sat with Matthew until visiting hours were over. Simona couldn't bring herself to leave; she didn't feel right going home. She decided to stay the night and slept in the waiting room around the corner of the Intensive Care Unit. She ended up staying another three days and two nights without ever leaving Chicago Medical. All she had were the clothes on her back, her wallet, keys, and cell phone.

She couldn't bring herself to do anything like watch television, laugh, or think of tomorrow; she was living in her own *coma.*

Her days were spent with family; her family, church family, and friends of Matthew's. Her nights were filled with fitful sleep, every hour or so sneaking her head around the corner to ask about her brother, pacing up and down halls, and trying not to cry.

The whole family was on pins and needles, anticipating a change, no matter how small. They were constantly watching with bated breath for any sign: a flick of an eyelash, a motion of a finger, the movement of his mouth; they were grasping for any little indication at all. It was so heart-wrenching, waiting, and feeling so helpless. Regardless of the hours that were swept away with no response from Matthew, the family still talked to him as though he could hear and understand every word.

It had been five days when Matthew's eyes finally opened, but not in a conscious state; more like he was still *dreaming.* His eyes were glazed over, but Alayna saw it as a sign he would be "awake" by morning, so she stayed overnight at the hospital with Simona. The two talked most of the night about Matthew; Alayna was grueling over the guilt about the way she had treated him.

"I was a terrible girlfriend. I can't blame him for cheating on me. I wasn't satisfying him the way a girlfriend should and if I would have treated him better, he may not be in here right now."

Simona tried to comfort her, "We never know how our actions are perceived by others. You were caught up in school, work, and taking care of Jett; it's easy to overlook the little things like a kiss or touch. I know he loved you, even when he was with Junie, or else he would have never called you just to talk before he went to that party. Don't beat yourself up; he knows you're here now."

Alayna tried holding back her tears; the guilt was eating her up and her eyes were opened to how much she really did love Matthew. She wanted another chance to prove her love and she knew now just how much she wanted to spend the rest of her life with him.

Simona was feeling a bit guilty, too, and asked Alayna, "Did Matthew ever say anything about me . . . If I was an awful sister? I mean, I was a teenager, but I was always on them, you know? I yelled at them, sometimes even spanked them, and I wonder if he ever held any anger in him about me being hard on them. Just be honest."

Alayna replied, "Matthew had nothing bad . . . ever . . . to say about you. He talked you up and told me how you were hard on them, but that he learned by it. He was respectful to everyone, Simona. He would bend down to play with this little handicapped boy and that little boy's face lit up. That is who Matthew is; his nature is truly gentle and kind, that is why I love him so much. He's not like any other guy I know. You did nothing wrong in helping your mom raise him. He loves you very much and I thank you for how he turned out."

Simona smiled and said, "I never knew . . . I'm glad he turned out that way."

It was after one o'clock in the morning and the two girls tried to get comfortable to sleep. Simona was used to the chairs in the waiting room, but Alayna had to lie flat on the floor. By the time morning came, the waiting room was filling up with people whose loved ones were going into morning surgeries, so the girls had to get up.

Alayna was exhausted, "How in the world did you do this for two nights? I'm so tired; I have a headache!"

"I just know I couldn't sleep anyway if I went home because my mind won't turn off. I just know I have to leave tonight. After four days and three nights, I need a shower and some clean clothes."

When Alayna and Simona walked in Matthew's room, his eyes were losing the "glazed" look and becoming *glassy.* Yet, he still was inside himself; still in an unconscious state.

That night, Simona was filled with guilt driving home.

The next day, Simona had brought Matthew a soft, cushy, lime green frog, because she noticed how Matthew would keep his hands tightly clenched. She had to work at prying his fingers open to hold his hand, while explaining what she was doing, in hopes that he would understand and respond. Simona could tell that her brother was relaxed with the little frog in his hands; plus, Matthew's hands didn't get as clammy and chapped, because all the moisture was consumed by the stuffed animal. Seeing how well his hands were doing, Simona picked up a baby-blue bunny of the same texture so he could hold one in each hand.

The beginning of the second week, Simona went up to see her brother and noticed the drapes closed to his room. She walked in to find two police officers standing at the end of his bed; one officer had a camera in his hand and Matthew was completely uncovered and naked.

Simona was livid, "What are you doing?" she asked as she went to cover her brother back up.

"We are investigating Matthew's incident and came up here to ask him some questions."

"He can't speak; from what we're told he never will. Why was he uncovered?"

"To examine if there are any other marks. We took the pictures as evidence of any unusual cuts or bruising. I see his knee is red and his knuckles scraped."

"I'm sure he got a hit in."

"We believe Matthew fell and hit his head."

"No, he didn't just hit his head. The doctor told us he has *numerous* bruising on different parts of his brain. If he fell there would only be one bruise–my brother was *attacked!*"

The officers were talking among themselves when Simona asked, "Why didn't you stop the party? I know you know when a party like that is going on and it was right there on North Street. I see cops drive by there all the time; you didn't notice all the cars on that small street?"

The officers became quiet and one finally spoke up, "We are investigating officers, we are not patrol."

The response sounded like an excuse, and Simona folded her arms to demonstrate she disapproved of his statement.

The officer cleared his throat, "I understand your concern and I'm really sorry this happened to your brother. We will try and find those who did this to him and they will be punished."

Simona didn't like being patronized and responded with, "If you come up again to take pictures, cover him up next time when you're done."

Before the officers left, one walked toward her and handed her his card, "Call me if you have any questions or information."

Simona stayed until Alayna relieved her so she could go to work. Simona hated leaving Matthew, but she knew she could trust Alayna to take good care of him and let her know if there were any changes. When Simona got into her vehicle to head off to work, she put on the radio like she always did, but this time a strange feeling came over her. The music was picking at her nerves and she felt agitated and uncomfortable. If she drove without music, her mind would race, like a million voices in her head were talking all at once and she felt herself wanting to cry or scream. She began pushing buttons on the radio to find something to sooth her and make her calm before she had to deal with work. Suddenly, she heard a song pull at her ear that stopped her finger from flicking the channel. Before she realized what station she was on, a peace came over her, and her heart stopped pounding. The music put her mind at ease. The song was called, "I Don't Want to Go" by Avalon. She was on a Christian station that played modern gospel music. That station became the only station that came through her speakers for months to come; along with Avalon's, *Oxygen,* compact disc (which she had to go out and buy). The songs that she heard, day after day on that station, driving back and forth to the hospital, work, and home, gave her strength and filled her with comfort. Avalon, Steven Curtis Chapman, Michael W. Smith, MercyMe, and many other Christian artists' songs spoke words, in volumes, in Simona's heart; helping her to be clear in dealing with a tidal wave of emotions that were making her spiral into depression. Driving in her vehicle became her time with God. She began praying and asking Him for the ability to deal with all these circumstances that were pushing her over the edge.

Chapter 11

"Behold, I will bring it health and cure . . . and will reveal unto them the abundance of peace and truth."
(Jeremiah 33:6)

The second sign of joy is . . . Hope.

More Bad News

By the middle of the second week, Matthew had developed an infection. It was getting harder for him to breath. The doctors approached Cynthia and asked if they had permission to give Matthew a tracheotomy. This frightened Cynthia and a feeling of despair overcame her. Although she had the support of her family, church family, and friends at work, she was losing the battle with hopelessness and could only think the worst.

Everyone grew concerned and confronted the surgeon. The doctor, who performed the brain surgery, brought Cynthia, Alayna, and Simona into an office and showed them Matthew's brain x-rays. He began to explain, pointing at the blackness in the middle of Matthew's brain, or lack thereof. The slide showed what it looked like–nothing - there was no more brain. The damaged brain broke down, became fluid, and absorbed into his spine. This dumfounded the women and they couldn't comprehend that Matthew had a "space" in the center of his brain.

Alayna asked, "Will it fill back in . . . grow back?"

"No . . . my best advice is to find a nice facility to set him up in where he'll be comfortable."

"Like a nursing home?" Cynthia asked.

"If that is what's good for you."

"What about Matthew? Will he 'come back' to us?" Alayna asked.

"My opinion is he will never talk or walk again. I believe he will be . . . in a bed."

"Like a vegetable?" Cynthia asked.

"Yes."

This was not what they wanted to hear and couldn't imagine Matthew in a vegetative state. They went back to Matthew's room and he was just lying in the bed, so still, not even knowing who or where he was, and unable to respond to all their love and pleading. The thought of him being like this the rest of his life was too big of a pill to swallow. Yet, the family clung to believe Matthew would soon come out of his current status, and that they wouldn't have to deal with arranging a facility for him to just exist in.

Mandy, being the matriarch of the family and having a deep and close relationship with God; became surprised by her own feelings to have a question for Him–*why*. She would never admit it aloud, but mentioned the word to Simona, in a passing phrase. Simona had never, ever heard her grandmother question God, even slightly, and it was chilling to hear such words come out of her grandma's mouth. Simona was raised by her grandma to believe in God, trust in God, have faith in God, and never question God, never curse God, and never deny God. Even though Mandy expressed her inner feelings for a mere second, (if to get it out of her broken heart), she picked up right where she left off with her Lord and began trusting Him like she had been for nearly 40 years.

Simona, on the other hand, seemed to have seen the grandma that she may have had, if Mandy had never found the Lord. For that instant, a fear overcame Simona and she thought, "If she can have her faith shaken - where does that leave me? I'm not even near to having such a close walk with God like she has."

Down deep in Simona's soul, she was so thankful that her grandma was a Christian and lived by those beliefs. If it weren't for her prayers, her teachings (no matter how much Simona disagreed at times), and her many at-home-sermons that sometimes made Simona uncomfortable or bored; she would never have wanted her grandma any other way.

Alayna lost her job at the nursing home, because she had a hard time leaving Matthew and would be late for work. The nursing home wouldn't work out a specific schedule for her; they were always changing her hours, and making it impossible for her to have enough time to spend with Matthew. She was worried where she would get the money to pay rent, bills, and take care of Jett. She refused to stay away from her son's father, even for a day, and had faith that he was going to fully recover.

"He *will* be back to normal!" she would state positively and made sure no one dampened her hopes.

She would show up and try to make Matthew look at her while she talked to him; trying to break through the obstruction which hindered him. No one wanted to face the fact that Matthew had a part of his brain that was not there. Alayna looked up on the internet on how to work with brain injuries, and was given even more hope by what she read. Since Matthew was young, brain cells can continue to grow and multiply until the age of twenty-five. Matthew was only twenty. Alayna saw this as a challenge; she became determined to help Matthew come back to her. She and Simona would talk to him, encourage him, and explain everything that was around him. They explained whatever the doctors, nurses, or they, themselves, were doing; to help him understand that no one was going to hurt him. The family believed just because Matthew could not respond, didn't mean that he couldn't comprehend.

Cynthia saw the persistence Alayna was taking, in helping Matthew, and knew he needed her during this very crucial time. As they sat with Matthew, Cynthia talked to Alayna about moving in with her. With all that was going on with Matthew, they both needed each other as a support system. Cynthia would rather have Alayna dedicate her time to Matthew, instead of looking for a job and a place to live.

"I know you're independent, but if you are unemployed and can't make your rent, you can always move in with me. At least, until Matthew gets better, then you can find another job. Jett, too, needs a stable home and to feel secure . . . I'm sure his little mind knows something is not right, being that you are away from him so much."

Alayna felt relieved.

By the middle of the second week, Matthew had a piece of life come back to him; he now would enclose his fingers around the hand that was holding his. He held the hand gently and every once in awhile, would give a squeeze. The family was exhilarated, and a new hope came to light. By the end of the second week, Mandy asked, "Matthew, can you hear me . . . blink your eyes, if you can hear me?"

Matthew would lie still as night, but he built up the force to *slowly* close his eyes, and *slowly* open them back up. It was though he wanted his grandma to *know* that what he done was *not* a reflex, a mere involuntary blink, but a controlled movement to say, "Yes, I heard you."

The family seemed to feel Matthew was moving right along with his progress, and felt he soon would be talking.

In her free time, Alayna was moving in Cynthia's house, but eventually needed help lifting her furniture. Alayna's friend offered her assistance and told Alayna that her boyfriend would help with the heavy things. Alayna didn't know her friend's boyfriend was African-American, and the boyfriend brought his friend, who was also of the same race; she didn't care, but the police sure did. Alayna saw police lights flashing on her side mirror. She looked down at the speedometer and noticed that she wasn't speeding; so she pulled over to let him pass. She was taken aback as the police car stopped behind her.

The officer approached her side and asked Alayna for her license and registration.

Alayna began to explain that the truck was her fiancé Matthew's, that he was in Chicago Medical Hospital fighting for his life, and that she was moving her things to his mother's.

The policeman didn't care; he ordered everyone out of the vehicle.

Alayna and her friend got out, while the two young men got out of the back of the truck bed. Alayna couldn't understand what was going on, but her instinct let her know it had to do with her and her friend being white and the two guys being black. Alayna was embarrassed and began to get upset. She tried to let the officer know that she needed help moving, and that they were friends, but the cop was ignoring her as he leaned into the truck, yanked out her purse, and began sifting through it.

"What are you *doing?*" Alayna screamed.

Alayna felt violated. When she stood up for herself, the cop backed off, but with stern warning. She was so mad, she could barely see, and wanted to turn him in.

When she got to Cynthia's, she could hardly keep the words from running together as she explained what just happened, and asked hypothetically, "Why was he looking in my purse anyway; what did he expect to find? I'm going to call his superior!"

Cynthia tried to calm her down and rationalized the outcome, "I'm afraid it would be all in vain; after all, it seems the police don't care much for the Gioia family from past experiences."

Moving Out

By the third week more bad news befell the family; the hospital couldn't keep Matthew there anymore. He had to be moved to a long-term care facility that carried ventilators. The family thought they had more time; they couldn't believe that the hospital was giving up on Matthew so easily. They knew how much Matthew had been trying so hard to "come back," and hoped the hospital would reconsider letting him stay. Matthew had no health insurance;

therefore, he had to leave. The thought of Matthew moving from a hospital, where doctors could care for him, to a facility where care would be questionable was uneasy to deal with. The family tried to find a nursing home close to home, but there was no place available. Instead, Matthew was moved to a State Hospital, which was still about an hour north from Kankakee.

Once Matthew arrived, he was in a large room with five other residents. Compared to some of the other patients in his room, Matthew looked bad and this brought on a sinking feeling in the family's soul. Matthew's eyes focused on the ceiling and when he looked around, he hardly ever made eye contact with his visitors. Although it seemed he couldn't even grasp a single thought, Simona believed he was scared. At Chicago Medical, when she would hold his hand, Matthew was gentle; now when she took his hand, Matthew squeezed so hard Simona would shriek in pain. Matthew wouldn't let go either and Simona had to pry his fingers back to release her hand. She knew Matthew was trying to ask "what is going on?" in the only way he knew how.

Simona, Alayna, and Cynthia would often explain to Matthew just what was going on and that he just needed to get a little better before he could come home. Everyday they would express how good he was doing and to keep up the hard work. They would tell him things to look forward to: sleeping in his own bed, driving his truck (which he loved), seeing the Chicago Bears (which had recently moved their training camp to Bourbonnais), and having family dinners at Grandma's house (another thing Matthew loved was his Grandma Mandy's food).

Just because Matthew was now being transferred to a long-term care facility, it didn't change anyone's commitment to be there with him. Matter of fact, Matthew being there had caused the family to want to be there more. Alayna and Simona still went everyday, and Mandy tried to go every other day. Unfortunately, Cynthia's hours at the Post Office were hard for her to make it up to the hospital as often as she would have liked. It would often overwhelm her, and she would sit at her desk and pray for her son several times a day. She would call Alayna at the hospital to keep informed on his condition just to make it through work. When Cynthia had a day off, she would bring a book and sit beside Matthew to let him know his mother was near.

Adjusting to Change

One day, Tony went up to see Matthew at the same time his mother, sister, Alayna, and Jett were there. Alayna took out her camera to take pictures of Matthew. She wanted to document his developments. Cynthia told Tony to stand by Matthew to take a picture with him and Tony shook his head "no."

Cynthia pushed and told him, "He's your brother, take a picture with him."

"I don't want to." Tony said with a slight cry in his voice.

Tony was struggling and he felt uncomfortable with this proposal. His brother was injured, damaged, and predicted to never be the same. He just wanted to come see him, and be there for his brother, not feel pressure to act like "this" was *normal.* No one knew how anyone else was feeling deep inside, how each one was dealing with this abrupt, horrible change in their life, and trying to strive for resolution.

Later on, Shannan, Tony's fiancée, told Cynthia how she would wake up in the middle of the night to find Tony sitting on the couch, with a picture of him and Matthew on his lap, crying. Cynthia realized she hadn't even thought of what her other son was going through and how he could be suffering. She was too drowned in her own grief to realize it.

She felt bad and thought, "How could I not see past myself—past Matthew?"

Matter of fact, everyone was guilty of that, but it was to be understood. When such a tragedy happens; chaos explodes. It was so easy to forget major things like simple priorities, random responsibilities, and even something as simple as asking, "How are you?" Everyone was so within themselves that such little amenities were forgotten.

Simona and Alayna came to see Matthew on a weekend. One of the nursing assistants mentioned, "He had company last night."

This was actually frightening news; what if it had been Matthew's attackers to finish the job? They were outraged and ordered the hospital to keep non-family members from coming in to Matthew's room. Unfortunately, the nurse and assistants couldn't promise anything. After all, they were there to take care of Matthew; not be his bodyguard. As Alayna and Simona walked in Matthew's room, they found provocative pictures of guys and girls getting drunk.

Alayna couldn't identify one person in the pictures and said, "I know *all* Matt's friends, and none of these losers look familiar."

It frightened Simona, because she remembered how the police pulled off Matthew's blanket and clothes to take pictures, and she feared that Matthew could've been assaulted. "They could have touched him, and Matthew can't even defend himself. What did they do, just gawk at him?" Simona hypothetically asked.

This outraged Alayna; Simona had a point and the same fear engulfed her.

Alayna got on her cell phone and made some calls; she knew just who to contact to spread the word, "You better get out a warning that if we find out *anyone* comes up here to see Matthew . . . the law will be involved!"

Alayna's threat apparently worked. It was later found out that the company Matthew had was only curious acquaintances. This was even more frightening, because they wondered, "How did they find out where Matthew was?"

Days turned into weeks and Alayna never tired of visiting Matthew, giving him sponge baths, changing him, and monitoring his reflexes, blood pressure, temperature, and cleaning out his trachea. Although Alayna was not in nursing classes yet, she believed she knew more than the nurses. Matthew was getting to a point where he was breathing on his own; the monitor read that he was taking in practically all of his own oxygen.

Alayna asked if the trachea could be taken out and was told a firm, "No." Case in point, if he should code, the trachea already inserted in Matthew's throat was easy access to open his lungs.

Within that same week, Alayna and Simona arrived to see Matthew; he had pulled out his feeding tube and the tube in his throat. Alayna used a little vacuum attached to the monitor to suck out the phlegm from his throat and Matthew gagged more than usual.

She told Simona that she read that once the gag reflex comes back to someone with a trachea, that it was time to take it out. The two changed Matthew's sheets from them being dirty, mostly caused by liquid food and mucus from his throat. While putting on the clean sheets, he pulled out the tube from the trachea again. Alayna told him to keep it in there and not to touch it, but every few seconds, Matthew would have his hand to his throat again trying to pull it out.

The following day, Alayna asked the nurse again about removing the trachea; this time explaining that the tube in his throat was causing him discomfort. The nurses and assistants never had someone question their procedures before and were getting quite upset with Alayna. She didn't care; Alayna knew Matthew didn't need it anymore. Matthew was gagging, coughing, and every chance he had would try to pull out the tube, but instead of helping Matthew to be comfortable, the nurses brought in restraints and tied Matthew's hands to the bedrail. He thrashed about; he hated the restraints.

Alayna finally met with the doctor by the end of June. She told him her concerns about the trachea, but he responded with "We'll see."

The beginning of July, the doctor took out only the tube of the trachea, but kept the hole in his throat open, along with the bracket still stitched into Matthew's neck, just in case the tube had to be used again. The doctor still wanted Matthew to have oxygen and placed a mask over the opening; but Matthew would pull the oxygen mask off and hold it in his hand.

It seemed he was becoming a little more attentive; at least now he would actually look at someone when they spoke to him, although he couldn't focus on them for very long. This little change was so exciting for the family, but this was a characteristic of short-term memory loss. Since Matthew was off the ventilator, he was able to be moved to another room. This was so convenient, because now everyone could feel at ease, have a place to sit, and visit and work with Matthew more privately.

While Matthew was being transferred to his new room, Cynthia and Alayna were sitting in the waiting room and were introduced to another family going through a similar situation. They began talking to a Latin family, whose son Greg, (same age as Matthew) was also a victim of an attack. Greg was beaten, and his attackers hit him repeatedly over the head with a golf club. He and Matthew suffered the same injuries, ended up in the same hospital, and on the same floor. Cynthia and Alayna heart's bled for this family with complete compassion and empathy. They tried to get the hospital to put both boys in the same room to give each other support, as well as work with them together. The hospital ignored their wishes, but the families would acknowledge each other in the halls, visit one another's sons, and keep each other updated on their procedures and progress.

One day, a doctor approached Alayna and suggested Matthew receive shots as therapy, "Day after day, lying in bed and unable to exercise, these shots would help prevent the constricting of his muscles."

Alayna refused the treatment and told the doctor, "No way! I exercise Matthew; he only needs me."

Alayna was indeed giving him exercises, moving his arms and legs daily. One thing about Alayna, she was confident, to the point of arrogance, but she believed she was the only one who could help Matthew. She was determined and always second guessed the doctors, and that is what Matthew needed. She was not going to have Matthew be a guinea pig. She watched every little thing the hospital did or didn't do. Alayna was very diligent about Matthew.

As for Greg, his family agreed to the treatment, but unfortunately, the shots only made his muscles worse. His therapist hardly ever came in to work with him. Within a couple of months, Greg's muscles ended up constricted to where he was curled up, stiff, and unable to be limber. Matthew's family was angry at the hospital for what they put Greg through, knowing that his family was unable to be there as often as they could; they felt the doctor misled the family into a false sense of obligation.

The family had adjusted to driving up to see Matthew; they had stepped up to the plate. They had bonded together, worked together in helping and supporting Matthew and each other through this awful situation.

The church family knew members of other churches throughout the United States, and those churches knew members throughout other countries, had requested prayer for Matthew. Prayers were being sent to Heaven all over the world. Matthew's family gained strength through prayer and love offerings from the church. They accepted that Matthew would only be healed by the grace of God, if He should grant such a healing.

In a different way, they were unaware how God was healing them. They forgot about themselves, concentrated more on the Lord, by thanking Him for the little improvements Matthew made. They no longer vented what *they* were going through or how this was affecting *them*. They were there for Matthew, and encouraged *him* to try everyday to say a word, react to a touch, or follow an instruction like blinking his eyes or turn his head to follow someone around the room.

A goal was set before them and they weren't giving up. Everyday Matthew was challenged as he began to master responding to their commands.

Alayna put a washcloth on Matthew's face and told him to pull it off. He lay there, hearing everyone talk to him, and to each other. His arm would move, but not far enough to take it off. Alayna told him again, "Take off the washrag, Matt, you can do it."

A couple of minutes went by, and it was like Matthew was building up the capability. When all of a sudden his arm bent straight up, his hand landed on his face, his fingers clenched the cloth, pulled it off, and his arm fell, tiredly, back to his side. Everyone clapped and cheered at his accomplishment, and the corners of Matthew's mouth lifted for a slight smile; he knew they were proud of him and he was proud of himself, too.

A Setback

When Matthew was sent to Chicago Medical that night on May 12, the doctors were so concerned about the trauma to his head and brain that something seemingly minor as his kidneys never was an issue. The alcohol Matthew consumed at the party was never entirely drained from his kidneys and the alcohol turned into a sugary substance, which then turned into stones. After the few days when Matthew wasn't waking up from his drug-induced coma, a catheter was inserted, since he was unable to get up and use the restroom on his own.

Now, several weeks passed and the catheter was still inside Matthew. As he began moving more, he felt the thin, flexible tube against his legs that would sometimes get tangled around them, causing him to pull at it. The snake-like feeling served as a problem to a confused and curious brain-injured patient. Again, like they did with the trachea, the nurses had to tie Matthew's hands to the bedrail to prevent him from pulling out the catheter. He would get so mad and pull at the bedrail. It broke everyone's heart to see the begging and pleading on Matthew's face. He was in so much misery and could not utter a word; only communicate with his eyes, appealing to his family to remove the straps from his wrists. The pain he felt as he struggled with the restraints did not break his spirit to stop trying to be unconfined. The family took them off, but they knew as soon as they left, they would have to be fastened once again.

Matthew seemed to be looking so good, making great eye contact, and following simple orders like turning on his left side or lifting his head. He knew his right from his left, his leg from his arm, and he even began to point.

When Simona came in to see her brother on her way to work, Matthew was actually reclined in a Geri chair surrounded by pillows; he had on a pair of sweat pants, a t-shirt, and a bandana on his head. He looked happy to be sitting up and dressed in clothes, instead of lying down in a hospital gown. With Matthew's face glowing from excitement, he even looked healthier. It was such a wonderful day for Matthew that Simona felt bad she had been running late, and could only spend an hour with him. She cried on the way to work, because she hated to leave. She was so happy to see another step forward in Matthew's development.

All the nurses and assistants absolutely loved Matthew; they would talk to him, sit with him, and he would smile at them. Unfortunately, there was always going to be someone working at a hospital or nursing home who worked just for the paycheck. It's sad, but it's true. It was easy to tell when Matthew's nurses and assistants were on their day off.

The next day, Simona came to find Matthew in bed. It looked like he was sleeping, but when she moved closer; he looked like he was dying. She panicked, because the way he looked reminded her of her Pappy Sam that night she lost him. Matthew was yellowish, almost ashen; his eyes were slit and his mouth was open and dry.

Simona called on the nursing assistants and asked, "What's wrong with him?!"

"He's just tired."

"NO–this is not right–something is wrong with him! He looks like he's dying . . . Please, help him!"

"He's okay. I'll be back in a few minutes."

The girl didn't come back in a few minutes and Simona's heart was racing. She began praying as her skin became clammy and her body anxious. She couldn't sit still and she tried talking to Matthew, but ended up pacing the floor; back and forth from Matthew's bed to the door looking for someone to help her brother. It looked like he had reverted back to his coma state. Finally, Alayna came in and Simona screamed out, "Thank God you're here! Look at him! Something is not right!" Simona believed Alayna would know what to do, if not, she knew Alayna would demand some answers.

In the meantime, Cynthia and Mandy came up to see Matthew. They heard how well he was doing the day before, and was looking forward to seeing him sitting up in the chair. Their hearts dropped when they saw Simona and Alayna's concerned faces.

The four women were beside themselves, and it seemed the nurses and assistants thought they were over-reacting. Simona and Alayna had been there everyday with Matthew, and knew his little behaviors inside and out. They knew something was seriously wrong.

One assistant came in and told them the same thing, "I'm here everyday with Matthew and he's fine. We can't just wait on him all day, we do have other patients."

From 7 A.M. to 2 P.M., Simona waited for an answer to why her brother was in this kind of condition. Alayna was disgusted at the way the staff was not attending to Matthew. Cynthia and Mandy sat by Matthew's side, praying and shaking their heads; it seemed no one cared to respond to their pleas. It appeared that the more worried, the more they asked, and the more they tried to have someone at least take five minutes to check him out, the more the staff ignored them. Matthew laid in that condition for the *whole* first shift!

Simona was ready to phone work and call off, when the second shift nurse came in and looked at Matthew's catheter bag. She looked at his last output in the chart-book, and noticed there had not been a change in output. She pulled back the covers, lifted up Matthew's gown, and pulled out the catheter. There was a small kidney stone, the size a bit larger than a grain of sand, blocking the urine from coming through the tube. Once she inserted the catheter tube back into Matthew, he filled up a whole catheter bag and half of another, in a matter of a few minutes! Soon, the color in Matthew's face came back into his cheeks and his eyes tiredly opened. He could have died that day; his kidneys or bladder could have exploded and poisoned his body. If only the first nurse would have just taken the time to figure out what was wrong, Matthew wouldn't have suffered all day (including his mother, grandmother, sister, and girlfriend).

After the relief that Matthew was going to be alright, the anger set in; Simona and Alayna were so furious at the first shift that they wanted to sue.

Mandy tried to calm them down, "Just be thankful that you were here."

"We were all *here* and they didn't do anything–no matter how we begged!" Simona screamed.

"Yeah, I know, but he made it and we have to be thankful he's okay." Mandy assured.

"This is why we have to be up here everyday. They don't care about Matt or anyone else in this place; they're just here to take home a paycheck." Alayna accused.

The day was so pressure-filled that by 3 P.M. everyone was exhausted. Cynthia and Mandy went home soon after Simona left for work, but Alayna stayed to help Matthew.

It set Matthew back in his recovery, and took about another week until Matthew was back up to where he was that first good day; that good day when he was sitting up and dressed.

Chapter 12

" . . . we glory in tribulations . . . knowing that tribulation worketh patience."
(Romans 5:3)

The third sign of joy is . . . Faith.

The Verdict

Alayna, Simona, and Tony went to court for the hearing of Li'Mex. Since they were unaware of all the other court hearings, (as if they were being deliberately kept from them), Matthew's girl-friend, sister, and brother, were not going to miss this one.

As they sat in the courtroom, they watched him; Li'Mex didn't seem like someone who looked remorseful as he glowed in his orange jumpsuit.

Just before the proceeding, an attorney approached the three on Matthew's behalf and asked them to follow him. He sat them down in a small room away from the courtroom, and explained that every single witness that were there at the party, gave numerous and different statements. They began to read them, as Alayna and Tony knew some of the witnesses.

"Why would they come back here and keep changing their story?" Alayna asked.

"This is why I brought you in here. See, Mr. [Li'Mex] wasn't mentioned in these statements and we have no proof he was there or even did it," the attorney said.

Everyone on the street admitted that Li'Mex was indeed there that night and participated with Doughboy and the Bolton brothers; how did he avoid being in these statements?

Simona asked, "How come we didn't know about the hearing of the others?"

"You *were* informed by mail."

Meanwhile, Li'Mex was confessing his involvement to the beating of Matthew on the stand.

When they left the courthouse and went home, they asked Cynthia about the notices in the mail.

Cynthia responded, "Yes, here they are . . . they all came by mail, *after* the hearings."

Alayna said, "We should have been at every trial! We should have testified on Matthew's behalf."

"Yes, we should have been able to express our grief, so they would understand what they did to us." Cynthia stated.

The end verdict was that Doughboy was to serve the most time, because he was arrested while on probation. Li'Mex was served less than a year in jail. Since the other boys were under age, they served time in detention, and were out when they turned eighteen–which was less than two years. All convicted for indictments on Mob Action.

Darcy was never arrested; her name was never linked to the beating, *according* to the police statements. The family was at a loss over the injustice.

"Can't we sue for restitution?" Simona asked.

"Those kids have no money." Cynthia said.

"Yeah, but it would be taken out of their paycheck for the rest of their life, as a reminder to what they did to Matthew." Alayna added.

"They are going to have a hard time getting jobs, because no one is going to hire them. If they do get a job, they'll never last very long, or they'll just collect unemployment. Besides, the two young boys . . . I know about their mother, and she has had a difficult time with them. They're always in trouble, and I can imagine the hurt she is going through. Tony and Matthew could have easily been like that. I wouldn't sue. I won't . . . I just won't. Money isn't going to bring Matthew *back*."

What Cynthia said didn't stop Alayna and Simona from visiting different lawyer's offices and asking for their help. Over the next year, each one turned them away; not really refusing their services, but explaining to them that it would be an expensive, useless trial. The boys that did this to Matthew were going to get what they were going to get–little time in jail. The main response they heard was " . . . the only way they would get hard time is if they killed him."

Alayna and Simona would argue over the television. Alayna wanted to watch her soap, while Simona wanted to watch *People's Court,* so they would alternate shows. During an episode of *People's Court,* Simona thought that she would write Judge Marilyn Milian and explain the injustice of what happened to her brother. Not really expecting a reply, she was surprised to receive a letter from Judge Milian. As heartfelt as the letter was, the Judge had explained that being unaware of the facts between both parties and the laws of Simona's state that she could not help her quest. Although, she pretty much told her that the lawyers Simona spoke to were honest enough to inform the family to save their money. Simona was very grateful that Marilyn Milian had taken time out of her schedule between her family, court cases, and television to answer her letter. Alayna was very impressed that Judge Milian wrote and stopped making fun of Simona's addiction to the show.

The Cell Phone

Cynthia knew how much her son loved his cell phone and decided to bring it to him. As Cynthia and Alayna sat with Matthew, Cynthia pulled the phone out of her purse and gave it to him to hold.

Just then, a nurse came in and saw the device in Matthew's hand, and sternly told the women, "Cell phones are *not* allowed in here!"

"It's not charged," Cynthia explained, "I just gave it to him to hold."

They all noticed how Matthew looked at the phone. He slowly pushed the buttons as if he was calling someone, and then slowly put it to his ear. They were excited that Matthew remembered what to do with it.

July 21, Alayna went up to see Matthew and she forgot to turn off her cell phone; it rang and she pulled it out of her purse to talk. Matthew put out his hand to hold the phone and Alayna put the phone up to his ear; suddenly she heard him whisper out a "hello." Her eyes became wide with shock and she started jumping up and down. She knew she had to call his mom and have her hear Matthew talk.

She called Cynthia at work and told her, "Talk to Matthew."

When Alayna put the phone to Matthew's ear, she covered his trachea with gauze, and again he said "hello," but this time he managed to say it a little stronger, since the hole was covered up. When Alayna took the phone back, the two of them screamed with excitement; Cynthia and Alayna had tears of joy rolling down their faces. Matthew was talking and they finally heard his voice for the first time in over two months. Their prayers were being answered.

Cynthia told her, "I can't wait to see Matthew tomorrow!"

It never dawned on Cynthia and Alayna that a phone would be a start to him talking. The question on their minds was "How long has he been able to talk?"

Wednesday was Cynthia's day off. She and Alayna had their hopes high that Matthew was going to be talking to them when they walked in the room, but Matthew was quiet and never made a sound. They tried to get him to talk, directly to them, but it was just like he had been for the past three months. They felt discouraged, but then Alayna pulled out her cell phone to see if Matthew's talking the day before was just a fluke. Alayna called Tony to talk to his brother.

When Alayna handed Matthew her phone, Matthew heard his brother's voice on the other end, his eyes lit up, and belted out a "Wuz up?"

Just then, Simona walked in and Cynthia and Alayna both burst out telling her the good news. Simona spoke to Matthew, but he just looked at her with the same reaction he had been giving his mom and Alayna. It seemed that if Matthew was on the phone too long, he would stop talking, as though he was bored. Cynthia and Alayna wanted Simona to hear Matthew talk, so they hurried Tony off the phone to call Mandy, because they didn't know how long Matthew would keep this up. When Matthew's grandma heard him say, "Hey," everyone could hear her through the phone screaming joyously. Simona's face lit up, along with a big smile, until she could hardly focus on Matthew anymore through the tears filling her eyes. Cynthia wiped away a few tears herself. The thrills of those precious moments were too great for words.

Matthew couldn't hold a conversation while he was on the phone, but he did answer soft, simple responses, like "yes" or "no," to the ones asking the questions on the other line. Once he was off the phone, he never said a word, as though he couldn't speak again. It was like he just went through the motion of what he was supposed to do on a phone.

It was a start and they knew it was going to take time, patience, and a lot of work to get Matthew to speak face-to-face. It was a *boost* for them, because when it seemed like working with Matthew was effortless, a hidden miracle would take place for them, reminding them to be steadfast, and not give up on him. All the prayers going up for Matthew weren't just for him to "get better"; they also prayed to help the family keep their faith alive. The family and the doctors didn't know if Matthew would ever speak again, and the cell phone was a miracle; it motivated Matthew to talk. Matthew may never have started talking as soon as he did, if at all. It was like a series of fortunate events: Cynthia giving him a cell phone (something Matthew loved), giving him a feeling of familiarity sparked him to "know" what it was used for. Alayna leaving her cell phone on, getting a call, and giving Matthew the phone - he *knew* to be heard, he had to speak. This was a monumental breakthrough, not just Matthew to talk, but for the family to experience joy once again. It was a ray of warm sunshine burning through the dark clouds they had been living in for nearly ten long weeks. Thank God for His mercy. It was a sure sign that Matthew was recovering.

Matthew Responding

After much repetition and coaching, Matthew was now able to give gestures like, "thumbs up," "high-five," and "flexing his muscles." Alayna began sitting Matthew up on the edge of the bed, while she stood in front of him. She helped him get his balance to sit up and strengthen his back. She wanted him out of the bed, out of the Geri chair, and able to sit in a wheelchair. One day, while Alayna had him strengthening his back, by having him sit on the edge of the bed, Matthew decided to stand up. Alayna's eyes got big and became almost scared of what he was doing. Matthew was strong and persistent on wanting to stand. Alayna held on to him tight and let him stand, but knew he had to sit right back down since his ankles were weak from suffering foot drop, which was caused by not putting any weight on them for so long. When she let Matthew stand, he was so excited; he felt invincible and went to put his foot forward to walk. That showed Alayna, his mind was thinking.

Alayna screamed out, "NO, Matt!" and made him sit back down on the bed.

Matthew looked upset and tried to force his way back up, but Alayna put her weight on his shoulders and tried to explain, "You're going too fast, Matthew. You need to ease into it slowly, your body isn't ready for you to stand or walk, yet."

Matthew's expression was comical, it was fairly easy to read what was going through his mind; his mouth closed tight, partially rolled his eyes, and his shoulders went down as he let out a quiet sigh–he was irritated. Yes, he was definitely coming back.

One morning, Alayna and Simona had arrived at the same time. When they both walked in and saw Matthew, Alayna immediately hit the call light. Matthew was dirty, had dried food on his gown, bed, face, and hands from last night's dinner. He was strapped down, his gown was twisted around his stomach, and his catheter bag was full. (Again, it was the day off of the nurses and assistants that loved Matthew).

When a nurses' assistant walked in, Alayna tried to be calm and show her how Matthew looked, but the assistant began arguing, "I just got here, and I have other patients I have to check on first . . . He is *not* the only one in this hospital!"

Alayna refused to be talked to in such a manner, and told the assistant to show her some respect, but the assistant demand she show *her* some respect. The two kept bickering on "respect" that the issue at hand was not being addressed–Matthew.

Simona stood there, speechless, at the end of Matthew's bed. As her eyes darted back and forth, like watching a tennis match, when she finally looked down and noticed Matthew's expression. He was clearly upset, and unable to convey it any other way except his eyes. He pleadingly looked at them to cease the dispute, but those two weren't looking at him.

So, Simona raised her arms to referee, "Hey . . . Stop . . . Okay, okay . . .", but neither of them paid her any attention; matter of fact, they just got louder and leaning in closer at each other. Suddenly, Matthew tried to sit up in the bed, but couldn't get his balance, so he laid back and hoisted his leg up in the air to try and stop them; he felt the tension between them and it was making him nervous.

Simona yelled, "Look at him!"

They both stopped fighting.

Alayna leaned down, sifted her fingers through Matthew's hair, and noticing his dismay, consoled him, "Its okay, Matthew."

Simona tried to set things in perspective, "I know you both get the point of respecting each other–you just kept *repeating* yourselves," she turned to the assistant, "We just wanted to show you what was going on. We weren't blaming *you*," and then Simona turned to

Alayna, "She's only one person and obviously this happened on third shift. Look, Matthew is the one who needs the respect. Can we just start over here?"

Alayna apologized to the assistant. The assistant apologized to Alayna and stated, "I will definitely let someone know about Matthew" and she helped Alayna clean him up.

There were other times when the family felt like Matthew was neglected–and there were words–it just never got *that* heated. Alayna began to watch her temper, but word got out to "Watch out for the girlfriend."

Physical Therapy

Because the news got around that Matthew *talked,* all the nurses and assistants were ecstatic that he may actually be coming out of this "vegetative" state. Mary, who was a short, Eastern Indian woman, was Matthew's physical therapist. She was more than excited to get Matthew started with therapy. Although Matthew was still not walking, focusing his eyes on anything for more than a couple of seconds, or showing signs of total understanding or emotion; it didn't matter, he had given faith to everyone in the hospital to "work" with him.

As soon as he had a day off, Tony came up to see his brother; he strolled in the hospital with a white and blue Hawaiian shirt on and his sunglasses on his forehead. He joined Alayna and Simona, who were sitting in the day-room with Matthew. Matthew was sitting in a Geri chair, with a pillow behind his back, and bandana on his head to cover the deep indentation from where there was no skull bone.

While waiting on Mary, Tony tried talking to Matthew, but he didn't respond. He just stared intently what he was seeing behind his own eyes. Tony sat in an empty Geri chair, beside his brother, and faced him. He grabbed Matthew's hand and held it, shook it, and tried to make Matthew play thumb war, but Matthew would just lie back in the chair and closed his eyes like he was going to fall asleep. Tony gave Matthew his cell phone, then hid behind his brother and pretended he was on the other line. Matthew looked at the phone, dialed some numbers, and put it to his ear as though he knew just who he was trying to contact. Even though Matthew's mouth would be open, his eyes looking far off in the distance, they could see certain little expressions on his face that his wheels were turning. Matthew was trying to fight the powerful force of his detriment to come back to the world he once knew.

Meanwhile, Alayna tried to make Matthew hold his oxygen over his trachea.

Simona handed Alayna the video camera for her to use on Matthew's first day with Mary. She kissed her brothers goodbye, and left for work.

Tony asked Alayna for her cell phone, so that he could call Matthew. She handed Tony her phone and after he dialed the number, Matthew got a funny look on his face.

"What'd you do?" Alayna asked.

Tony laughed, "Phone's vibrating . . . pick up the phone, Matt."

Alayna and Tony were trying to get Matthew to look at them, but he was just sitting there. Finally Alayna told him, "Hey Matt, give me a high-five!" Matthew resting his left hand on his chin, reluctantly lifted his right arm to touched Alayna's hand.

"Yeah," said Alayna.

Meanwhile, Tony looked in Alayna's phone index and asked, "Who's this guy on your phone?"

"A friend of my mine," Alayna said.

"From where?" Tony pushed.

"I was talking to him when me and Matt were broke up. Why are you looking at my phone numbers?"

"Wanna see my phone numbers?" Tony asked.

"No, I'm not nosy like you." Alayna refuted.

"Yeah, okay." Tony said sarcastically.

They were always bickering at each other; Tony and Alayna had a love-hate relationship. Just then Mary walked in the room and Alayna yelled out, "Mary's here!"

Matthew was able to graduate to a wheelchair, but since his oxygen tank couldn't attach to it, Mary brought a machine to measure Matthew's oxygen every few minutes. Once Matthew had the trachea out, he was able to breathe on his own, but the hospital wasn't taking any chances.

Mary wheeled him down the hall, and talked to him, leaning over him in a fashion for Matthew to see her, "We're turning right . . . okay, and you'll be coming this way almost every day now for therapy. Do you like going places?"

Matthew nodded his head up and down twice and Mary told him, "Say, Yes!"

Mary wanted Matthew's first day with her to be a tour around the hospital, to help familiarize him before the actual therapy.

Alayna and Tony followed Mary to the physical therapy room to show Matthew where he would be exercising; then wheeled him to the recreational room. In that room were plants, a television with a Nintendo and video games, fish tanks, and a radio playing overhead.

Matthew looked like he was confused and frightened, but he was just concentrating and absorbing where he was. Tony went on the other side of the aquarium to get Matthew to look at the fish.

Alayna saw the look on Matthew's face, and bent down calling his name, "Hey, Matt?"

Matthew eyes just got wider and Alayna shook his arm to get his attention, "Matt?"

Alayna asked him, "Do you know what those are?" as Matthew's head tilted side to side. "Those are fish, a fish tank," she said as she pointed to them.

Matthew's mouth moved, but nothing came out.

"What is it? Are those fish? Can you say, 'fish' . . . 'fish?'"

Matthew looked intently into Alayna's eyes and mouthed the "sh," and then barely whispered, "*fish.*"

"Yeah, you know what they are."

At the end of the tour, Matthew's big surprise was that he was able to go outside.

Alayna had set her purse on Matthew's lap, and took the video camera to record his reaction to the sun on his face, "Hi, Matt! Smile for me."

Mary checked his oxygen, "97, its good."

Matthew sat up, grabbed the purse with both hands and lifted it up.

She told Tony, "He's gonna throw my purse . . . he will."

Tony told him, "Hold it for her, Matt. Leave it there."

Matthew put the purse down and slumped back into the wheelchair. It was easy to tell he was not happy about having to hold it. Alayna once again told Matthew to smile. After several prodding from her and Mary, Matthew gave them a big smile, as if to patronize them. His actions spoke much louder than words. When Tony knelt down in front of Matthew to talk to him, he handed Tony the purse.

By the end of July, Matthew became restless and strong enough to pull himself out of the bed. He was confused and wanted to walk. The nurses and assistants refused him for his own safety, and began strapping his wrists down on the bedrails at night. That caused him to be combative. Matthew would get so angry about the straps; he would pull so hard that his face would be flushed red and his body clammy from perspiring from the force of trying to break them loose.

One day, Alayna and Simona arrived early and saw the straps around his wrists; they also noticed a change in his behavior. They believed Matthew had suffered a small stroke. He wasn't responding well like before, wasn't making eye contact, was sluggish with his reactions, and the right side of his face looked droopy and he was no longer using his right arm. The two girls were furious and demanded answers. Finally, a nurse came in and criticized them for wasting the nursing assistant's time with silly questions.

"He has a brain injury. My staff cannot be in here 24/7 to make sure he doesn't get out of bed and fall. The straps are for his *own* safety and as for a stroke . . . like I said, he has a brain injury; this is the way he is."

"NO!" Alayna scolded right back, "Matthew has been doing great; alert, responding. Look at his face, his mouth is sagging on one side and he's not using this arm!"

The nurse shook her head and said as she was walking out, "You all just overreact. He's fine."

Alayna called everyone with power in that hospital to make sure this would never happen again. It was over a month before Matthew started *trying* to use that arm again. From then on, a nurse was assigned to Matthew's room on every shift–Alayna got her 24/7.

The family noticed how Greg was always outside. Alayna had to struggle just to take Matthew outside his *room.* She couldn't believe how rudely the nurses approached her every time she would attempt to take him out. Yet, she tried to understand that the hospital was just being cautious. The family wanted Matthew to have fresh air, instead of sitting in his stuffy hospital room. They figured the staff knew them by now to trust Matthew in their care, but it was always an encounter as they wheeled Matthew toward the exit. The family would take him out to the picnic tables and visit on the beautiful lawn. When Alayna could, she would bring Jett to visit his dad on a nice day, so that they could go outside. This way the little, active three-year-old wasn't cooped up in the hospital being bored.

One day, Alayna, Simona, and Mandy walked in the hospital. Alayna saw Matthew sitting in the hallway, with a long-sleeved, starchy, "factory" shirt on, and his wrists strapped to the arms of the wheelchair. She noticed his face was beet red and sweat dripping off his brow. Simona didn't even recognize him.

Alayna asked, "What is this? I bring him clothes and t-shirts; why does he have *this* on? Can't you see he's burning up?"

She wheeled him into his room and changed his clothes, and then told the nurse she was taking him outside.

"Are you going to take responsibility for him?" the nurse questioned.

"Of course, we've been taking responsibility of him." Alayna said nicely, trying to restrain herself from rolling her eyes.

Mandy and Simona waited for Alayna and Matthew to come out and sit under a shade tree. Matthew was getting better at focusing his eyes and was no longer staring off into space.

Mandy asked him, "How come you're so cute?"

She pulled up her chair and asked, "Do you like to be outside? Thumbs up?"

Matthew looked at her and put his thumb up; Mandy, with her thumb up, pointed to herself and said, "Me, too. I like to be outside."

Matthew was so attentive now that he always sat forward in his wheelchair and looking up, down, and all around.

Alayna told him, "Hey, Matt, those guys down there, they like your truck. They said, 'we like your truck' and I told them 'it's my fiancé's truck."

Mandy exclaimed, "You're a really handsome guy; I think I'll keep ya!"

Alayna asked Matthew, "Give me a kiss."

Matthew kept his head looking at the parking lot as Alayna knelt up to him and said, '*hey*' to get his attention. Matthew looked over at her and saw her lips puckered; he puckered his lips and then turned his head back to the parking lot.

Everyone let out a sound of disapproval, and Mandy said teasingly, "Shame on you, Matt, you better give her a kiss . . . I want to see it."

He just kept his head turned away.

Mandy asked, "What are you looking at, Matt?" Matthew scratched his ear and turned his head back to Alayna; Mandy said, "Now he's ready."

Alayna leaned in and Matthew softly kissed her. Then turned his head right back to the parking lot. Alayna figured out that Matthew was looking out for his truck; he was always so protective of it and hearing someone else liked it, kept his eyes fixed on it. Alayna gave him her keys and asked him, "Which one is your truck key?"

This helped deter his concentration on the parking lot and more on what was in front of him. It was the little signs to show that Matthew was training his brain. Although he couldn't express vocally what he was doing, he was focusing and worrying about his truck. It was so slight that no one really picked up on how hard he was concentrating. With all the distraction from his loved ones around, vying for his attention, Matthew responded to them, yet keeping his mind and eyes on his truck.

Mandy reminded Simona about the time, "You better get going; I don't want you to be late or speeding to work. You have to allow for traffic and accidents; it's 25 after!"

Simona hated to leave; it was a beautiful day and she enjoyed being around everyone, but she had to be at work by 3:00 P.M.

After Simona left, Alayna built up the courage to ask Mandy a favor. Since the accident she had with an elderly couple, her insurance had gone up to an SR22 which was more than she could afford at the time. Her insurance was canceled; therefore, her license was revoked. She wanted her license back to avoid the fear of being ticketed, or maybe even arrested, every time she drove up to see Matthew. Alayna presented her case to Mandy.

Being Mandy was truly grateful for everything Alayna had been doing for Matthew, she smiled at Alayna and asked, "How much do you need?" and promptly supplied the funds.

That day, it was Grandma Mandy's turn to escort Matthew and Alayna to therapy. Matthew's legs were getting strong enough to sit in his wheelchair and use his feet to scoot himself around, so it was time to be vertical. Mary pushed Matthew's chair to the bars for him to stand, but because they put him in the chair so early, Matthew was very tired and wanted to shut his eyes. Mary was so good at encouraging him, and getting his attention, so he stood up for her. As she held him, Matthew gave walking a try, while another therapist wheeled his chair behind him in case he should fall backwards. He concentrated so hard that his mouth stayed agape and his pinkie would rigidly stick out from his fist. Matthew's brain wanted to walk with one foot over the other, like he wanted to cross his legs; this concerned Mary, so she wanted to work with him to undo that habit next. Matthew walked between the bars three times, and everyone clapped and cheered for him *every* time. Then he sat back down in his wheelchair.

Mary playfully exclaimed, "Chase me, Matt!" as she backed up in another wheelchair.

Matthew would use his feet, scooting to follow her, but he kept crossing them. Mary placed her foot between his feet to discourage him from doing it. After a few times around the room, Matthew got the hint. So, Mary began teaching him how to turn in the wheelchair; when he finally did it, everyone cheered again. Another exercise, Mary worked on Matthew's hand-eye coordination by bouncing a big, plastic, pink and white ball to him. She had Matthew catch it and bounce it back to her, and that seemed to really "wake" him up. Everyone had a blast watching and participating with Matthew by playing different games with the ball. He was having fun and the smile on his face showed it. That was one of the most successful therapy sessions Matthew had.

Therapy was helping Matthew even get better at expressing himself. He knew when he was being "cute" and would slightly smile at his actions. He liked to tease. One example, Alayna told him to put the shaving cream on his face so she could shave him, and he went to put it in his mouth. Simultaneously, Simona and Alayna yelled, "NO!"

Matthew put his hand down and gave a great, big, smile like he was laughing.

Matt's Truck

On August 2, 2002 Tony and Alayna took Matthew outside to let him sit in his truck. Tony had drove it up to the grass and Matthew actually pulled himself from his wheelchair into his white, Dodge Ram; even with his catheter still very much a part of him. Tony turned on Matthew's cd player and they listened to the rapper Nelly's song, *Country Grammar.*

Matthew looked around, mouth agape, and pointed forward; he wanted to take a ride.

"Going for a ride, Tony?" Alayna asked.

"No!"

"You're not? Why not?"

"Can we?"

"I guess. Just go, like, go down, and around the parking lot, and come back."

"I gotta buckle him up," Tony insisted.

While Tony leaned up and over his brother to pull down the seat belt, Alayna realized what was actually taking place; she let out a huge sigh and warned, "You better be careful, because I'm *so* responsible for this," and nervously laughed, "I can't argue my way out of this one."

Tony drove very slow around the parking lot and came back. Matthew looked at his brother and his head nodded in approval, like "Thanks for the ride."

Alayna approached the passenger side of the truck to face Matthew and asked Tony, "Did he like it?"

"He looked straight ahead the whole time," Tony responded.

"Did he?" and she turned to Matthew and asked, "Cool, huh? Yeah? Do you remember your truck? This is what you gotta fight for . . . things like this . . . to go home and get your butt out of this hospital. Right?"

Still worried about the drive in the parking lot, Alayna told Tony, "I guess its okay as long as we didn't go off the property."

As Tony and Matthew sat in the truck, Tony pulled open the glove compartment, the ashtray, the cup holder, and had Matthew pushed them closed. They went through different compact discs and Matthew enjoyed listening to his music. He even tried to head bang, by bobbing his head, and even moved his mouth as though he was singing.

Tony put sunglasses on Matthew, but Matthew lifted them up on his forehead.

Alayna knew he liked "jamming" in his truck with his brother, and she was filled with delight at his joy and exclaimed, "I love you! I want a kiss!"

Matthew kissed her, and when she asked for another one, he leaned in again.

Alayna saw the Matthew she loved coming through. She fondly placed her hand on his chin to turn him in her direction, "Hey, look at me, I'm going to try and get you a pass to go home on your birthday," she said, lovingly rubbing his back, "How's that sound . . . wanna go home for your birthday, and Thanksgiving? You should be home by Christmas, huh?"

When Alayna asked about a pass for Matthew, she was overjoyed that they let him come home over a week later.

On August 11, Matthew was able to come home for one night on the weekend.

The drive home was exuberant for Matthew; riding in his truck, looking around at the world; it was the most alert and focused he had ever been.

When Alayna entered Bourbonnais, she began asking Matthew, "Which way do I go?"

Matthew pointed for every turn and straight ahead; he knew where home was.

Alayna pulled up in the driveway and pulled out his wheelchair from the back of the truck. In the meantime, Matthew slid over to the drivers' side; he wanted to sit behind the wheel. Suddenly, Jett jumped up on the passenger side and sat down beside his dad.
Alayna told Matthew, "Babe, I'm hot, let's go in the house, come on . . . over here," as she pointed down at the passenger seat.

Right when Alayna told their son, "Jett, move, so Daddy can come . . ." suddenly Matthew opened the driver's side door to get out. Alayna shrieked, "No, Matt! Ooh! Matthew, you can't come out on *this* side, I was standing over there. You scared me."

Alayna held on to Matthew, and decided to let him walk in the house. She told Cynthia, "He's always in the wheelchair; I want him to feel free of it while he's home."

Alayna asked Matthew if he wanted a bath, and he nodded his head in agreement.

The whole family came over to welcome Matthew's first weekend home: Mandy, Julie, David, Diana, Candice, Krystle, Jonathan, Simona, Tony, and Shannan.

Since Matthew was used to the quietness of a hospital, whenever there was an abrupt noise (like the slamming of a door), he would just shake his head in annoyance.

During this time, Simona moved in with her mom as suggested by her family. Cynthia had her own room, Alayna had Matthew's room, Jett had the middle room (which *was* Cynthia's office), and Simona had the front room–she slept on the couch. All of Simona and Alayna's furniture and belongings were stored in the basement. Simona would lie on the couch at night and her mind would reel with questions. She found herself wondering about Matthew—if he was going to get better, and what if he didn't, how long would she be living back at home? She was used to living alone and although the family's main focus was on Matthew, she felt guilty thinking of her own selfishness. She liked her alone time and missed having her own place.

Later on, Simona finally moved herself down the basement. It had been unused for several years, so it was full of pill bugs, earwigs, and different kinds of spiders. She paid for an exterminator to come and spray; then she set up a corner of the basement as her own little domain. What she didn't realize was bugs were the least of her problems. The basement leaked and she could tell mold was growing behind the walls, because her allergies were acting up. One night, she was asleep and awoke at 2:30 A.M. to the sound of water. She turned on the light to find a waterfall gushing out of the east wall. She frantically pushed her furniture away from the sudden flood and grabbed a broom to sweep it toward the drain. The wearing away of the basement wall was just another added stress to the family. The contractors, who came to do the work, promised the whole basement would be waterproof and mold-free in less than six months. (To this day, the basement is still not completely finished and still leaks).

While the family was visiting, Cynthia was upset about Matthew's truck payments. When Cynthia took Matthew to buy that truck, the salesman suggested disability insurance. Although she would have never dreamed that would actually happen, she did spend the extra $1,300.00 for it. Apparently the salesman never dreamed that it would happen either, because the insurance was bogus. Cynthia was furious, because now she was responsible for Matthew's truck payments. She talked with her family on what she should do, because she personally knew the owner. Everyone suggested she get a lawyer to intervene between her and the owner of the dealership and force him to make the payments. Cynthia did just that, but on and off the owner did whatever he could to not pay. He made late payments and skipped months to try and discourage Cynthia to just pay them herself, but she wasn't falling for that; she just called up her lawyer again. The owner gave many excuses to his tardiness, but was still bound to make the payments until the truck was paid off.

When Matthew went back to the hospital the next day, the doctor finally removed his G-tube out of his stomach. Matthew had been eating some pureed food over the past three weeks, but the doctor kept the feeding tube in for bags of nutrients to build up his strength. While home, Matthew ate solid food. If the hospital would have known, they would have had a fit.

Chapter 13

" . . . count it all joy when ye fall into divers temptations; knowing this, that the trying of your faith worketh patience."
(James 1: 2–3)

The fourth sign of joy is . . . Strength.

Reunion

It was the Saturday before Labor Day, and it was the annual Harris family reunion. This was Matthew's mom's side of the family; his grandma Mandy's side and the only side he knew well. Matthew was able to get his weekend pass for the event, and the extended family was so surprised to see Matthew there. They all were in awe of the miracle that God performed for him and the family rallied around him to shake his hand, hug him, kiss him, and encourage him. He was so surrounded by love and felt it that he would laugh, and his laughter made everyone at ease. Matthew was still not saying any words; he only shook his head "yes" or "no." He now had the catheter out and was able to use the restroom. The trachea was also finally removed from his throat. The doctor who removed it admitted that it was in for way too long and might be why Matthew wasn't speaking. The length of time it was in had damaged certain vocal cords and left a prominent scar.

During the picnic, Matthew had so much attention that Alayna wanted to spend some one-on-one time with him. She walked Matthew to the "look out" of the Kankakee River, and Tony took Jett down the hill to throw rocks in it. Matthew and Alayna were beaming and happy to be together. Shannan was so happy for them that she took some pictures of the couple before they headed back to the picnic.

Cynthia had brought a blanket and pillow for Matthew, in case he became tired and wanted to lie down. Sure enough, after his walk to the river, he was ready to relax. Tony put one arm around his brother's waist and led him to the blanket that Alayna was spreading out under a huge shade tree. Matthew had become so thin, it looked like Tony would be able to pick him up and carry him. The pillows and blanket looked so inviting that Mandy came to lie down beside her grandson for awhile, so did Simona, and then Jett. Jett enjoyed racing around with his "new friends," but every once in awhile, he would come up and check on his dad.

Last Straw

Matthew was moved into another room, closer to the rehabilitation area. Rehab was an important part of his *learning* and the next step for him to be able to come home. Because of the intense "training," no family members were able to be with him during his therapy. Matthew was now walking by himself, but still dragged his foot. To be able to walk, yet have no short-term memory was dangerous; Matthew still needed to have a nurse present in his room.

He was able to say words out loud, but he was very selective in what he said; it was like he was always second guessing himself and afraid he might say the wrong remark.

The family would take Matthew outside and play cards with him; this taught Matthew how to recognize numbers again, add, subtract, and follow directions.

Since Matthew was now going through rehabilitation, the administrators, physicians, therapists, and nurses of the hospital who dealt with him, had a meeting with the family on his progress. These meetings, in the past, were usually accompanied by several questions along with much disagreement, mostly from Alayna. Sure, the personnel were just trying to do their jobs by setting certain rules, but they talked to the family like they knew nothing, and treated them as though they were incapable of taking care of Matthew. The family didn't know if they talked like this to everyone or if the hospital really thought they were inadequate. Needless to say, this infuriated Alayna. After all, she began college classes to become a nurse, and was studying everything she could about how to care for a brain-injured person—especially the man she loved. Besides that, she spent nearly every day observing his every move and progress.

When Matthew would come home on weekends, he would eat dinner like everyone else, but at the hospital, they were still pureeing his food. During the meeting, Alayna had brought this up, and asked if the family could order a pizza for Matthew's birthday. Since his birthday landed in the middle of the week, he was declined a pass, so they couldn't take him home or out to eat. The personnel started scolding Alayna on giving Matthew solid food and that they couldn't trust the family to take him home on the weekends anymore.

Alayna told them, "He eats just fine!"

"And if he chokes?" one of the therapists asked.

"I could choke," Alayna stated, "Matthew is never out of our sight and it's not like we don't know how to use the Heimlich. Besides, have you ever watched him eat?"

Although the meeting seemed like a waste of time, by dinner Matthew's food was ground up, a thicker texture instead of pureed.

Alayna was pleased that a point had been made.

The following early evening, as Cynthia, Simona, and Alayna sat in the front room discussing Matthew, Alayna said, "I just can't wait until he's out of there. I want him home so bad; I miss him. I'm going to call him to say 'goodnight.'"

As she was connected to the nurses' station, she asked, "Can I be transferred to Matthew Gioia's room, please?"

"He's outside with his nurse having a cigarette."

"Is the nurse having the cigarette or Matthew?" Alayna asked very concerned.

"I think both."

"All right, I'll call back later." Alayna got off the phone and tried not to jump to conclusions, but she didn't like the fact someone was smoking around Matthew.

The nurse liked Matthew and took him wherever she went; she thought Matthew smoked because he reached for one of her cigarettes. Matthew's long-term memory remembered that he smoked and he knew how to inhale. The problem with this is that the nurse should have known better; cigarettes constrict the blood vessels and with such severe trauma to Matthew's head, he needed blood to flow freely to his brain.

About a half hour later, Alayna called back and was connected to Matthew's room. She asked his nurse, "I called earlier, but was told you both were outside having a cigarette."

"Yes."

"Did Matthew smoke?" Alayna asked curiously.

"Yes," said the nurse as though it was very normal.

"What?!" Alayna exclaimed.

"Why, I thought he smoked; he reached for it."

"He doesn't smoke and we don't want him to start!" Alayna was ready to sue the hospital, she had enough of all the little mistakes and mishaps Matthew had been going through, like unnecessary pain, being pinned down, and kept from coming home on the weekends. Now having someone with a medical background purposely give him a cigarette was the last straw. Too much effort had been taking place—working with Matthew's damaged motor skills, teaching him how to count, say the alphabet, and focus on one thing more than just a few seconds - he was supposed to be safe at a hospital.

Matthew's twenty-first birthday had to be spent at the hospital and Alayna ordered the pizza. Cynthia, Jett, and Simona joined the celebration and enjoyed watching Matthew get so excited opening his gifts. The best gift was being told that he'd be able to come home the next week–October 4, 2002.

Home

Matthew living back home was challenging. He could not be out of anyone's sight for a minute. Matthew seemed to have developed a similar condition to OCD–obsession compulsive disorder. He would pace back and forth, from one room to another, like a caged lion. He couldn't stand to see a drawer slightly open, or shoes not lined up together, and he always smelled his food or drink now before ingesting. If a dirty plate or glass was sitting on the table, Matthew had to pick it up and put it in the sink, if a tissue or piece of paper was lying on the floor, he had to pick it up and throw it away. Sure it was wonderful to have a "butler," but it was an obsession with him to the point where he could not sit still. If he was told not to worry about it or leave it there, Matthew would look hurt or disgusted. He needed to be doing something *all the time!*

Then, there was another problem; he was ALWAYS going to the bathroom. The toilet wouldn't have time to finish refilling, when Matthew would be flushing it again. At first, everyone thought it was because he was bored or maybe the slightest sensation to urinate would prompt him to run to the bathroom; but it ended up being something very wrong. He still had kidney stones and they were too big to pass. All the scar tissue from the catheter being pulled out and reinserted several times during the course of his hospital stay had blocked any chance a stone (depending on the size) would be able to pass through. At this point, the family was unaware of what Matthew was going through, as the flushing of the toilet every ten minutes became annoying.

One night, Cynthia, Simona, and Matthew sat on the couch, watching television, and eating a slice of homemade peach pie. As soon as Matthew was done eating it, his hands were sticky from the filling. (He still was not very good at using utensils and sometimes would use his fingers to push the food onto the fork or spoon). He stood up to put the empty plate in the sink and rinse his hands.

Cynthia heard the clanging of the plate against the bottom of the sink, a few seconds later, she heard clicking.

Click . . . click . . . click . . .

Suddenly, she frantically jumped up screaming, "Matthew!"

Simona jumped up and followed her mother to check on her brother. With Cynthia yelling, it startled Matthew to stop long enough to see what his mom wanted. Matthew was just about to "wash" his hands in the flame from the stove. Matthew had become confused when it came to the burner, and misconceived it for the faucet. Cynthia looked at Simona with relief as she led Matthew to the sink and turned on the water. Matthew looked like a light bulb went off; he smiled and lightly laughed as though he was embarrassed for making such a mistake.

The family noticed when they would give Matthew math problems to solve or to sign his name he would have his chin on his chest to see the paper, so Alayna went to have Matthew's eyes checked. After the Optometrist showed the test results, Alayna just became angrier at what those people did to Matthew. When Matthew was hit by the shock absorber to the back of his head, it was where the two optic nerves met, and that damaged his peripheral vision. The doctor told her that she should be thankful that he didn't go blind.

Fund Raiser

Alayna and Dee (mother to one of Matthew's friends) decided to throw a fund-raiser for Matthew. It was to be held at a club in Monee; this did not make Mandy very happy. A bar was not appropriate for church members, and therefore felt attending was unacceptable. She thought it was a bad reflection on a church-going family, especially when the church had given generous contributions to Matthew. The heavy metal band performing was called, *Dissolved Mind;* this was too ironic to Matthew's condition. Mandy, Cynthia, and Simona feared Matthew's noise tolerance, now that he suffered from headaches all the time.

Alayna was upset by the disagreements and said, "Matthew's friends want to see him and it's *going* to happen; we already have money invested and the band wants to do this for him!"

Matthew did have a lot of friends, who were all now 21 years old, and this was the one place, and chance, to see them all together.

During an interview for the newspaper, Alayna stated, "Matthew has worked so hard to get to where he's at now. I praise him everyday."

Dee added, "I would hope that people would come and support the benefit. This is just an awful thing to happen to anyone."

On October 6, 2002, Cynthia, Simona, Matthew, and Jett arrived for the fund-raiser in Monee. Once people outside the nightclub noticed Matthew was there, the place nearly emptied, and everyone came out to see him and hug him. Cynthia and Simona's eyes began to tear up as they watched how his guy friends cried and hugged him. Girls came up to Matthew giving him kisses and he thought he was in heaven. When they all finally went back inside the bar, it was a party; a celebration that Matthew had overcome the odds. It was funny seeing tough guys with tattoos and piercing acting like little boys, so excited to be hanging out with their friend once again. The benefit was mostly packed with Matthew's friends, but also a few who read Matthew's story in the newspaper and wanted to show their kindness.

The fundraiser consisted of raffles and items to be auctioned off to help Matthew and his family financially. Matthew's aunt Julie had donated a pottery piece that she had made, Alayna's grandma donated a blanket she had sewn, as well as Dee's grandma, and a local diner donated gift certificates. Plus, there was a pool tournament. Just before the raffle numbers were to be called, a couple of Matthew's friends, and his brother, Tony, brought Matthew up to the D.J. booth.

Seeing Matthew up on the platform above the crowd, the whole bar started cheering, "Gioia . . . Gioia . . . Gioia!"

Each boy gave a speech about Matthew, and thanked everyone for supporting and celebrating with them. Tony went a step further by acknowledging the obvious, " . . . so, let's not forget that we are all adults here, and not let the partying get out of hand, okay? This is a joyous occasion and we are grateful to use this place to celebrate my brother being home."

While Tony was talking, Cynthia and Simona could tell he was holding back from crying, as he went to hug Matthew; they almost missed what happened next - Matthew took the microphone and gave a speech of his *own.* Now, this was shocking to the family, because this was the first time Matthew had said more than just one word, and without being prompted by a question. Cynthia and Simona looked at each other as their jaws about hit the floor, heard the sound of Matthew's voice calmly expressing his gratitude, "Thank you for coming . . . I really appreciate it. I love you."

Tears fell from the eyes of those who knew that Matthew had not spoken in such length, while the crowd went nuts, screaming, cheering, whistling, raising their glasses, and chanting once again, "Gioia . . . Gioia . . . Gioia!"

It was a great evening, but it was obvious that Matthew was growing tired, so the family thought it best to take him home. Everyone gathered around hugging and kissing Matthew goodbye, encouraging him to keep up the great work, and to get better. Matthew was all smiles that night, beaming when he was approached by one familiar face after another. Since his brain could no longer recall recent memories, his whole night would be erased by the time he got home. The proceeds from the fund-raiser did help expenses a lot, and the family appreciated all who made it successful.

Breakfast

Sunday, October 27, Alayna sat with Matthew on the couch in the family room, trying to make him talk, "Say, 'HI.'"

"*Hi*" Matthew would whisper.

"Louder."

"Hi."

"I love you."

Matthew smiled and nodded his head, "yes."

"Say it."

"You love me."

Alayna laughed, "No, I mean say 'I love you' silly."

Matthew got up off the couch and walked away, and Alayna noticed he was walking better and not dragging his foot as much anymore. When Matthew walked back, Alayna told him to sit at the kitchen table, which was about two feet away of the family room. She put two bowls on the table, two spoons, and a box of *Berry* cereal and milk.

"Pour your cereal."

Matthew shrugged his shoulder; his eyes shown he was scared and confused.

"Pour your cereal."

Matthew grabbed the milk, with the cap still on it, and tipped it over his bowl.

"Stop being silly; you know what comes first."

Matthew's face turned sad, his eyes cast down, and he slightly shrugged his shoulder.

"You don't know?"

Matthew put out his hand, palm up, and pointed to Alayna's bowl.

"Oh, you want to do my bowl?" Alayna asked as she pushed her bowl toward him.

Matthew's eyes became wide, he shook his head "no," and he started pointing his finger back and forth, from her bowl to his bowl. What he really wanted was for her to do it, so he could see how it was done.

Alayna told him, "I want some cereal!"

Matthew's face fell again. He took his left hand and started opening the top of the cereal box, and then placed it in his right hand, to unravel the bag inside with his left. (He still barely used his right arm, after that hand restraint incident, which caused the small stoke).

When he looked at Alayna, he knew by her face that he was doing well; he smiled. Alayna giggled seeing his face light up again. He poured the cereal in Alayna's bowl first and then his. As he went to put the box on the table, he stopped himself, looked inside, and noticed the bag was still open to expose the cereal. He immediately started to roll the bag down into the box and shut the lid. When he sat the box back on the table; the next process escaped his mind. He became confused and paused.

"What's next?" Alayna asked.

Matthew stuck his hand in *Alayna's* cereal, nervously adjusting the colored corn balls, just as she asked, "Now what do you do?" then stated, "I hope your hands are clean," just as Matthew pulled his hand out of *his* cereal.

Matthew shrugged his shoulder as he pushed Alayna's bowl toward her.

"What goes next?" Alayna asked profoundly.

Matthew's mouth dropped open, his head kept shaking side to side, and his hands would raise palms up. Grabbing his bowl and shifting it away from him, and back toward him again, as a means to tell her that he didn't know what went next. Finally, he became so frustrated that he grabbed his spoon, scooped it in his cereal, and went to take a bite.

"Hey, I want milk in my cereal!" Alayna said.

Matthew bit down on a spoonful of dry cereal, and Alayna groaned. Matthew's face looked surprised and he grinned real big.

Alayna started laughing and asked him, "Wouldn't that taste better with some milk? Put some milk in it, silly."

Matthew unscrewed the lid with his left fingers and poured the milk in his cereal, then Alayna's. He smiled and nodded his head up and down happily, feeling he accomplished something big and was able to enjoy his breakfast.

A Third Surgery

Toward the end of October, Alayna had called Chicago Medical to schedule a day to put Matthew's skull bone (that they cut out in May), back in his head. The lady on the other end of the phone scheduled the surgery for the 31st–Halloween. Just as Cynthia was about to make arrangements for taking off work and booking a room at a hotel, the hospital called back with some disturbing news; they lost Matthew's skull.

"What?!" Alayna shrieked, "Lost it? How is that possible?"

As the hospital apologized and assured that they would do everything in their power to find it, Alayna told Cynthia and Simona what was going on.

Cynthia was upset, "What else can possibly happen to him?"

Simona was rocked, "This is ridiculous! They *better* find it or else we *will* sue–Christian or not!"

Alayna agreed and said, "I've about had it the way these hospitals don't care about Matthew."

A few days later, the family received a phone call from Chicago Medical saying they found Matthew's bone.

Alayna said, "They found it in the back of the freezer."

Simona was already skeptical, "What freezer?" Simona sarcastically stated, "Are you sure it's Matthew's? After all, the way they're losing body parts, it could be anyone's!"

Simona believed that she was starting to learn how everything happens for a reason. When her job announced they were closing, she took that as a sign that this was where God wanted her to be since Matthew needed eyes on him at all times. She felt that by her family encouraging she come back home and help with Matthew was God's way of giving her a place to live before work dropped the axe. Because her job closed, the state had offered to pay for college. (Simona decided to study Law Enforcement to eventually become a Juvenile Officer.) She was trying to follow the path that was in front of her. She was excited about her new career choice and tried to be optimistic (which was something new for her). She filled up all her time to ignore the anger that was building inside her. The short fuse she suffered suddenly had no wick at all.

She began feeling useless when it came to Matthew, plus she was jobless, moneyless, and lonely; these things were taunting her.

Being back at home, she saw her old friends and cousins that were married with children, but she had dedicated all her time to her job. Now she was living back with her mom and felt her independence slip away.

Alayna knew for Matthew's surgery that they would have to shave the area on the left side of Matthew's head, follow the scar to cut and peel back the skin, and attach his bone back to his skull. She figured it would be best to just shave his whole head, so that it would be easier on the surgeons, and that way his hair would grow back all at once. Matthew's hair was so thick and wavy; it was a shame to have to shave it all off.

When she was finished shaving Matthew's head, the indentation was so great and almost fake. Matthew looked like he had no left side of his head. The thought that behind the skin was his brain chilled the family; there had been nothing to protect it for over five months. It was frightening to think that if he might have fallen anytime during that course and hit his head; it could have killed him.

On the 30th, Cynthia, Simona, and Alayna escorted Matthew to Chicago Medical. He had to arrive the day before the surgery to be prepared and observed to make sure nothing would cause complications. They were brought to a small cubical where there was only a curtain, two chairs, and a bed in-between. After they had settled in the "room"–time stopped. Maybe every two hours someone would come in and take Matthew's blood pressure, or a doctor would show up to answer questions. Matthew was getting restless. Cynthia tried reading a book, but with Matthew always trying to get up, it was hard to concentrate. In his condition, Matthew couldn't be still; let alone to be enclosed in such tight quarters that faced only a curtain, barely a foot from the end of the hard hospital bed. Alayna tried to keep him calm by explaining their plans to take Jett trick-or-treating, and Matthew's eyes lit up like a pumpkin–he was excited about the candy.

"They could at least put a T.V. in the corner," Simona said.

Around ten hours later, finally the surgeon came in and explained the pros and cons of surgery; he sounded very hopeful that everything would be fine. Visiting hours were almost over; Matthew was being sent for some tests, and to get a good night sleep before the morning surgery. The women hated to leave him, but lovingly hugged and kissed him goodbye. The women were a bit worried, but they tried to make the best of it. They ate dinner that night in the hotel restaurant where they were staying, and the next morning went out for a big breakfast.

When they arrived at the hospital just before noon, Matthew was out of recovery and sitting in his room with his head bandaged and a big smile on his face strapped to the chair. One of the nurses greeted the three women and informed them that Matthew had already walked up and down the halls twice, and tried to "escape" that they had to secure him. Matthew hated to stay in one place, especially if he had to sit or lay down.

The first thing Alayna wanted to do was take off the bandage and see Matthew's head.

She unraveled the gauze, exposing stitches where the last stitches had been, as dried blood stained his scalp. He was so happy to see his family, but after about a half-hour, Matthew got on the bed and curled up in a fetal position. He put his hand on his head and became very still; he had a headache.

After a couple of hours later, Alayna was getting restless, along with everyone else.

Cynthia asked, "Where is the doctor . . . can't they release him yet?"

Alayna went to the nurse's station to ask them to page the doctor. "We have to get home. I promised our son that I would take him trick-or-treating."

Finally, the doctor gave the go-ahead.

By the time they arrived home, Matthew's head was already starting to swell. He would sit on the couch looking so pitiful. His damaged eye (from the hit by Doughboy) was once again black and blue, and also swollen shut. The more time that went by, Matthew's head looked like a basketball; the stitches made him look like he actually had on a mask. Once the trick-or-treaters began ringing the doorbell, they would take a look at him and their little eyes would get as wide as saucers. Since Halloween is no longer for the little kids, some teenagers approached the door.

A girl asked, "Is that real?"—referring to Matthew's head.

Alayna responded warningly, "Yes, that is what can happen to you when you drink."

The girl's mouth dropped open, and she and her friends took off relatively fast.

Alayna told Simona, "You know, I should take Matthew to all the High Schools and show them just what can happen, if they drink or do drugs."

Simona added, "Yeah that would be a good idea. It might just change someone's life."

A Promise Kept

The family brought Matthew to church, and the church members were thrilled to see the miracle before them. Matthew walked in with a big smile on his face and confidently stuck his hand out to shake the men's hands as they welcomed him. When the ladies reached out to shake his hand, Matthew gently leaned down and kissed the top of their hand. Oh, what a gentleman!

The church family was so pleased to see how God had heard and answered their prayers. Matthew's presence in church helped the members of the congregation strengthen their faith, too. Besides just praying, they kept a basket in the front of the church to hold an offering for Matthew. This money helped Cynthia so much with the travel expenses, a motel a couple of times, and hospital parking. The offering was indeed a God-send for her to pay for things she normally would not be able to afford during the last five hard months.

Simona kept her promise and went to church. Simona went a step further; she stood up and testified how thankful she was that God helped her brother and how far the Lord had brought Matthew–further than expected.

Mandy was overjoyed that her whole family took up the whole pew beside her. All she ever wanted was her family to be saved and in church.

Chapter 14

"Know ye that the Lord he is God: it is he that hath made us, and not we ourselves . . ."
"For the Lord is good; his mercy is everlasting . . ."
(Psalms 100: 3 & 5)

The fifth sign of joy is . . . Thankfulness.

Holiday Dispute

Through Thanksgiving and Christmas, the family felt the joy of having the whole family together; they truly had so much to be thankful for. Matthew was now speaking clearly, but never started a conversation and was unable to keep one going. The one thing Matthew had no problem with was eating, he loved to eat, and his thin, frail, frame was now getting thicker and healthier looking. Matthew sat at the end of the table, where his grandpa used to sit and asked, "Where's Grandpa?"

Everyone became quiet, they didn't know if they should tell him the truth or not.

Simona told him, "He passed away."

"He died?" as Matthew looked shocked and saddened, because he truly loved his grandpa Sam.

"We carried his casket after the funeral. You, Tony, and I were pallbearers." Matthew shook his head in disbelief, and looked unhappy about being unable to remember.

On New Years Eve, Cynthia and Alayna had a run-in; a disagreement about Matthew. Cynthia wanted him to be in church with her for night-watch service.

Alayna, on the other hand, wanted Matthew with her and her family for the night, and put up a fight, "If Matthew wasn't hurt he wouldn't spend his New Year's in church!"

Cynthia defended, "I want him in church with me. God saved him and he needs to be there so He can keep blessing Matthew with good health."

The verbal fighting began escalating into drudging up the past, and turned into a bunch of hateful and hurtful words toward each other. Alayna got her way.

Simona, unaware of the dispute, happened to call her mom to tell her that she would be spending her New Year's Eve with some friends. Cynthia began crying and told her what happened. Simona knew that she couldn't leave without trying to patch things up between her mom and Alayna. On her way to her friends, she had a feeling that Alayna and her family were eating at their usual buffet restaurant. She drove into the parking lot, and sure enough she saw Alayna's car. She walked up to the table where Matthew, Jett, Alayna, and Alayna's family were sitting and asked her if they could talk.

Right away, Alayna became defensive, "How dare you track me down and ruin dinner with my family!"

Simona was calm and just wanted to ask Alayna's side of the story to smooth out the friction, because it bothered her to see her mom and Alyana at odds with each other.

Alayna stood up and told Simona, "Let's go outside!"

Simona apologized to Alayna's family, and wished them a Happy New Year. Seeing Matthew sitting there with them, she felt strange to go up and kiss him for the New Year in front of Alayna's family.

When Simona and Alayna were outside, Simona tried to explain that her mom just wanted Matthew with her at church, " . . . it's nothing against you."

"He is *my* fiancé and he wouldn't want to spend his New Year's in church from eight to midnight."

"I understand that, and I agree with *both* of you. Matthew is just one person and it's like he is being pulled, but it's not a bad thing. It shows that he is loved knowing his mom and fianceé want to spend as much time with him as possible. You two shouldn't fight over him–compromise."

Alayna changed the subject, "How dare you, track me down like this! Do you have some kind of radar on me?"

"I just drove by and know that this is where you always eat; it wasn't like I hit every restaurant in town. If you weren't here, I was just going to head out and meet my friends." Finally, Alayna backed down a little, so Simona continued, "It's not about who is right here, Alayna, it's just that you want to spend New Year's with Matt, and so does my mom."

It was tough, but Simona thought she made her point; Alayna just wanted to feel right and have someone agree with *her.* Alayna became quiet and Simona found it as an opportunity to give her a hug and end the bickering, "I don't want to come home and you two still mad at each other, okay?"

"Well . . ."

"Go, back in there and enjoy your dinner. Have a great New Year and tell your family I'm sorry about the intrusion."

Simona believed that maybe she made a difference that night, but this was a picnic compared to what she would be dealing with in the future.

Music and Matthew

By the end of January, after playing with Jett outside in the snow, Matthew called snowballs . . . shells. So Alayna started going around the house pointing to objects and asking him what they were. He gave about two-thirds of the correct answers; Alayna told

Cynthia and Simona about what happened. Therefore, everyday someone would take the time to help Matthew recognize objects around the house.

With Cynthia the only one working, Alayna and Simona had to divide their college classes, so that someone was always with Matthew. Jett would sometimes go to pre-school to be around kids his own age.

At night, the family would gather around and watch television. When the second season of *American Idol* started, it was a show everyone looked forward to watching. Matthew and Jett loved music, Cynthia caught the last season's finale and was curious to watch this one from the beginning, and Alayna and Simona missed the first season because of work. Everyone already had their favorite singers; Cynthia liked Kimberly Locke, Simona liked Clay Aiken, and Alayna couldn't make up her mind between Kimberly Caldwell and Josh Gracin.

Week after week, everyone voted for their favorite. Simona liked Clay, because he resembled the guys she had crushes on growing up. She found out that he had recorded music prior to the reality show. She heard him sing songs she used to sing in church like *The Blood Will Never Lose Its Power* and *I Know Who Holds Tomorrow.* Then there were songs Clay sang, originally sung by Avalon, Steven Curtis Chapman, and Michael W. Smith. Some of these songs were the same ones she held close to her as she drove to and from the hospitals where Matthew stayed.

Simona also read about how Clay Aiken was a teacher for children with autism and special needs. Until now, Simona was unsure of how to deal with Matthew being in the position he was in and found she felt very uneasy. She loved her brother and was told several times that she babied him. After reading about how Clay dealt with those children with disabilities, Simona knew she was taking care of her brother all wrong. She needed to treat Matthew like *he* would like to be treated and not like her *baby* brother. She finally came to terms with realizing that just by "watching" Matthew was not *helping* him.

Cynthia told Simona and Alayna about a dinner that went on every year, for the Post Office credit union members, and asked if they would like to go with her, "I never go and I should, but I feel uneasy going alone."

"Sounds fun," Alayna exclaimed, "Sure, we'll go!"

On that night, Cynthia, Simona, Alayna, Matthew, and Jett got all dressed up and went to the dinner. There was dancing, too; and Matthew *took* Alayna's hand. She became a little flushed at the way he was so dominant. Matthew loved listening to the music and dancing with Alayna. Simona and Jett joined them to do the *Chicken Dance* and Matthew laughed at how funny everyone looked doing it.

Later, Alayna and Matthew danced to a slow, romantic song. After that dance, the couple came back to the table. Without any prodding from anyone, Matthew shocked everyone by getting on one knee, holding Alayna's hand, and asking, "Would you marry me?"

Everyone's face lit up, "Wow!!"

Alayna hugged him and said, "Yes, Matthew!"

It was then that Matthew began to get a little more confidence in himself and say words aloud when he thought of them.

Seeing how much Matthew loved music, Simona would sing and dance with her brother when it was her day to watch him. Every song Simona would sing to him, he could finish by whistling, humming, or sometimes singing the words. (She couldn't believe how many songs he remembered.) He had perfect pitch, except for certain octaves due to the damage from his trachea. Singing helped Matthew "talk" more, because he was getting used to *hearing* himself. She also made him say words or sing loudly to get used to his voice. Simona loved to make him laugh and purposely vocalized the *Chicken Dance,* Matthew laughed while he clapped and stomped his feet during the song. Simona felt that by acting foolish, she helped Matthew feel relaxed and know that it was okay to express his emotions. So far, Matthew had only expressed happiness, even when he felt pain, or embarrassment.

Matthew had become paranoid since he was home, and now was learning to express his feelings. His pacing and looking out the windows and doors was something the family thought he did because he was bored and wanted to go somewhere, but one night he really scared Alayna. Jett was in bed, Cynthia was at church, and Simona was invited over to friends, and Alayna and Matthew were the only ones in the house.

Matthew looked out the window and had this frightened look, "Someone's out there."

"What!" Alayna exclaimed.

"They're trying to get in."

Alayna panicked, but then realized that this is what Matthew had been doing all along. He always was checking and rechecking the front and back doors to make sure that they were locked. She sat him down and told him, "You are safe here. Nobody can hurt you anymore."

Matthew nodded his head, agreeing, and trusted Alayna's words.

The Dog

The beginning of March, Alayna came home with a birthday gift for herself, a female cocker spaniel, which she claimed Matthew had bought her. She walked in and handed the puppy to Simona, "Isn't she cute? I just couldn't walk out of the pet store without her." Alayna knew Cynthia was going to have a fit, but bought the canine anyway.

Simona's stomach was in knots seeing that dog and all she could do was roll her eyes, "How much was she?"

"Six hundred dollars," Alayna said in anticipation of a reaction.

Simona's eyes lit up in disbelief that Alayna would fork over that much money for a dog.

"I don't care what your mom says . . . I'm keeping her."

It was as if Alayna wanted Cynthia to yell at her so she would have an excuse to fight. Simona knew there would be one and she just couldn't handle the anxiety. She needed to put the fire out *before* it started. Simona tried to ponder a solution, as Alayna left to take the puppy, along with Matthew and Jett, to show her mom.

When Cynthia got home from work, Simona asked her mom if she would like to go out to a Chinese restaurant. During dinner, Simona broke the news to her mom.

Cynthia asked, "Is this why you suggested we go out for dinner . . . to prepare me?"

"I just can't take the fighting and it's like she's wanting one . . . you know?"

"All I know is that I find it very disrespectful to buy a dog, and have it live in my house, without asking my permission."

"I know and I agree, but what's done is done, and there's no need having a bad night if there's nothing we can do about it."

"How much did it cost?"

Simona held back, "Now, it. . . . it's . . ."

"Was it over a hundred dollars?"

"Uh . . . more . . . like . . . uh . . ."

"Three hundred?" Cynthia asked with a higher vocal in her voice.

Simona cleared her throat, "Si . . . six . . . hundred."

"WHAT? She complains she can hardly pay for new shoes for Jett. She's always borrowing money from her dad - he's practically at our house every week."

"I know . . . that is why I thought I'd let you cool off before we go home."

Alayna called Simona on her cell, "Where are you?"

"We went out to eat."

"Is she mad? Did you tell her?" Alayna asked excitedly.

"No . . . uh, she thinks it'd be nice to have a dog around the house."

"Yeah . . . right. What did she *really* say?"

"Seriously, she's okay about it."

When Cynthia and Simona arrived home, Cynthia leaned down and gave the puppy love as she ooh'd and awed over it. Alayna's face was very doubtful of the whole act, but Cynthia was not going to give her a fight; her daughter made a special effort to avoid one and she was going to honor her request.

After Shocks

On March 24, 2003, something happened that no one was prepared to face. Alayna and Matthew were in the backyard with Jett. Alayna wanted to plant some flowers and Matthew was picking up some broken branches that fell off the tree. It began to drizzle outside and Alayna told Matthew and Jett, "Let's get inside before it starts to rain."

Alayna was walking in front of Matthew; Jett was already through the patio door when Alayna turned around and saw Matthew looking up to the sky. Alayna called his name, but Matthew didn't respond. When she went toward him, Matthew started to twitch. She knew just what was going on—Matthew was having a seizure.

Alayna screamed to Jett, "Get me the cordless!"

Jett was startled. He couldn't understand why his daddy was lying on the ground and his mommy was not leaving his side. He ran back outside toward his mom, as the screen door slammed shut.

Alayna demanded, "Go in the house and get me the phone!"

Jett was so scared that he had a hard time getting the screen door back open. Finally, he opened the door and ran inside, grabbed the cordless phone, and ran it to his mom.

Alayna hated that Jett was seeing his dad this way, but she needed help, so she ordered Jett, "Get Simona! Tell her it's an emergency!"

Alayna was on pins and needles as the seconds felt like minutes ticking away. Simona was still in bed, asleep, when Jett opened the basement door and screamed down in a trembling voice, "Monie, hurry! Come quick, it's an emergency!"

Simona jumped up from the sound of Jett's cry, "What, Jett?"

"Hurry, Mommy needs you, it's an emergency!"

Simona ran up the stairs as Jett pointed and led her, "They're outside!"

When Simona saw Matthew lying on the ground and Alayna beside him, as a soft rain fell, everything faded out of focus for her, except that very image. Although she was running out of the house toward them, it seemed like she was moving in slow motion. She didn't know what happened, she thought Matthew had fallen and hurt himself. He didn't look stiff, his body was more of a shiver than a shake, his eyes had more a frightened look to them, and his bottom lip quivered as he moaned. When she dropped to her knees beside him, Alayna told her that he was having a seizure. Fear engulfed Simona to where she thought she wouldn't be able to catch her breath. Out of the corner of her eye, she saw Jett standing at his daddy's feet, and she found the strength to put on a brave face. Simona held Matthew's hand with her right and with her left hand she nervously ran her fingers through his hair.

Alayna kept repeating to Matthew, "It's almost over, Matt. Relax."

Simona bent down to assure her brother, (and herself), "Its okay, Matthew," then turned and asked Alayna, "How long has this been going on?"

"It's been almost five minutes. The ambulance is on its way."

Soon they heard the siren and Alayna turned to Simona, "Are you okay to be here with him while I show them where we're at?"

"Yes." Simona said confidently.

Alayna opened the gate which faced the street and waved the paramedics over.

Simona began humming the "chicken dance" to Matthew and he turned his head and looked right in her eyes, "You're going to be okay, Matt," and she began to hum to him again.

Matthew's breathing was getting back to normal; he loosened up and began trying to move around.

"No, Matthew, wait for them to check you over," Simona calmly stated.

When the paramedics leaned down to help Matthew, Simona stood up beside Alayna.

"Can you stay and watch Jett while I go with him to the hospital?" Alayna asked.

"Of course," said Simona, shocked that Alayna would even have to ask.

As Alayna followed Matthew and the paramedics into the ambulance, Jett and Simona stood on the edge of the driveway and watched the doors close. The ambulance didn't take off right away, because the paramedics had to take Matthew's vitals and some blood.

Meanwhile, Jett stood staring at the vehicle and asked his aunt, "What are they doing with my daddy?"

"They're going to take him to the hospital."

Now, Jett just got used to his daddy being home, and knew the last time he was in the hospital was a long, long time. He leaned down and picked up a rock and threw it at the ambulance, walked down the driveway and threw another one, and then another one.

"Jett, stop it." Simona said, "Come here."

Jett reluctantly approached her and Simona took him by the hand, "I know your upset, but they are going to help your daddy. You're mommy is with him, and you know that she'll make sure everything is okay."

Jett pulled his hand out of Simona's, turned around, walked a few steps toward the ambulance, and sat down.

Simona knew he was hurting and confused, so she told him, "Let's go inside, Jett. I'll put on some cartoons for you."

Meanwhile, Alayna called Cynthia at work to meet her at the hospital. Alayna was a wreck; she wanted answers. After some tests, they found what provoked the seizure. It was the initial blow to Matthew's eye and the aneurysm from behind it. Since the brain runs on electrical *charges,* with some of Matthew's gray matter disintegrated, there was a "dead end" that the charge hit and caused the body to convulse.

The doctor came in to explain what to expect, "We have to monitor his levels and figure out the best dose of medication for him to keep the seizures under control."

Matthew was in the hospital for two days for observation when they finally let him come home. Jett was happy his daddy was back, but it was obvious what he had seen made him grow up; his mannerisms were more adult-like and he seemed to take his dad under his little wing. He was now getting out of hand. All the commotion was just too much for a three-year-old to digest. Alayna was getting nervous when it came to dealing with him.

She sat down with Cynthia and Simona and told them, "I worry about Jett, he is getting so hard to handle. I used to tell Matthew, and with one look, Jett would straighten up. I can't do this by myself. I give you permission to help discipline him, spank him, or ground him; whatever it takes to keep him under control. I just don't know what to do."

Exactly a month later, Matthew suffered another seizure. It was early in the morning when Alayna and Matthew were down the basement in the shower. Suddenly, Matthew began acting strange. Alayna knew what was happening and tried to get him out of the shower, but he became too heavy. Her main concern was getting him on his side. Most of Matthew's body was now on the floor, except for his ankle. As he was convulsing, it was banging on the ledge and against the shower doors, causing his foot to swell.

Cynthia was the only one in the house, besides the couple, and *fortunately* was running late for work. Alayna screamed for help, but Cynthia couldn't make out what she was saying. Usually the two are always laughing and joking around, but somehow she felt it was different this time. She stopped to listen and heard Alayna scream.

Cynthia went into the kitchen and opened the basement door, "Alayna?"

"Call an ambulance . . . Matt's having a seizure!"

Cynthia ran to the phone and called for help. The paramedics just happened to be in the neighborhood when the call came through. Before Cynthia had a chance to tell Alayna they were on their way - they were there. Cynthia guided them to the basement and before Alayna could be warned, the paramedics were heading to the bathroom. Alayna scarcely heard them coming toward her (since the water was still running in the shower), and barely had enough time to grab a towel and cover herself. As the paramedics covered Matthew and brought him upstairs, Alayna gathered his clothes so he could get dressed in the hospital.

Once at the hospital, Alayna demanded to know why this happened again.

The doctor instructed her, “Don’t panic, it may take a few times before we can figure out the right dose of medication for Matthew.”

“What about his levels?” she asked.

“His levels are fine, but like I said before, seizures can still happen if the charge has no where to go. Even if we find the right amount, it may hold them off for awhile, but there is no guarantee that he’ll never have one again.”

This was an addition to the worry the family had been going through. Just when it seemed everyone was comfortable with caring for Matthew in his current state, seizures were a condition that had to keep them on their toes. With Simona being afraid to take her eyes off her brother before, she was now faced with that fear again. Even Cynthia was finding herself feeling on edge whenever Matthew would move suddenly or make a funny noise.

Although Matthew looked perfectly normal to people; it was when he would answer with one-word replies or a confused “huh?” that gave his disability away. He was still dragging his foot once in a while and the re-attachment of the bone in his skull, which was frozen, *shrank.* This caused a large indentation that was very grotesque and visible when his dark hair would be combed back or if his ball cap matted his hair down. The muscle on the left side of his head detached and fell to the side of his face. This generated a dreadful, loud popping noise when he would yawn, throwing his jaw out of place, and causing him severe pain and panic as he tried to pop it back in. He still struggled to remember his family member’s names, and appeared shocked when told that Jett was his *son.* In Matthew's mind, he still thought that he was 18 years old and looked confused when told he was 21. Matthew knew he was different than before and often would shake his head "no" or say "I can't anymore" when asked about his capabilities. The overall condition of Matthew broke the hearts of his family and made some angry.

Alayna declared that the town and those who did this to Matthew should be informed of his struggles, "They need to know what he is going through–what we are going through!" and called the paper to run a story.

A reporter came by to do the article on Matthew which would be run on Father's Day. The reporter asked questions and took statements from the family. Alayna noted, "Matthew is forever going to pay for what *they* did."

Simona injected, "He came a long way, and it has a lot to do with Alayna being there."

Cynthia replied, "She loves him more than anybody I ever knew could love somebody."

Alayna stated, "He was perfectly healthy before this. He had nothing wrong with him. Now he has heart problems, bladder problems, and seizures."

Cynthia told the reporter, "All the family's put their lives on hold, because we have to take care of Matthew twenty-four hours a day. We're crammed in here. Sometimes it gets tense and stressful, but we all love one another dearly. We do."

"I think this brought me to realize how much my family means to me," Simona said, "I feel like this all changed our perspectives somehow."

When the reporter asked Jett what he felt, the boy replied, "Mad at those bad people. I want to be a policeman, so I can put away the bad guys who hurt my daddy."

Alayna ended the interview by sending a message to the assailants who attacked Matthew, "God knows what you did, and *you're* going to pay for it."

Out of the blue, Matthew began to ask for someone. No one was able to figure out who Matthew was asking for, because he had a hard time getting out the persons last name. Matthew's persistence went on for a couple of months when Alayna figured it out. Matthew was asking for his best friend Todd; he wanted to know where he was. Alayna promised Matthew that she would try and find him.

Dad Returns

Chuck had been writing Cynthia for awhile to see how Matthew was doing; unfortunately he was writing from prison, again. He had been reading his Bible, going to church, and praying often while incarcerated. He asked Cynthia if he could come back to Illinois to help out when he got released. She was undecided and talked it over with the family.

Alayna was thrilled about it; she knew how much Matthew loved his dad, and she looked forward to meeting him. Simona was just the opposite, along with Mandy, who did not want him to come back. They didn't trust him and there were still some pretty raw feelings that hadn't healed. Cynthia thought Chuck would be a great help; she remembered him as a guy who used to cook and clean. She believed that he had truly changed and could be a considerable asset to Alayna and Simona, who were burning the candles at both ends with studying, cleaning, mowing, and taking care of Matthew.

Cynthia wrote Chuck back and told him they would make room. He would be sleeping on the couch in the living room.

Chuck came back to Illinois in June. He returned hurt; Tina, his only daughter, had "cleaned house" while he was in prison. Chuck had many things coming to him once his parents died. Charles died years ago, but Myrtle died while Chuck was behind bars, and Tina took everything out of the house. What she didn't keep, she sold. This hurt Chuck deeply. There were many things he owned as a boy, and things he had collected, that were rightfully Tony and Matthews to inherit. Not one cent went to Tina's brothers; Chuck felt she was very heartless. He figured that Tina didn't want him to have anything, but Chuck didn't care about what *he* was out; he wanted his sons to have it. (Now Matthew didn't know what he was missing, but Tony did. He tried finding his sister, but gave up).

Chuck was also very distraught over what Tina took of his parent's things. While living in California, he was able to love his parents like a son should. He realized how the circumstances must have been when he was a baby and how much they truly loved him. Charles and Myrtle never gave up on Chuck; they loved him and he finally grew up enough to understand their sacrifice. He missed them and Tina taking away those memories, if only in material belongings, hurt him deeply. He knew he had to pray to forgive her or else it would tear him up inside.

On the Go

Matthew's restlessness had gotten the better of him. He was not used to staying at home all the time; he was always a guy on the go. He was bored and his mind carried his legs. Simona was down at her grandma Mandy's. Alayna was cleaning and thinking that Matthew was sitting outside on the swing (where he usually sat; often looking like he was trying to remember *something*). When Alayna called for him, he didn't come. She began to look in the bathrooms and then outside, but Matthew was no where to be found. She began to panic and called Mandy's house; asking if Matthew walked down there.

Mandy called out to her granddaughter to look outside to see if Matthew was in sight, but when Simona ran out front, she didn't see him anywhere. Everyone's blood ran cold. Where could Matthew have gone? If someone stopped him, would he get in their car?

Alayna jumped in her car to go toward the highway. Simona ran to the park, down the hill, heading for the river below, and praying every step of the way that he wasn't down there. Suddenly, Simona's cell phone rang; it was Alayna. She found Matthew eight blocks away, walking toward the YMCA. Who knows where he was headed, but Matthew could have got lost and end up missing.

That day didn't stop Matthew from wandering off. Simona found him walking toward the highway the following week. When she went to retrieve him, Matthew became upset with her. He stood in the middle of the street and refused to turn around. Simona tried to understand him and asked him, "Where are you going?" Matthew shrugged his shoulders, he didn't know, he just wanted to go *somewhere.* After about ten long minutes of debating, Matthew finally gave up and reluctantly headed back toward the house.

Matthew loved his wallet and hated to be without it, so Cynthia made sure he always had a little money in it. One day, Matthew seemed to leave after everyone checked on him. By the time the family realized he was gone, he was on his way back home. He had went to the gas station and bought a Reese Peanut Butter cup and a strawberry crush. Simona suggested getting an alarm system. Although they could have used one, Cynthia declined the idea. She just couldn't afford another expense while supporting everyone. (The family ended up getting an alarm a year later. When Simona began working, she paid for it).

Chapter 15

"When thou art in tribulation . . . if thou turn to the Lord thy God . . . he will not forsake thee . . ."
(Deuteronomy 4: 30&31)

Change in Guardianship

Matthew had been in and out of the hospital over his constant urinating, or lack thereof. Alayna always ended up taking him in the evening or late at night, and every time the hospital would give her a hard time about signing the order and release papers. She would come home and complain to Cynthia that she was tired of fighting with the hospital on her right to sign forms on Matthew.

One night, Matthew seethed in pain from his abdomen and bled from his penis. Alayna and Simona took Matthew to the local hospital, but after hours there, the E.R. doctor suggested the girls bring him up to Chicago Medical. It was closing in on midnight and to drive over an hour up north was going to put in for a long night. They decided to stop by the house before the trip, to change, and fill Cynthia in on what was going on. When the girls told Cynthia what they had to do, she asked if they wanted her to take him.

Alayna told her, "Its okay, we'll take him. It's just Jett, is it okay he stay's here with you?"

"Of course," Cynthia chuckled. Jett was already asleep beside her as she continued, "If you're going to be home after 9:00 in the morning, then I'll call work and let them know I'll be coming in late."

Once at Chicago Medical, Alayna and Simona waited on Matthew's tests and x-rays, and then were confronted on signing papers for procedures. Alayna went to sign and was asked if she was family, "I'm his fiancée."

As the doctor and nurses looked at each other with concern, Alayna pointed to Simona, "That's his sister."

The papers were set in front of Simona and a wave of panic came over her. What if she signed and something happened to her brother, she would never be able to forgive herself. She looked at Alayna and knew that *she* would sign, so she took the pen and signed her name. As they waited on Matthew's procedure, Simona told Alayna, "That is the most terrifying feeling . . . to be *that* responsible for someone."

Matthew came back very groggy, and as he laid there trying to fight sleep, the girls waited on his results. The doctor told the girls that Matthew's kidney was full of stones and would have to be removed by surgery and with the obstruction of scar tissue that there was no way he would ever pass them. "I advise you call and make an appointment to get this done as soon as possible." Matthew was released a little after 5:00 A.M.

Cynthia was the only one working: maintaining the mortgage, utilities, food, and household things for a family of six people on just *her* paycheck. Alayna had agreed to pay Cynthia rent on her unemployment checks. Simona had agreed too, but her unemployment was running out since she didn't have any dependents to claim. Needless to say, the tension in the household was silently and intensely mounting. Since Matthew was disabled, he was actually a ward of the state. A woman by the name of Sally was Matthew's guardian ad litum, which was someone who looked after Matthew's best interest. Alayna told Cynthia about an idea she had about *them* being guardian over Matthew. This way she could sign the papers when she took Matthew to the hospital, yet Cynthia would still be in *full* control. (The way Alayna presented the information; it sounded what was supposed to be *power of attorney*). Trusting Alayna, Cynthia agreed. After all, Alayna was unemployed and studying nursing–she was an available asset to Matthew. She had *time* for him, *educated* to care for him if something should happen, plus she *loved* him; there was no reason not to believe this was wrong.

Alayna invited Sally over and discussed the issue; Sally informed Alayna the stipulations of guardianship, but Alayna never informed Cynthia. Cynthia believed that she was just giving Alayna the right to sign in her absence; she didn't know she was signing for her to *be* absent.

When Cynthia and Alayna went to the lawyers to get it in writing, the lawyer looked at Cynthia and asked her, "Do you understand?"

Cynthia trusted Alayna and the lawyer, and thought if there was something unstable about what she was about to sign, they would have told her. In the end, Cynthia was guardian, but only over Matthew's estate; Alayna was guardian over Matthew's body. Cynthia thought she was doing right by Alayna, seeing how well she took care of Matthew and loved him. She loved Alayna like a daughter, and believed that she was doing right by Matthew and the family. Besides, Alayna had grown into the family, expressing a desire to be apart of the family, wanting to marry Matthew, and become a branch on the family tree. She wanted to have another child with Matthew; in hopes that the cells in the umbilical cord could be used to help Matthew grow new brain cells when it came to stem cell research.

What Cynthia did not know was that she was signing her rights away, and it was just a matter of time, before her considerate decision with her "daughter" would come back to bite her.

Soon after Alayna had "rights" to Matthew, it seemed she was taking things Cynthia would say and do judgingly. The two were always nit-picking and snapping at each other so much that Simona couldn't take it. Matthew and Jett felt the tension in the house as well, and their behavior began to change with the mood. Matthew wouldn't smile and his face would always look concerned. Jett was acting out more by screaming when he didn't get his way, crying, throwing things, and even hitting.

Simona suggested a family meeting; they would sit around the table, and Simona would be the mediator. Most of the time, someone would take what the other said out of context, or feel it was a personal blow. Once talked out was discovered that it wasn't toward the other one at all. Simona noticed that Alayna and Cynthia were alike in a lot of ways; each believed they were right, both would see a situation the same way, but in their own perspective. They were different sides to the same coin. Simona knew that for her sanity, everyone had to get along and work out their problems as soon as possible. The meetings helped, and eventually were being used for decisions regarding Matthew and Jett. This way, the whole family could be on the same page, and agree with the development of both boys. It worked for a while . . .

Family Outing

Alayna suggested taking a family trip to Lake Michigan. Unfortunately, as much as Cynthia wanted to go, she was unable to get the time off work. Cynthia felt a little apprehensive about them going, because of all the medication Matthew was on. They were always unaware when the next seizure might strike, and the fact that they would be in a different state and not close to any hospitals was a little scary.

"Please be careful." Cynthia pleaded.

"We have to go on with our lives. We can't just stop having fun because of Matt's condition." Alayna stated.

Cynthia knew that and she wanted them to have fun, but just wanted them to keep it in the back of their minds to be aware of Matthew, and Jett for that matter. The long drive, keeping an eye out for crazy drivers, being far from home, and knowing anything can happen was all Cynthia was trying to convey; her concern . . . out of love . . . for everyone in the car - her family.

Alayna packed her, Matthew, and Jett's things while Simona packed up Alayna's car with the tent, pillows, sleeping bags, cooler, and folding lounge chairs. This was going to be a little vacation for the two girls before college classes started again, and precious time spent to relax.

Once they arrived, Alayna began to take pictures, Simona started to put up the tent with Matthew's assistance, and Jett ran around out of excitement. After everything was settled, all four loaded up in the car and drove to the lake. The waves were huge, crashing onto the sand, and a red flag was up to warn that it was unsafe to swim.

Alayna was just so excited to see the lake and asked Simona, "Is this anything what the ocean looks like?"

"With the waves as big as they are for such a small lake, yeah, you could say it looks pretty close to how an ocean would look, but the ocean is so much more breathtaking."

Alayna couldn't help herself; she had to put her feet in the water, and of course Jett was curious, too, and wanted to be right next to his mommy.

"Oh, my God, it's so warm!" Alayna yelled.

Now, Simona was one who did not like getting wet, and a bit afraid of the water, since she didn't know how to swim. She wanted to take a chance to feel the warm waves push up against her, and forced herself to stand in the lake, knee high.

Matthew walked toward the edge of the lake; Alayna met up with him, took his hand, and brought him with her into the choppy water. He laughed and laughed as he felt the weight of the water push him backwards. Matthew's laughter made Jett so happy, his daddy was having fun. Jett wanted in the middle of his parents and held their hands; he felt so secure for the first time, and Alayna and Simona noticed relief overcome his whole body. Jett let himself be a kid.

Alayna told Simona, "This was such a good idea! Jett is having the time of his life and Matthew can't stop smiling and laughing."

Simona wanted to join in the moment. She built up her nerve, and walked out further into the lake until it was up to her shoulders. The waves came and easily went over her head. Simona pushed the fear down deep inside of her and thought, "I'm fine . . . I'm going to be okay" as she focused on Jett and Matthew having such a great time.

She was not going to think about her fear of water. She was going to concentrate on playing with her brother and nephew, letting it burn into her memory. They rode the waves for well over an hour when they decided to go back to their camping site. Once they started walking toward the car, they realized they hadn't planned on getting *in* the water. Therefore, here they were fully dressed, soaking wet, and no towels. It was a spontaneous act and they accepted it as a *vacation* thing.

They each took turns in the tent getting dressed in their sweats to sleep in later. Simona built a fire and Alayna started to get dinner ready. Suddenly, Alayna received a phone call from her brother, Tom. He and his friend wanted to join them. Simona really didn't want them to come, nothing against Tom, it's just she wanted it to be only her, Matthew, Alayna, and Jett. If they came, she knew she wouldn't feel comfortable. She tried to give excuses at first that the park was packed and that it was getting late, but Alayna begged her to go ask the front desk, so Simona gave in. The park told Simona, "no," and she felt relieved, but Alayna told her brother to come anyway and see if they wouldn't let them in. Less than two hours later, Tom and his friend pulled up to their camp site.

Later on, after Tom had up his tent, everyone sat around the fire. The fire was in a two foot deep pit surrounded by thick concrete. Matthew was sitting the furthest away from the tents and near the logs of wood. Since Simona was halfway around the fire pit, she could barely see her brother in the thick of the night. As Matthew went to get up, he lost his balance and fell. Simona jumped up as fast as she could and ran to him. She couldn't tell why he fell; did he trip on the logs or was he in the midst of a seizure?

Tom made the comment, "He's alright. He's a man, he can take it."

When Simona reached her brother, he seemed to be okay, but was touching his leg and repeating the word, "Ouch."

Simona let Tom know, "It's dark and he can't see well anyway. He could have easily lost his balance by tripping on this wood and hit his head against the concrete."

The guys just laughed and Simona noticed that Alayna didn't even look concerned. Simona brought Matthew into the tent and pulled up his pant leg to look at his shin. The skin was scraped and would easily turn into a bruise. She was mad at the way no one seemed to care if Matthew was alright. Here they were, hours away from home, no doctors, and she felt it to be her responsibility to make sure Matthew didn't get hurt.

She heard Tom exclaim to his sister, "She babies him too much! She's going to turn him into a wimp."

Simona refused to feel embarrassed or ashamed by comforting her brother. She was shocked that Alayna could brush Matthew off that easy, especially after seeing her fight with doctors and nurses when *they* wouldn't make Matthew their #1 priority.

What floored her the next day was that Alayna told her, "Well, you did overreact."

Simona was hurt. She did not look forward to spending the day at the lake with Tom, but she knew if she let him get to her that she would just be ruining it for herself.

Simona didn't say much the rest of the day, and barely went near the water like the evening before. She stayed on her chair in the sand, and watched everyone else enjoy the water. That night, they folded up the tent, packed up the car, and headed home. Alayna talked of the fun they had and doing it all again, but Simona was not agreeing to anything.

Tension Builds

Chuck didn't seem the man he used to be; he didn't drink anymore, but he didn't really clean or cook either. After being in prison on and off for so long, he had a calloused outlook, he wasn't as humble, and his words were cocky, arrogant, and sometimes very cutting to those who heard them. Chuck was not a picture of health; he looked ashen, was very thin, and could hardly breathe from years of smoking. Still, although he may not have been feeling well, he hadn't learned how to interact with his disabled son.

He knew Matthew had no short-term memory, and when Matthew would come up to him to shake his hand in a gesture to say "hi," (after about the 3rd or 4th time), Chuck was getting irritated, "You already shook my hand!"

Matthew would walk away hurt, but having no short-term memory, forgot and would go up to him again. Chuck appeared to have lost all patience and couldn't handle the behavior his son had. He was even sharp when answering Matthew's questions.

Matthew asked, "Can I have some?" when he saw Chuck making lunch.

"NO! It's just for me," Chuck would say sarcastically, but Matthew didn't pick up on the sarcasm, and took it literally; his face would drop, his eyes look downward, and it was obvious Matthew was hurt and sad.

Finally, Chuck would slightly hit him in the shoulder and say, "Of course you can have some; I'm making it for you and Jett."

Then Matthew would smile and laugh. Chuck's teasing was not meant to be cruel to say the least, but when Alayna or Simona would overhear; it infuriated them. Alayna and Chuck would get into arguments, but Chuck defended himself by saying that he was just playing.

"Well, he doesn't know you're just playing!" Alayna grabbed Simona to tell Cynthia hoping she could help back her up.

"I know Chuck is just teasing, but Matthew doesn't know that!" Simona said.

"I heard him today, but if I'm not here, then what does Chuck say to him?" Alayna asked and exclaimed, "Its abuse!"

Simona stated, "Seeing Matthew's face was like watching his heart break."

Cynthia became angry, "He hasn't been there for his boys all the time they were growing up; he needs to learn to start having some compassion!" When Cynthia confronted Chuck, he would have his "usual" attitude and sulk.

The tension was progressively growing in the house.

On October 17, Simona was trying out for the police department at the college. She had passed the requirements for stretching, lifting weights, and sit-ups, but when it came to the 5-mile run, she ran into problems. Simona was not in the best athletic shape to take on such a run; she became winded just running a half-block to her grandma's house. She was confident and ready when they set the mark. Simona began to run, but it wasn't even a minute when she began to tire. Her breathing was all wrong, her heart was beating fast, and her legs were weak; Simona's vision was even becoming blurred. She pushed herself harder, but her body was not used to the stress. She managed to make it almost 4 miles when she felt extremely nauseous; then suddenly her feet gave out beneath her. She lay on the ground and felt the earth spin around her.

One of the officers approached her and asked if she was okay, while another told her, "If you get up and walk–you can still make your time."

Simona wasn't going anywhere except to the hospital. She had never been in an ambulance before and this was going to be her first ride. The paramedics gave her oxygen, but once in the emergency room, the doctors were puzzled. They asked her if she suffered with asthma or was already sick, but Simona was perfectly healthy prior the run.

Meanwhile, after receiving a call, Mandy hurriedly arrived to support her granddaughter. She sat with Simona in anticipation of finding out the cause of such a reaction.

After the hospital ran a series of tests, they found that Simona had air in her stomach and that her bronchial tubes were constricted. Since she was not breathing correctly in the crisp morning air, her bronchial tubes closed and she developed instant bronchitis. The doctor wanted to give her a shot of steroids to relax the tubes and release the constriction, but Simona refused. After *much* prodding from the doctor that it was just a *small* dose of steroids to help her breathe; Simona finally agreed to the shot. Then she was admitted.

When the family arrived to make sure she was not dying, Matthew, on the other hand, acted as though she was. His eyes showed grave concern as he sat by his sister's side. He took her hand, kissed it gently, and asked in a whisper, "Are you okay?"

"I'm fine. Don't worry; I'm going to be okay." Simona said smiling to ease her brother's mind.

"I love you . . . so much." Matthew said softly. Matthew couldn't take his eyes off Simona the whole visit. He was confused and his face showed his worry. Matthew may not have been able to say what he was feeling, but his emotions wore clearly by his expressions that night.

Simona had noticed how Jett was playing everyone. If he didn't get his way from his mom, he'd go to his grandma, if that didn't work, he'd go to his grandpa, and if that didn't work, if possible he would ask his dad to get it for him. Matthew didn't know any better; he just did what he was told. Jett was *also* trying to compete with Matthew. If Matthew got to stay up late, he should, too. If Matthew had two pieces of chicken and fries, he should, too. If Jett was told he couldn't have any candy because he didn't eat his dinner, and Matthew got a piece, Jett would cry and have a fit. Soon, it seemed that Matthew was being denied things so that Jett wouldn't get *jealous.*

Simona had seen that was unfair, since Jett was a child and Matthew was his father. Jett would have to learn that he couldn't always get his way *and* to respect his dad. Simona tried to teach her nephew this, while it was her day to watch him and Matthew, but was soon to get undermined. Mandy had made a huge, homemade spaghetti dinner and a fruit and vegetable tray. As the tray sat on the counter, Jett and Matthew would go in the kitchen and eat off it.

"Don't eat it all! Get out of the kitchen; we are waiting on the rest of the family." Simona told both of them.

Matthew sat by Simona and she noticed how Jett kept going back into the kitchen.

She got up and scolded him, "What did I say? If you keep eating this, there won't be enough for everyone else! Listen to me and get out of this kitchen!"

Soon, Alayna came in the back door from school; Matthew and Jett went back into the kitchen to meet her. Matthew leaned in to kiss her, and Jett went to follow her into the bedroom. When Matthew went to follow them, he saw the tray on the counter and took something off the tray. Just as Matthew put a piece of food in his mouth, Jett turned around and saw him.

Jett screamed for his mom and said, "Daddy keeps eating off the plate!"

Alayna came back in the kitchen and yelled at Matthew; his eyes lowered. Just when Alayna walked out of the room, Jett threw his hand up and grabbed something off the tray and ate it.

Simona glared at him, "You know what you *just* did was wrong! You *know* to wait, your daddy doesn't remember."

Jett grinned, and stuck his tongue out at her.

"I don't need this" and she growled, "I hate how he plays everyone."

Jett ran to his mom and told her that Simona said, "I hate you."

Simona went outside to sit on the front porch and was talking on her cell phone venting to a friend. Alayna opened the door and told her, "We need to talk . . . right now!"

Simona hung up from her call and Alayna yelled, "How dare you tell Jett you hate him; that is not how you talk to little kids!"

"*What?* I never said *that!*" and Simona thought, "Here we go again."

Alayna went off on Simona. Simona knew there was nothing she could say; Alayna was going to believe what she wanted. After hearing Alayna tell her what a terrible aunt she was, and how she doesn't have any kids to know how to raise one; she had her fill.

"He keeps everyone up in arms around here, playing everybody, and he gets away with things and he *knows* it!" Simona screamed as she got up and drove off in her vehicle.

Soon, the family was arriving and it was time for dinner; Simona was still gone.

When she came home, her grandma approached her to eat something. "Let it go. Just say you're sorry and forget about it."

"This is just another instance on top of the last . . . too much has been building to just forget it. I have nothing to apologize for . . . she comes home and Jett knows that he can say whatever he wants, and she'll yell at *me* instead of him." Simona just wanted Jett to respect his dad. She knew she didn't have any children and was sick and tired of hearing that line. It was like Alayna was throwing it in her face that she had a child by trying to make Simona feel less of a woman because she had never experienced pregnancy or birth.

Simona knew that everyone felt sorry for Jett because of what happened to Matthew. She knew how his mom was balancing school *and* taking care of his dad. Simona felt sorry for Jett too, but he was getting away with too much. It didn't matter what anyone said, Jett would constantly contradict them. Everyone needed to be on the same page when it came to disciplining him. It had to be dealt with or he was going to just get worse the older he became. Regardless, Jett was still a child in the learning stages, and it didn't matter what circumstances surrounded him, he needed to know boundaries - he had none.

Simona was just trying to do what she felt would help him in the long run; instead she was being put down and ridiculed. She may not have had children, but she helped raise Tony and Matthew and both her brothers knew respect. They stumbled through their growing up stages of learning from their mistakes, but neither one ever put down their sister, nor ever complained, or expressed detest on how she treated them. Plus she had never heard them, *ever,* talking back to an adult and she knew their respect exceeded the limits of just their family.

After dinner, the whole situation still upset Simona and she felt condemned by her beliefs. She apologized to Tony for being too strict when he was growing up. She asked him to forgive her on any mistakes she made "raising" him and Matthew.

Tony looked at her and said, "You kept us in line. You don't need to say you're sorry. Matt and I feel you did a great job. Besides, Jett needs to learn to respect Matt. Matthew is still his dad! I love Jett, but he's spoiled and gets anything he wants. Don't worry about it."

Later on that night, Cynthia called Simona up to have a family meeting. When Simona sat down, Cynthia and Alayna *both* criticized her on how she handled Jett.

Simona looked at them and asked, "This isn't fair . . . you're *both* ganging up on me! Who's the mediator? This is not a *just* meeting . . . I'm out of here!" She ran back down the basement feeling totally alone.

Alayna came in to contact with Todd and told him how Matthew had been asking for him. Todd agreed to come by and visit. As soon as Matthew laid eyes on his friend his whole face lit up. At first Todd was distant, unsure how to interact with Matthew, but put on a smile to make him feel at ease. Todd's presence meant everything to Matthew.

A Love Loss

Alayna told Cynthia that she was going to study with a classmate she met in college, Erica. Every week Alayna would go to her house or she would come over to Cynthia's. It wasn't long until Alayna's new friend, Erica, asked her to go out to the bars for a couple of hours. Alayna claimed she had no interest in bars or drinking, it just wasn't her thing. Yet Alayna seemed to spark an interest in going out. She sat down and talked with Cynthia about it and Cynthia tried to show her some support.

"Going to the bars doesn't necessarily mean you have to drink. I know you've been dealing with a lot with taking care of Matthew and Jett . . . and going to college. I know you need to go out sometimes and let off some steam. Get away for awhile. Relax."

"Are you sure? I feel so bad having Matthew fall asleep without me."

"One night shouldn't make you feel bad."

So, Alayna went out. She left at around 9:30 P.M. after Matthew and Jett went to bed. Soon, she began going out more often and it was becoming a habit. She seemed to leave freely, without guilt, and going out more than just one time a week. Pretty soon, she was going out earlier and earlier, even when Jett was still up. After Thanksgiving, it was to a point where she was going out before dinner.

One night, Jett was getting defiant, and refused to go to bed until his mom was home to tuck him in. Cynthia tried to read him a bed-time story, but he kept asking for his mom.

Simona walked in the bedroom and told him, "Go to sleep, Jett. Quit giving grandma a hard time!"

"I want my mommy!" as Jett screamed and cried.

Cynthia tried to calm him down, "Why don't we call your mom and you can tell her goodnight, okay?"

"Yeah," Jett agreed excitedly.

"Then will you go to sleep?" Simona asked.

"Yes."

Cynthia tried several times, but Alayna never picked up her phone. "She probably can't hear it," Cynthia said, recalling how loud bars could be.

Simona went to Jett's side, "Look, your mommy is out with a friend. Grandma and I are trying to get you and your daddy in bed and it's already going on midnight. So if you go to bed, when you wake up she'll be home; then you tell her how you feel."

"I want her here . . . NOW!"

"I know you do, she's your mommy, but we're here, too. You're not alone." Still, Jett was screaming and vying for attention.

Simona told her mom, "We've done everything we could; maybe we should just ignore him."

Cynthia agreed, and after 20 minutes of Jett carrying on, he finally fell asleep.

After dealing with Jett having a temper-tantrum, Cynthia knew it was time to confront Alayna about leaving the boys so early in the evening. "I don't care if you go out, but you have a responsibility to be here for your son."

"Oh, sure, one minute you tell me 'go out . . . have fun' now you're putting me on a guilt trip that I'm ignoring my kid?" Alayna asked sarcastically.

"You don't understand Alayna; you're leaving in the evening and not getting back until early in the morning. Jett misses you. He cries for you."

Alayna felt everyone was ganging up on her. Not only was Cynthia concerned, but even Alayna's own mother, Linda, had recently cautioned her on going out as much and as often.

"So! Now I have a curfew?" Alayna asked defensively.

"No, but you are guardian to Matthew's person! What if he has to be taken to the hospital and you're out, and I can't get a hold of you like last night? I tried calling and you didn't answer. This is why I felt when we went to see the lawyer that *both* of us would be able to be guardian for Matthew, just in case one was not available. Now, here we are–do we have to go back to the lawyer and reverse this?"

"Fine, then I'll stop going out!"

Cynthia rolled her eyes and Alayna saw her, "What? How come I go out and everyone acts like I'm doing something wrong? I don't need your attitude and I don't need to live here anymore. I go to school, take care of Matthew and Jett, clean the house, cook dinner, and when I go out once in a while, I get 'attitude'! It's too crowded and I feel like I'm going to go nuts if I stay here any longer. I go out to help me deal!"

"I understand that Alayna, and no one is telling you that you can't go out. I'm just saying to go out later, after Jett goes to bed, like you did before, and to call or check your phone in case anything happens here that you need to know about."

It was getting tense in the house and everyone was feeling like the walls were suffocating them. Simona was upset how much Alayna had changed. Additionally, she still harbored the agitated feelings from being ridiculed on Jett's behavior. Unaware of how

Simona felt toward her, Alayna tried to convince her that by going out she wasn't doing anything wrong; how going out helped take her mind off the anger she carries from what happened to Matthew.

Simona had to express her feelings, "What about me? Where do I go to take my mind off what happened? I hate the bars, I don't drink. I'm not working, so I have no money to go out or to a movie. My friends are married or busy. I don't have anyone in my life to take *me* out or someone to hold me when I want to cry with what *I'm* going through. You said you hated to go out, hated bars, but you go. I know you need to get away, but *I* don't have an outlet. I enjoy the time we all spend together and get my strength off that."

"Well, I need to get out of here and get a place for just me, Matt, and Jett."

Simona knew it didn't matter what she said, Alayna was thinking only about herself. She started to walk away when Alayna said, "Your mom better understand that Matt is *mine* and is going with *me*."

"Where?" Simona asked. "You don't have a job. How are you going to get a place?"

"I get paid to take care of Matthew, plus money from the state for Jett; I can afford a house."

Simona knew that Alayna was dreaming, after all, who would approve her for a home loan when she didn't have a job? (Although, her "job," was taking care of Matthew, Simona didn't consider that a "stable" job).

"Matthew is still recovering. He needs *all* of us." Simona said.

"Well *I* don't need THIS! I will get a house for us–*I* AWAYS GET MY WAY!"

Simona was getting mad, "Matthew needs to be here with us; mom, me . . ."

"Your mom signed him away! What kind of mother does that?"

"What? She didn't sign him away!"

"I am guardian over Matthew; she is guardian over his money. I know how money-hungry she is so I let her *have* his money."

"She's not money-hungry!"

"Yeah, right, you always hear her how she cries about us not giving her enough money."

"Yeah, she's taking care of five people here who aren't working!"

"Anyway, I would *never* give my child away!" Alayna screamed.

Simona was fuming and couldn't believe the words coming out of Alayna's mouth. If she could say these words to *her*, Simona wondered what she was saying to others about her family. Simona walked away and hit the walls on her way down the basement.

Alayna screamed down, "Real cute, Simona. You know you have an anger problem, and I don't think my son needs to be exposed to your rages!"

Simona held her tongue from screaming back and said under her breath, "Better the walls and not you."

Cynthia and Simona were dumbstruck; Alayna had turned into someone else. Sure the living situation was getting unbearable, but all this hate hanging in the air was villainous and unhealthy.

Chapter 16

"A soft answer turneth away wrath: but grievous words stir up anger."
(Proverbs 15:1)

Division

By the beginning of December, it was obvious to the family why Alayna was acting out the way she had - it was out of guilt. She had been meeting Todd, her ex-boyfriend and Matthew's best friend, at the bars. She would talk about Todd nonchalantly, as if nothing was going on, but Simona had caught on to her little act, and was unsettled about how she was treating Matthew. Alayna was the one who would always ask the question, "What would Matthew do?"

She wanted to keep Matthew "alive" in every way possible. Believing she knew him well enough to know what he would like or disapprove of, she knew (and everyone else did too) that by sneaking off with Todd would make Matthew mad.

Todd was now separated from his wife and never really got over Alayna. He was grasping the opportunity to get the girl he wanted, but instead of trying to win her, he began defacing his best friend. He began filling Alayna's mind with all the things Matthew *used* to do; leaving Matthew unable to defend himself. Alayna heard, (and allowed herself to hear), how Matthew would go with this girl, and that girl, and she began to build up resentment. She didn't seem to remember how much she and Matthew were on and off all the time. Todd didn't give her specific days, yet Alayna began to turn on Matthew, treating him differently, and losing patience. The family noticed she was changing.

One night at dinner, Matthew used his hands to pick up his food. He was hungry, and it was hard for him to struggle with the fork, so he would get frustrated and use his fingers. Alayna snapped at him and smacked his hands. Alayna's behavior had got the best of everyone lately, and Cynthia confronted her on it.

"I'm trying to teach him not to use his hands!" Alayna said, defending herself.

"I understand that, Alayna, but lately you've been losing patience with him."

"It's been long enough, and he needs to learn . . ."

"I know, but you keep snapping at him . . ." As the two bickered back and forth, finally the truth came out.

Alayna let a little statement about Matthew's womanizing surface, "All that I do for him! Why? He never gave me any respect. It was just one girl after another. He used me."

"*What?*" Cynthia asked, "Where is *this* coming from?"

"Todd told me how much Matthew cheated on me all the time."

"And you believe him? You're mad at Matthew . . . *now?* You want to turn your back on Matthew after something Todd said when Matthew can't even defend himself? Grow up! That is history."

Alayna became angrier and stormed into her room, got changed, and went out.

Cynthia and Simona talked about what had happened. Cynthia expressed her concern, "I don't want her to mistreat Matthew because of something he did years ago."

"What I don't understand is they were broke up when he got hurt . . . she pushed herself back into his life, and now she is mad at him for dating other girls? She sounds like she is just making excuses to be with Todd." Simona said.

"I understand Alayna is a woman with desires and she needs a man in her life; if she wants to be with Todd, I have to support her."

"She's just a hypocrite! 'Oh, Matthew would want it this way . . . Matthew wouldn't want to go there' . . . now she apparently doesn't care anymore what Matthew thinks or *would* think."

A week later, Alayna didn't care what anyone said about her hanging out with Todd; she kept insisting they were "Just friends" and that Erica was always with them.

That night, after everyone was in bed, Simona was still up. She couldn't sleep and noticed how Alayna wasn't home yet. It was going on 2:30 A.M. and she had a sick feeling that Alayna was *with* Todd. She knew that she shouldn't care, but she also knew how hurt Matthew would be. After all the things Alayna had done for Matthew, wanting to marry him despite his disability, and having such faith and love that he would overcome this obstacle. Wow, now to turn her back on him so fast from hearing a few "stories" from Todd–she didn't know who to despise more. Simona's respect for Alayna was dissolving. The two girls had become so close over the past year and a half or so Simona thought. If Alayna was longing to be with a "whole" man, and/or beginning to tire of the responsibility, Simona would have understood if only Alayna had come to her and expresses those feelings. Instead, Alayna denied any feelings for Todd or confess she may have taken on too much with the guardianship. Yet, Alayna's behavior was stiff and cold, and the only feelings she expressed were anger and hostility toward everyone, including her *own* family. Simona interpreted it as guilt.

Alayna walked in at 6:30 A.M. and Simona approached her, "Where have you been?"

"I went to watch a movie at Todd's and fell asleep."

Simona felt Alayna was lying and bottled up her emotions from going off on her throughout the day. Later on, it was obvious that something was eating at Alayna, because she was very agitated. She was complaining under her breath, stirring about the house, and snapping at everyone. Earlier, Alayna's mom, Linda, had told

Alayna that it was wrong of her to be with Todd and that it was betraying Matthew. Linda loved Matthew and had even noticed a change in her daughter, even in how she was treating him. Alayna, feeling no one was on her side, was about to erupt.

After dinner, Cynthia tried to ask her what was wrong. Alayna just kept saying how much she needed out of this house and wanting to get a place for just her, Matthew, and Jett. Cynthia didn't know where all this anger was coming from. The more Cynthia tried to console Alayna, the more Alayna became enraged.

"I've *got* to get out of here! I'm going crazy!" Alayna screamed.

"Then go . . . I don't want you feeling you *have* to stay here."

"I'm not leaving without Matthew!"

Simona was livid, and she brought herself into the argument, "Why do you want Matthew?"

The thing Simona couldn't fathom was why did she want Matthew when she wanted Todd? Then it dawned on her, Alayna was getting paid good money by the state to care for Matthew, being guardian over him was filling her pocket with over $2,000 a month. That amount also included the money from the state for Jett, since his dad could no longer work and support him. Since Alayna was not working, that would be the only way she could afford to move out.

Simona followed Alayna into the bedroom and asked her, "Why are you so mad? What you pay in rent here cannot compare to out there with utilities and food."

"I have to get out of here!"

Simona had to ask the question she asked earlier, "Why did you come home at 6:30 in the morning?"

"I told you I fell asleep at Todd's house watching T.V."

"I know that's a lie. When you're watching movies here, and there are like ten minutes left, if you're tired you'll get up, say goodnight, and go to bed."

"That's different, I'm near my bed."

"Yeah, then if you're that tired, get up, get in your car, and come home."

"I know what you're thinking, and Todd and I are just friends. He reminds me of Matthew, the way he laughs, his sense of humor, and just the little things he does reminds me of how Matthew used to be."

"Then if you want to be with Todd, why take Matthew? Why hurt my mom like that?"

"She doesn't want him . . . she signed him away . . . to me!"

"You tricked her–she didn't know that she was signing her rights away. She thought she was signing so you could take him to the hospital, and sign for his treatments without you coming home griping about how hard of a time they give you."

"*Still,* he's mine now, and wherever I go, he goes!"

"What if someone did that to you . . . took Jett away from you?"

"That would never happen because I wouldn't *let* it happen."

Simona knew there was no use arguing with her. Alayna was dead-set in her own thinking. The family thought Alayna obviously never really cared about them, knowing they were hurting by her actions; she just cared about herself and getting her own way. Cynthia hated the fighting; she couldn't sleep and would cry throughout the night.

She asked Simona, "How come we cannot have any peace in this house? First I had to deal with the signs in my yard, then with Matthew getting hurt, and just when I think things can't get worse, she threatens to take my son away from me."

Simona didn't have the answers; her mom didn't deserve this. Meanwhile, Alayna was torn–she loved Matthew and wanted him to be a part of Jett's life; Todd was a rock for her to lean on. She just didn't know how to handle her emotions nor explain them properly to Matthew's family. She just blew up.

Christmas Eve came and everyone met at Julie's to open gifts. It was tense, but everyone tried to treat Alayna like they always did and welcome her with open arms. She didn't know the family knew of her outings, but in their hearts they worried about Matthew and her plans - if she should be with Todd. New Year's Eve, Chuck and Cynthia went to night-watch service; Alayna, Matthew, and Jett went to her family's house, and Simona stayed home in her room.

Come New Year's morning, Chuck made pancakes for everyone to let them know he could be leaving for awhile. He heard that his parole officer never signed the release papers for him to leave the state and knew there may be a warrant out for his arrest. Chuck had planned to turn himself in on Monday the 5th, but the police saw him walking to the store on Friday and picked him up. Before Cynthia had a chance to give him a change of clothes and his Bible, Chuck was already on his way back to California.

No sooner than Chuck was gone, Alayna asked Cynthia for a favor, "Todd's mom has been really giving him a hard time, she's such an alcoholic and she takes all his money . . . could he stay here for awhile?"

Cynthia couldn't believe Alayna was asking such a request. Cynthia loved Todd; he was like her own kid. She practically raised him. He was always over, growing up with Matthew, and her love for Todd was very deep. Yet, the feelings were quite mixed, but she knew if she said "no" that she would have to deal with the wrath of Alayna. Alayna was hardly home enough as it was and Jett needed his mother to be home. Cynthia tried to justify that Alayna was young and still finding her way, and if Todd was here, then maybe things would calm down around the house. Cynthia even granted Alayna's request to let Todd use Matthew's truck for work. Simona was sick about it, and couldn't believe how Alayna could just bat her eyes and get her way. Todd stayed with them just over a week when Alayna announced that Todd was moving in with a friend.

A couple of days later, Alayna came skipping downstairs; unaware how much Simona had been fuming for the last few months over her obvious relationship with Todd. Alayna excitedly announced that she had *found* a house.

Simona wanting to scream, "WHAT?!" replied calmly, "I hope you're not trying to get it to have Todd move in."

Alayna jumped up as if she was just jolted with a bolt of lightning, "How DARE you say that! I thought you were on MY side!"

"You are the one that kept saying how much you want a place for you, Matthew, and Jett, so that you can be a family . . . I'm just saying, I hope you're not getting it for Todd to have a place to live."

"He's living with a friend!" Alayna screamed, desperately trying to convince Simona that she wasn't lying.

Alayna stormed up the stairs and yelled, "Come on Matthew!" Matthew looked at his sister and shrugged his shoulders. Simona smiled at him and opened her arms.

He hugged her and she told him, "I love you, Matt. She's just mad right now, everything will be alright."

Matthew smiled and laughed, "I hope so."

Simona knew she hit the nail on the head–full force! That was the beginning of the end of their friendship.

Betrayal

It was around the second week of January that Alayna came home and broke the news that she had *bought* the house. This was extremely shocking to Simona who couldn't understand who would possibly give her a loan for a home; she didn't have a steady job, and was already paying on a loan for her car - which Cynthia co-signed for her.

"What did she do . . . sell her soul to the devil? I can't believe they approved a loan when she's asking for money from her dad every week. She can barely pay what she owes now! When she says she always gets her way . . . I guess she must have some close connections to the man upstairs—or downstairs," Simona said.

Alayna accused Simona of being jealous, but jealousy wasn't the case at this point; it was the concern of Matthew's well-being. Simona knew that she was taking Matthew away now and there was nothing anyone could do about it.

Cynthia did everything she could to help Alayna get on her feet. She gave her utensils and other household things that she would need; they even went through and divided the food. Cynthia knew Alayna wanted her own place, she knew how strong independence is to a young girl, and that Alayna wanted to raise Jett without him having so many bosses in the house. Alayna tried to ease the move for Cynthia. She told her that she would still need help with Matthew and Jett when she had classes, and that they would still be able to spend the night. Alayna even tried to make Cynthia feel that there would be less stress of responsibility on her shoulders, and relieve the tension that has accumulated between them. Alayna made the statement that by her leaving the two may become closer. Cynthia loved Alayna and trusted her to juggle: caring for Matthew, Jett, her studies, her new home, and manage her own money.

Cynthia had put a lot of faith in Alayna, hung on her words, and believed that everything would be great. "She wants to experience her own family, and how it feels to be with the two men in her life," Cynthia said quoting Alayna's words to her.

Simona thought it would be wonderful if in fact that were true, but she disagreed about the two men in Alayna's life to be Matthew and Jett, but that Todd was an addition, if not, a replacement in that equation.

Alayna was still so angry at Simona for saying that she hoped she wasn't getting a place for Todd to move in, that she told Cynthia that Simona was not welcome at her house. Simona didn't care; she didn't want to be there, "Good . . . free of her at last! No more tension and little digs that I have to put up with. It just makes me wonder if Todd isn't a co-signer on that house . . . I just can't see how she was able to get a house approved of so quick."

Cynthia and Simona were now alone in the house and it was quiet, peaceful, and stress-free. Simona concentrated on her studies and Cynthia enjoyed being able to relax and watch a television show straight through without any interruption. The two would even go down to Mandy's for dinner; she enjoyed the company.

The Fight

January 27, 2004, Matthew had to go back to Chicago Medical for surgery to remove the kidney stones; the surgeon would have to cut a hole in his back to take them out.

On the way up, Cynthia took a wrong turn and had to turn around. She couldn't believe, as many times as she had driven up to the hospital that she still had a problem getting that turn right. It was worse on the way back home.

Cynthia got on the wrong road and as they were driving, Simona mentioned, "I didn't know we had a Hilton here," she didn't recognize anything and asked, "Are you sure we're going the right way?"

The two ended up over an hour out of their way and had to backtrack. Cynthia was so upset with herself, but Simona told her, "Hey, it's my fault, too, I remember what road you turned on, and I thought it was the right way."

Cynthia had problems seeing at night, shadows played with her sight, and she was now so stressed that she couldn't drive. So Simona drove the rest of the way home.

The next day, Cynthia almost made the same mistake again on the way up and told Simona, "You are driving home tonight."

When they arrived in Matthew's room, Alayna was sitting on the edge of Matthew's bed. Alayna asked, "Do you mind staying here awhile, while I run home to get a shower and see Jett? I've been up here all night and I miss him."

Simona rolled her eyes and thought, "Jett . . . right . . ."

Cynthia said it was not a problem, but she asked Alayna, "Please try to be here before it gets dark. We got lost on the way home last night. I have such a hard time driving at night that I don't want to go through that again." Just then Simona walked out of the room.

"Oh, I'm only going to be gone a couple of hours." Alayna assured Cynthia.

"Oh, good, plus Simona has school tonight."

"I don't care about Simona! I missed two days of school already, she can miss one!"

Cynthia was taken aback by the way Alayna snapped. Alayna kissed Matthew goodbye and left at 11:30 A.M. During their visit, Cynthia brought a book to read, Simona brought her school books to study, and between them tried to keep Matthew entertained.

When Matthew was given his lunch, Cynthia asked Simona if she wanted anything to eat. Simona declined, and Cynthia went and got a salad out of the vending machine. Not even an hour later, Cynthia started to get sick from it, "That salad must have been in there too long."

For the rest of the day, she was in and out of the restroom with a touch of food poisoning. At 3:00 P.M. Matthew's phone rang and Cynthia answered it; it was Alayna, "I'm going to be leaving shortly."

"Okay. Be careful on the way up."

When Cynthia hung up the phone, she let Simona know Alayna's plans. Then mentioned the odd way Alayna acted when she told her about Simona having class that night.

Simona's mouth fell to the floor, "You *what?* Oh, mom, you didn't throw me in there; now she's going to be late on purpose!"

"No, Alayna wouldn't do that."

"Mom, you don't know her . . ."

"You'll see . . . it's 3:00; she'll be here way before we have to leave. You have to be at school at 7:00, if we leave here at the latest 5:30, you'll make it."

"You want to bet on that?"

Five o'clock came and still no Alayna, Simona knew she wouldn't make it for school and turned on her cell phone to call her Sociology teacher to let him know she wouldn't be able to come to class.

By 6:00 P.M. Cynthia was worried because it was getting dark, "I hope she's alright, I hope she didn't get into an accident."

"Mom, please. This is against me, so that I won't make my class."

"No, she promised. She might have had an accident because she hasn't called."

Simona shook her head over the fact her mother was so *naïve.*

Ten minutes after seven o'clock, Alayna strolled in with a grin and waltzed up to Matthew to give him a kiss. Cynthia knew by Alayna's behavior that her daughter was right. She became hurt, grabbed her coat, and told Simona, "Kiss your brother, we're leaving."

Simona hated the fact she was right; she could see the hurt on her mom's face.

"You could at least say goodbye," Alayna said sarcastically.

Cynthia turned around and scolded her, "You promised you'd be here before dark. I told you I got lost last night and I didn't want to go through that again."

"Well plans changed."

"I worried that you had got in an accident."

"Yeah, right . . . I tried to call your cell phone to tell you I was on my way up."

"You know my cell phone is off . . . this is a hospital."

"I don't owe you an explanation. Just go, goodbye!"

Cynthia was so hurt and angry how Alayna was shifting the blame on *her* that she doubled up her fist in Alayna's face and stated, "I wish I could just hit you," and proceeded to turn around and walk out the door.

Suddenly, Alayna pushed Cynthia up against the wall, and began to lunge at her when Simona pushed Alayna away from her mother. "Don't you DARE touch my mother!" Simona exclaimed.

Alayna then pushed Simona and exclaimed, "Don't *you* push *me!*"

Before anyone could bat an eye, Alayna lunged toward Simona and pushed her toward the wall. Something inside Simona snapped; everything around her was in tunnel-vision and all she saw was red. Simona, who never been in a fight with a girl, (especially one who towered over her), grabbed Alayna's hair and pulled it down to where Alayna's face was in front of hers. While Simona was trying to pull Alayna down to her level by her hair, Alayna pulled Simona's to let her know how it felt. Just then, Simona had a clear shot and began punching Alayna on the side of the head. Alayna took her fingernails and scratched Simona's face on one side and then the other. The adrenaline was pumping through Simona that she didn't feel any pain. Simona doubled up her fist to knock the wind out of Alayna by socking her in the stomach.

Suddenly, out of the corner of her eye, Simona saw Matthew sitting straight up in bed, eyes glued on the two of them, and his mouth wide open. Simona also noticed her mom holding Matthew trying to calm him down. Simona came back to reality and felt sick to see her brother see such an act. She spread out her arms to surrender. By now, Alayna had Simona by the neck, her head faced down, and against Alayna's stomach.

Simona screamed, "Okay, I give up . . . stop, you win, you win!"

Just then, Simona saw Alayna's knee come up to strike her in the face, and Simona hurriedly brought her arms back in to block the hit. Alayna held on to Simona's head despite the request to stop, until a nurse walked in and observed the view.

The nurse reprimanded the two, "This is a hospital . . . we don't condone this type of behavior here!" and walked out to call hospital security.

Indignation

Cynthia and Simona headed for the elevator to leave, and were unaware that security had been called. Simona realized she had forgotten her school work in Matthew's room and they turned back around. A security officer approached Cynthia and Simona just before they reached Matthew's room. He told the women to follow him and guided them into a conference room. Cynthia looked over at Simona and was shocked by the sight of her face; it looked as though a tiger had attacked her. Simona didn't feel any pain, although she was picking clumps of hair off her shoulders that were pulled out from the roots.

The Security Officer began investigating what took place. He asked questions and seemed pleasant, but let them know that a Cook County Police Officer was on his way.

While Simona was explaining the events that took place to the security officer, at the same time a Cook County police officer was talking to Alayna outside the room. Suddenly, the door opened and a police officer walked in and toward Simona. He began reading her the riot act, shaming her for the act that took place, threatening to arrest her, and take her to jail.

Cynthia's mouth dropped and she told him, "She was defending me."

The officer began yelling at Cynthia, "There is no excuse to why she decided to pick a fight here in the hospital."

Cynthia tried to explain that Simona didn't pick the fight, "If someone pushed your mom, wouldn't you defend her?"

The cop, fully loaded on his big ego, responded, "No, I would call the police."

Cynthia couldn't believe that a son would let his own mother get pushed around, and not do anything, voiced what she was thinking, "Yeah, right, you would just sit there and let someone push your mom."

"That's the law! Your daughter could go to jail, because she broke the law!"

Cynthia knew that Alayna came back to the hospital late on purpose; putting the family through so much stress lately, and had pushed a button in Simona in a way she had never seen, since she attacked Chuck sixteen years earlier. Therefore, she had an uneasy time sitting there hearing the way this cop was making it sound like her daughter was a criminal.

Cynthia shook her head and the cop began reprimanding her, "You are no better and should be ashamed of yourself for threatening to fight, too."

Cynthia explained to the officer, "I'm Italian; my dad always did that to me, but would never hit me. Alayna knows that I would never hit her! It was only an expression."

"She didn't know that . . . you could be arrcsted too!"

Cynthia couldn't believe the denunciation; she was already feeling sick from the salad she had eaten earlier, and going through this interrogation was making her stomach turn. She got up and the officer pointed his finger in her face and demanded, "Sit down!"

Cynthia about to throw up from nerves, blurted out, "I have to go to the bathroom!" Cynthia walked out and saw Alayna in the hallway *acting* like she was so devastated. For the first time Cynthia had seen what Simona saw, and what Matthew would tell his mother every time she would defend Alayna when the couple broke up, " . . . but mom, you don't know how she is!"

Cynthia went to the restroom, and then snuck into Matthew's room to give him a kiss. He was smiling; he had forgotten what had taken place, and she apologized to him for bringing Alayna back into his life. She was heartbroken. Cynthia put Alayna on such a pedestal when she was nursing Matthew back to health, and now it was crumbling.

Meanwhile, Simona was being grilled over an open flame. She sat there taking every hit without becoming emotional, vocal, or disrespectful. When Cynthia came back in the room, Alayna followed behind her. Now, Simona was furious because Alayna was watching her being reproached and shamed by the police. Simona sat in the chair, going through everything she learned in her law enforcement classes, and tried to find the words to cut this cop down to size. What the officer was doing was wrong; he was not investigating what happened; he was *accusing* and had already made his decision that she was guilty. Simona knew Alayna had influenced him, and soon her anger wore away to frustration. Simona told the officer she was about to graduate college in less than four months for Law Enforcement. The officer let her know that if he took her in that it would ruin her chances in that career. The officer wouldn't let Simona get another word in; instead he claimed that he could arrest her for domestic violence if Alayna wanted to press charges. The officer looked over at Alayna and asked her what she wanted to do.

Alayna could've won an Oscar; she sadly looked at the officer and told him, "I loved her like my own sister . . . I . . . I just can't press charges."

Simona became filled with mixed emotions: anger, frustration, and hate–she didn't want Alayna to make a decision over her life; she would rather be arrested than let Alayna feel like she had the power. Simona's eyes filled with tears, they ran down her face, and she felt her face become hot, and knew everyone could tell she was crying. She was so mad that she couldn't control the flushness of her face, and the tears streaming from her eyes; she was not sad or happy, these were tears of revulsion and indignation.

Before the cop told them they could go home, he gave them one last instruction, "You are not allowed back here at the hospital," he told Simona, and she totally understood why, but then he made one last jolt, he looked at Cynthia. "Since Alayna is the guardian of Matthew; she has restricted you from coming up here."

Cynthia was devastated and cried, "That is *my* son!"

"By law, you can get arrested if you attempt to visit him."

Simona felt so bad to have caused her mom to be unable to see Matthew and it took everything inside her not to go berserk. When they were released from their temporary confinement, Alayna followed Cynthia and Simona to the elevator, along with a male nurse. Alayna announced how she was going to the emergency room to get her head checked. Cynthia and Simona both looked at each other in thinking the same thing . . . she *needed* to have her head examined. They tried to find some humor to submerge the destructive way they were feeling.

In the car, since it was after 9:00 P.M. Simona got behind the wheel to drive home. Cynthia was infuriated, "Why did she get on the same elevator with us? Why didn't she wait for the next one? Why did *you* forget your schoolwork?"

Simona knew the whole night was uncalled for, but she tried to console her mom, "What if I *didn't* forget my schoolwork? I may have had a warrant out for my arrest."

Cynthia calmed down, "You're right. You did fight in a hospital, and she may have very well pushed the issue . . . if we weren't there to give her *some* conscience."

Simona wanted to cry, over the feeling of being defeated, powerless, and over the fact that Alayna came out smelling like a rose - again!

Simona began to unload, "Isn't that how it goes? I could have been arrested! Well, I guess I could have pleaded temporary insanity. After all, she's been such a vindictive demon lately, and I've tried so hard to hold it all in. I'm getting to the point where I can't keep being the strong one. I'm human and I think I'm entitled to being weak once in awhile."

Cynthia couldn't agree more, "I can't believe how she has turned on this family."

Once they were home, Simona's body was still buzzing. When she was able to finally lie down in bed, the fight kept playing over and over in her head. Suddenly, it dawned on her that Alayna used to suffer seizures, after Jett's birth, from the complications when she was pregnant. Simona was filled with guilt and concern. She began to pray right away and asked God to forgive her for the angry blows from her fist to Alayna's head. She felt so bad thinking that she might cause Alayna harm by provoking a seizure. Then she thought about the fact that Alayna could be driving Matthew and Jett in the car and suffer one. For the first time, Simona thought her actions could have caused severe consequences. She wondered about if the guys, who caused Matthew to be disabled, ever felt such remorse the way she was feeling at that moment. Inside she wanted to call Alayna to apologize and ask her for forgiveness. But by morning, something was hindering her from carrying out her intensions . . . she *wanted* forgiveness, but did not *want* to forgive. She felt hypocritical, but she could not stop the anger rumbling in the pit of her stomach; especially every time she felt the sting from the scratches on her face.

Chapter 17

Not everything that is faced can be changed, but
nothing can be changed until it is faced.
(James Baldwin)

THC

Wednesday, February 4th, was Cynthia's day off. She asked if she could see Matthew, and to her surprise Alayna accommodated and let Jett see her, also. Cynthia was so happy to see the boys that she went to the Veterans sale where Mandy volunteered her service, so that she could see them, too. After Cynthia left the sale, she brought them to her sister Julie's, where Simona was babysitting Jonathan.

She told Simona, "Let Jett play, here, with Jonathan. I'm taking Matthew with me to my appointment to see a lawyer."

Simona was very proud of her mom for fighting to get Matthew back.

The next evening around 9:00 pm., Cynthia and Simona were watching *C.S.I.* when the telephone rang. It was Alayna on the other end, informing Cynthia that Matthew was in the hospital. Simona accompanied her mom to see Matthew; after all, they weren't at Chicago Medical, so there was no restriction to keep Simona away from seeing her brother. When they arrived at Kankakee Medical Hospital, Matthew was lying on a bed and Alayna and Todd were sitting on each side of him. Alayna couldn't hide the worry on her face as she tried to explain to Cynthia why they were there. For some reason, Matthew was bleeding profusely from his penis and the bathroom in Alayna's house looked like a murder scene.

After several hours, waiting on Matthew's tests results, Alayna mentioned that she had seen Cynthia's cousin in the emergency room when they came in.

Simona whispered to her mom, "That's probably why she called you. She probably figured that if she didn't call, word would get out, and you would know Matthew was here."

Finally, the nurse came in to let the family know that Matthew would be admitted, then mentioned that he had THC in his blood. Simona knew that meant Matthew had smoked pot. In Matthew's condition, any substances like marijuana could kill new brain cells that would help Matthew with his memory and recovery. Simona's eyes darted around the room to try and see a reaction, and noticed how Todd seemed to over-dramatize the *shocked* look. When he looked at Cynthia, he was preparing himself for her reaction, but the "THC" seemed to go over Cynthia's head. As for Alayna, Simona couldn't tell if she knew or not, Alayna kept a straight face. Simona was floored by such information, and couldn't understand why no one else seemed flustered. She was suspicious by Todd's reaction that he knew *something* about it. Her head was reeling as she followed her brother being taken out of the E.R. and toward his own room.

While in Matthew's room, a male nurse came in to prepare the bed. The nurse recognized Matthew from an earlier visit and asked Alayna, "I remember you guys . . . who are you again?"

Alayna responded with, "I'm his care-giver."

Simona was floored by her answer; normally Alayna was always calling herself "his fiancée" and hearing "his care-giver" set the tone for Simona that Alayna was indeed with Todd. She couldn't believe how unobservant her mother was as her blood begun to boil.

The more little innuendos that Simona noticed between Alayna and Todd, the more she feared for Matthew's safety. The thoughts crossed her mind, "giving him a joint might wipe out

Matthew's memory if he see them two together," "what if Todd was jealous of Matthew and tried to kill him," or "maybe since Todd was now Alayna's, maybe Matthew's not being cared for properly."

When Cynthia and Simona left the hospital, Simona told her mom, "I can't believe you didn't say anything about Matthew having pot in his system!"

"WHAT? I didn't hear that!"

"Mom, what do you think THC means?"

"Who said that?"

"The nurse said that . . . didn't you hear her when she came in to give Matthew's test results? You didn't see how suspicious Todd acted when she said that?"

Cynthia shook her head in disbelief for not picking that up and confirmed, "I didn't even notice . . . I didn't notice. I'll call my lawyer in the morning! I'm so glad you went with me. Thank God you heard that . . . I can't . . . I won't have my son live in that house."

The following day, Cynthia had to work, but asked Simona to go up and keep an eye on Matthew.

The doctor came in, confronted Alayna, asking point blank, "Do you know who could have given him marijuana?"

One thing about Alayna, she couldn't handle it when someone told her or made her feel like she was in the wrong; therefore she began to panic. Simona saw the fear in her eyes and wondered just what was going through her head. Alayna acted like the sky was falling. Alayna called her mother to come up, "I need you here, *now!*" then turned to Simona and asked, "Did you give Matt pot?"

"*You're* asking *me?* Alayna you *know* I don't do drugs . . . you *know* that I would *not* do this to Matt!"

Alayna was grasping for straws, "What about Tony or Cynthia . . . your mom had him Wednesday."

"Yeah . . . I know . . . they went to see my grandma and came to see me at my Aunt's . . . you *know* Alayna that Matthew didn't get any drugs from us. Did you ask Todd?"

Becoming very defensive, Alayna screamed, "Todd would never do that to Matt!"

Then, Alayna called her dad, "I have to ask you something; I won't get mad, just tell me the truth . . . did you give Matt pot?"

Alayna's mom and dad were divorced and the two despised each other. Alayna decided to let her dad back in her life when Jett was born, so that her son would know his grandfather. Alayna's dad, like Chuck, spent a lot of time in jail. When Alayna asked her dad about the pot, he admitted that he indeed let Matthew take a few hits - which by the way, was done in Alaynas' basement. Simona didn't know that Alayna's dad confessed. She still blamed Todd. She also blamed Alayna, even if she wasn't at home when the act occurred. In her mind, if Alayna was Matthew's guardian, then she should be the one to care for him. If she wasn't able to, then Alayna should bring Matthew home to his family.

In Matthew's hospital room, Alayna was on the verge of crying, her voice was high pitched, and her body screamed trepidation. She was expressing her fear to her mother, while Simona was still sitting beside her brother. Simona feeling uneasy as though she didn't belong in the room made herself stay right by Matthew's side and observed a side of Alayna that she had never seen. When Todd arrived and came into the room, Alayna got up to go talk to him. When the two came back into the room, Todd yelled at Simona and told her, "I didn't give Matt any pot!"

"Who said you *did?*" Simona asked. Simona wasn't admitting anything; she didn't want to get thrown out of this hospital, too.

Meanwhile, Cynthia had contacted her lawyer. That day, he sent out a letter to advise Alayna about his client fighting for guardianship of her son back. Later on that night, Alayna called Cynthia and admitted that her dad gave Matthew a hit off a joint, "I wasn't home. My dad is no longer welcome at my house."

Cynthia began to back peddle in her decision to fight Alayna. She now knew the truth about how Matthew ended up with THC in his system; she was relieved that Alayna and Todd were innocent. She went to call her lawyer the next day to cancel the notice, but her lawyer informed her that it was already mailed out. Cynthia displayed concern to Simona about how Alayna might react and felt she had jumped the gun. What Cynthia forgot to tell Simona was that Alayna's dad was the one who gave Matthew the pot.

Three days later on Saturday night, Alayna called to ask Cynthia if she could stay the night with Matthew at the hospital. Cynthia worked all day and was too tired, so Simona agreed to sit with her brother throughout the night. Simona had no idea what was in store. She figured she would watch *Saturday Night Live* and fall asleep in the chair beside Matthew, but she was dead wrong. Not even ten minutes after being in her brother's room, he began to show signs of anxiety. He couldn't be still and kept trying to get out of bed. Simona tried to explain to him that he had to *stay* in bed to get better, but it was as if Matthew couldn't hear, let alone understand her. The more time that passed, the more he became aggressive. After an hour of Simona trying to calm him down, Matthew suddenly grabbed his sister's wrists and pushed her backwards. He lunged forward as the needle from his I.V. pulled beneath his skin. Simona shouted to have him stay still, so he wouldn't pull the I.V. out of his arm as she reached for the call light to summon a nurse.

When the nurse walked in the room, Simona asked her what was going on. "Why is he acting like this?"

"He's going through withdraws." The nurse stated.

Simona thought, "Withdraws? Matthew wasn't an addict– what could he possibly be withdrawing from?"

Throughout the night, it was a constant battle. Simona was getting tired—not only physically, but mentally she was drained. She tried to talk to him, have him spell words, or answer math problems–anything to take his mind off the anguish he was suffering. Matthew was like a caged lion. He was physical, but his face and eyes showed complete exhaustion. His restlessness was beyond control and Simona couldn't take it anymore. She called the nurses station for the 10th time in over 5 hours for help, but this time asked if they could restrain him.

"We don't like doing that. As a hospital, we havc a policy to let the patient have rights. . . ."

Simona didn't want her brother in restraints anymore than they had their policy, but even though it tore her up inside she couldn't handle him and with a cry in her voice pleaded, "I love my brother. I don't believe in restraints either, but I'm tired and he just ain't letting up. Please, he needs to try and sleep. This is killing me having to fight him."

It was 3:45 A.M. and the nurses saw how frustrated Simona looked; they agreed to tie their patient down in bed. Once the restraints were on, Matthew continued to pull, but was going nowhere. His face was pale, sweaty, and his lips dry. Simona tried giving him a drink, but he only took a few sips. She wiped his face and talked to him sweetly as his eyes hung heavy, but he never fell asleep. Matthew didn't stop moving or attempting escape until 6:30 A.M.

Finally, he lay on the bed and rested, but still never closing his eyes. Matthew was indeed experiencing withdraws. It wasn't from the marijuana; it was from the barbiturates (his medication) that were prescribed from the physician at Chicago Medical. Alayna had never brought up Matthew's medication, because she figured the hospital would provide them to him. Unfortunately, two different hospitals and two different doctors didn't agree when it came to the medicine that was best for their patient. Therefore, Matthew suffered and being brain-injured could not explain his pain, and expressed his fear in the only way he knew how. Simona was worn-out, but was thankful that Matthew overcame the worst part of his withdraw and was going to be alright.

Come Monday, Alayna received the letter in the mail from Cynthia's lawyer and went ballistic. Right away, she contacted a lawyer of her own. Simona was sitting with Matthew when Alayna, Todd, and Jett came up there. When Alayna came into Matthew's room - she was ready for a fight. She acted real sweet to Matthew, but was throwing out snide remarks indirectly to Simona.

She was telling Matthew in syrupy tones, "Hi Mattie. Your mom thinks she's going to take you away from me, and she has no idea who she is up against." She was spitting out comments about Cynthia, knowing that Simona was defensive of her mom, "I got myself the most expensive lawyer in town and she is the *best* . . . your mom won't have a chance at taking me down! Like I said, 'I get my way, and I always will!'"

Simona was in motion to just walk out the door when she saw them come in, but she fell into Alayna's trap. "If you *ever* loved Matthew, maybe you should keep a better eye out on your boyfriend, and keep him from giving my brother pot!"

Suddenly, Todd became defensive and started to get in Simona's face; she was waiting for him to do something, and said, "He's *my* brother!" Simona should have known better than to say anything; her mind was telling her to bolt out of the room, but her mouth couldn't stop expressing what was in her heart. She wanted, so badly, for them to see that *she* was Matthew's family. She wanted them to see through her eyes, to realize from her point of view, they were holding Matthew hostage. Simona knew her actions could provoke Alayna to have her kicked out of the hospital by allowing Alayna to upset her. There was so much animosity between the two girls; nothing Simona said could have made the situation better.

Alayna demanded Simona, "Go kiss your brother *goodbye,* because you're *never* going to scc him again!"

Simona did as she said, and then bent down to kiss Jett. Suddenly, Alayna violently grabbed him and pulled him away from her, "Don't touch my son!"

Simona looked at Jett and said, "I want you to know . . . I love you, Jett."

"No she doesn't Jett . . . don't believe her!"

As Simona went to walk out of Matthew's room, she said, "You're raising him right . . . to be just like you!"

Cynthia was a wreck; unable to see her son and grandson, she second guessed herself, "Maybe I should have just let it go. I shouldn't have got a lawyer . . . I know Alayna . . . this would've passed and things would have been great again."

"Yeah . . . and then the next time she would just pull this again. Make you cry, keep you from Matt and Jett, scream and cuss you out, and then when she gets mad at her mom, she'll come back and be nice to you again. Don't you get sick of her games?" Simona asked.

Cynthia then blamed her daughter, "You should have just left the hospital room . . . you know how she is . . . she hates you and you just gave her more ammunition."

Simona knew her mom was right, but she hated living in the shadow of Alayna. Everyone seemed to fear Alayna; no one wanted to cross her. Oh, but Simona did, and she knew she had to stay away from her or else her mother would never see her son or grandson again.

Court

February 20 was their court date. The setting was something out of a *Lifetime* movie; Matthew sat in between Alayna and Linda, while Cynthia, Simona, and Tony sat behind them. Jett kept turning around to see his grandma Cynthia.

Alayna would make him sit down, "Stop looking at them!" she scolded.

Cynthia touched Matthew's shoulder, and whispered in his ear, "I love you, honey."

Alayna blurted out, "No, she doesn't Matt, or else she wouldn't be putting us through this!"

Matthew was so confused why he couldn't talk to his mom, sister, and brother.

Alayna looked at him and asked, "Do you love me?" Matthew shook his head "yes" and she told him, "Then sit here beside me and don't look at them . . . they are hurting *me*."

Matthew looked very sad, but he did as Alayna asked and faced forward. Linda was very upset and embarrassed by how her daughter was going about all this, but she was Alayna's mother and she was going to be there to support her. (Later on, Linda told Alayna that it was wrong how she made Jett stay away from his grandma Cynthia).

Meanwhile, the judge privately conversed with both lawyers, and when they came back to their clients it was obvious that nothing was getting started that day. Out in the foyer of the courtroom, the two lawyers discussed a way to settle some kind of truce until the next court date. Cynthia was not leaving until she knew that she would be able to see her son before then.

Alayna hit below the belt with an accusation that *she* knew was untrue, "I don't want him going over there . . . someone gave him pot, because he didn't get it from me and Matthew was over there before he ended up in the hospital."

Cynthia was shocked; her mouth fell as well as her heart. Cynthia knew that Alayna knew she would never do such a thing. Now to use such a blatant lie to keep Matthew for herself; it was devastating to hear.

Cynthia looked at Simona, "Can you believe that she just lied about me while I'm standing right here? Everything I've done for her, co-sign her a car, give her things for her house, was like a mother to her for years, and she lies about me. I'm really hurt!"

Simona looked at Alayna and could feel her insides turn to stone; this was beyond hate that she felt; there wasn't a word to describe it.

Cynthia blurted out, "I thought your dad confessed giving it to him."

"Well, he didn't." She turned to her lawyer, "If Matthew goes over there, I want him supervised."

Alayna's dad had recanted his confession as soon as he heard about the court battle. He was afraid, because he had given Matthew, (who was recovering from a brain injury), an illegal substance. Furthermore, he smoked the joint in Alayna's home, which was right across the street from a grade school. He was afraid, because that alone could have sent him back to prison. Alayna, no matter how mad she was at her dad, didn't want him to go back either.

Cynthia felt sick to her stomach and just kept shaking her head in disbelief. Her lawyer tried everything he could to comfort her, but this was so appalling to him that he told her, "I have never seen such manipulation . . . and I've seen a lot!"

When they left the courthouse, Cynthia was beside herself. When she got home, she confined herself in her room. She curled up in her bed and began crying; grieving her heart out. She wanted to die.

Simona was trying to hold it together, but when she got into her room, she hit whatever she could to feel the thrash of physical pain to dull the emotional pain she was feeling. Afterwards, she threw herself on the bed and cried; she cried so hard, so long, and so deep from within. Her body felt like it was in a vortex being beaten from the inside out. Her eyes were burning so furiously that she couldn't stand to open them; her throat was raw and tight as though she had been strangled. She was weak, her feet could barely guide her to the bathroom to rinse her face, and the heaviness of the weight she carried on her shoulders and inside her chest gave thoughts of taking a life . . . if not Alayna's, then her own. Then, she thought about her mom, her grandma, and her brother, Tony. If she felt like this, she couldn't imagine what *they* possibly were going through. She looked at herself in the mirror, cupped her hands under the running water, and rubbed it into her face. She wished she could just walk away and leave the situation, but knew she had to be strong, because she had to be there for them - her family.

Alayna, in the meantime, felt the earth give way under her feet. Her anger was getting the best of her, too. Her head called "for-the-kill" mode and it was literally making her sick. Alayna knew she had to start somewhere to ease her guilt.

Soon, she was allowing Cynthia to see Matthew on her days off, Wednesday and Sunday, but had strict times when he should come home. Jett was not allowed. Alayna told Cynthia that she wasn't keeping him from her; making excuses like he was playing with his friends or spent the night at her mothers. Cynthia was hurt and missed seeing her grandson. Matthew's family felt Alayna was not only greedy, but selfish and cruel to allow them to see him on her terms. They felt she had taken her power of guardianship straight to *her* head.

Chapter 18

"Thou wilt keep him in perfect peace, whose mind is stayed on thee: because he trusteth in thee."
(Isaiah 26:3)

Back Biting

In March, although Cynthia and Alayna were still in a state of war, Cynthia never thought she could lose. She and Simona went to Sally's office, (the previous guardian ad litum). Cynthia explained to her that she was unaware of the formalities of guardianship and pleaded with Sally to help her get her son back. Cynthia conveyed she was mistaken about the papers she signed; thinking that they were the formalities for power of attorney. She also expressed her concern over Alayna being able to care for Matthew without the help from his family and how she would keep him away from them. Simona added how she feared that Alayna was only using Matthew as a pawn to get a paycheck from the state, since she was now in another relationship.

Sally seemed very sweet and understanding. She promised that she would do whatever it took to help Cynthia, but with a twinge of five words, "It may be too late," in between the encouraging words. She promised a home interview to see how Matthew reacted in both Alayna and Cynthia's presence. Cynthia left feeling relieved, but Simona focused on the negative. Simona couldn't help but wonder *what* was *too late.*

Alayna was fighting with Linda and felt she had no one to turn to. She was one to turn on her own mother, just as fast as she would turn on anyone who did not agree with her. To Cynthia's surprise, Alayna called to talk to her and revealed she was sick. Alayna was suffering physically with an ailment and Cynthia became concerned about her.

"It's probably the stress of fighting in court. I'll hold off." Cynthia promised.

Alayna was taken aback and was astonished that Cynthia could be kind enough to put their differences aside. Alayna turned to the woman who was like a mother to her and Cynthia opened her heart, just like the story of the prodigal son in the Bible. Alayna was amazed by the forgiveness she was approached with, knowing everything she had done by putting Cynthia through such an unforgivable act. Alayna told Cynthia how Matthew and Jett would ask about her and how *she* didn't want to be the bad guy by keeping them from seeing their mom and grandma. This was Alayna's way of apologizing.

Then she began telling Cynthia all the things that her lawyer and Sally were trying to talk her into. Alayna repeated the exact statements that Cynthia and Simona had told Sally in confidence and how they were encouraging her to fight for *everything* of Matthew's, including his estate. Alayna was right, she had the *best* lawyer in town, Ann, and she was a ruthless, heartless, gold digger. Although Alayna was manipulative, she couldn't stoop so low to actually take everything away from Cynthia; she would be unable to look at herself in mirror. Cynthia was shocked that Sally would go behind her back like that and tell Alayna everything they had discussed in private. She couldn't believe that there were such cruel people out there; not to mention how humiliated she looked by being a complete fool to think someone was actually on *her* side.

When Cynthia told Simona what Alayna told her; Simona tried to warn her mother about falling into a trap, "What does that tell you . . . Sally telling Alayna everything we said and why would Alayna end up telling you? I don't know, Mom, maybe you should still keep your guard up."

Cynthia could tell her daughter was worried about more trouble and knew Simona was trying to protect her. Cynthia wanted to believe Alayna was trying to make up in her own way and hated to feel that she was being set up for more disappointment. Still, she figured it wouldn't hurt her to be cautious, "You're right. I'll still keep my lawyer on retainer. If Alayna should turn on me again, I will have no problem fighting 'til the end."

She knew she had to be patient and have Alayna earn back the trust in their relationship.

Meanwhile, Alyana was telling everyone how Cynthia was too afraid to stand up to her and took Cynthia's kindness for weakness.

Plans for Easter dinner were the same as they had been every year; Mandy would cook a homemade meal and the whole family would gather together after church. While setting the dining room table two days prior to the holiday, Cynthia had mentioned Alayna coming. The whole family spoke up in disapproval.

Simona stated to her grandma, "If she is invited here to eat, you all can eat without me!"

Julie, who recalled the image of her niece's scratched face, refused to come in the house if Alayna was there. Mandy loved her family and was not going to brush off their feelings and open her home to a girl who was keeping her grandson away from her daughter.

Cynthia couldn't believe the way her family was carrying on and stated, "You're supposed to be Christians and forgive!"

Mandy firmly stated, "I can forgive, and by prayer, forget, but I'm not going to open myself to hurt again. I helped that girl, gave her money to pay for her insurance to get her license back, and taught her how to cook." She choked back and continued, "I loved her and what she did to help Matthew . . . but she hurt this family, she hurt you, and I won't have her here if it's going to upset my entire family *and* Easter dinner."

Needless to say, Alayna wasn't asked to dinner, but she did send Matthew *and* Jett.

Less Hope

Simona graduated from Kankakee Community College with an Associate in Law Enforcement on May 15, 2004. The following month, Chuck came back from California. Since Alayna, Matthew, and Jett moved out, Cynthia decided to give Matthew's room to Chuck. Simona pulled up the carpet since Matthew's catheter leaked on it, pulled up the staples in the hardwood floor, washed down the walls, and painted the room a mint green to go with the dark blue curtains, comforter, and the blue and green painting on the wall. She managed to get the whole room done in one day.

Chuck was happy to be back and loved having his own room. After a few months, Chuck had gained a little weight. He began to fill out and color appeared back in his face. He wasn't looking as sick anymore.

One day, Alayna dropped off Matthew while she went to the doctor; Jett was at Linda's house. Cynthia was happy to see Matthew, but she had to leave for work. Matthew was all smiles being home and went down to wake up his sister. After Simona got out of bed, they sat on her couch and watched television for awhile. Matthew laughed at his sister making a fool out of herself, singing and dancing with him.

Later on, Alayna came in to pick up Matthew. She was all smiles and *friendly,* like nothing ever happened. Simona felt the anger rise up like a flame and burning her insides. Yet, through the battle of wanting to reach out and strangle her, Simona smiled and returned the "friendly" banter. The oddity between them was thick, pretending to converse as though they were closer than sisters. Simona felt the mask she was wearing was transparent and thought Alayna could see right through the act, but Simona kept smiling. When Alayna left, Simona's smile disintegrated.

She let out a grunt of frustration and turned to Chuck as she filled a glass with ice, "I *hate* this . . . having to be nice to her!"

Chuck agreed and replied, "Yes, but it's for Matt and Jett."

Simona filling up the glass with water, said, "If *I* do anything, she'll punish Mom and keep them from *her* . . . I feel trapped," and she took a drink of the ice cold water to drown the flames inside her. "They shouldn't be kept from this family, based on what *I* think, feel, say, or do!"

"I'm glad I wasn't here when things went down. I'm sure I would have been the blame for the pot in Matt's system." Chuck said.

"Yeah, well, it sickens me how she just kept him from us, while she's shacking up with Todd. I mean, Matthew's *our* family. If she wants to be with Todd, fine, but don't keep your boyfriend and your lover under the same roof. I'm sure all this confuses both Matthew and Jett."

Simona placed her glass in the sink and went back down to her room. She kept hearing everyone's advice to her over the last few months, constantly repeating how this anger was going to destroy her more than it would Alayna. She was on her knees every night asking God for strength to take away this anger, but her words fell too lightly when she told the Lord, "I lay this burden at your feet."

She didn't leave her burdens behind. She kept carrying them and God couldn't truly *take* them, if she wasn't willing to freely *give* them to Him. Resentment was closing in on her. She looked back on the life she had just a couple of years ago, and time passed so quickly. Here she was still living with her mom, jobless, even with a degree, and alone. Sure, she had her family, but the main reason to be home was to be with Matthew. Now that he wasn't living under this roof, she had no reason to stay. Unfortunately, without an income, she was discouraged and lonely. She had concentrated so much on her career over the last thirteen years, on her brother the last two, and trying to find and start a new career scared her. It didn't bother her that she wasn't married, but she did miss a special someone being in her life. She now became petrified of being in a relationship, because she felt her heart had become hard and seemed to forget how to interact. She lost her self-esteem and realized she was so quick to anger; she didn't want anyone to have to deal with her being so broken.

"It is of the Lord's mercies that we are not consumed, because His compassions fail not."

(Lamentations 3:22)

The first week of July, Cynthia looked on the front page of the newspaper to find out that her fight to get Matthew was less hopeful - her lawyer had put a gun to his head and killed himself. She looked at Simona and said, "Do you get the impression that maybe we shouldn't be fighting for Matthew? Nothing seems to be going in our favor."

Simona felt like she had the wind knocked out of her, "*Unreal* . . . what else could possibly be stacked against us?"

"Well, I guess we're just going to have to let the Lord fight in our place," Cynthia said.

Simona recalled the Bible scripture in Exodus 14:14–"The Lord shall fight for you, and ye shall hold your peace." She realized that she was trying to fight something that she had no control over. She wanted justice, but it wasn't the right time; it wasn't going to happen on *her* time, because this was not *her* fight to win.

Simona misinterpreted her being home. She felt she was sent home because Matthew got hurt; to help him and be there for her family. She believed that she was sent to win Matthew back from Alayna, but she put way too much credit on her shoulders. The lessons to be learned were not just *for* Simona, but for Cynthia and Alayna as well—compromise, forgiveness, faith, and trust.

Cynthia didn't want to fight; she wanted peace, and the closeness that she and Alayna used to share. Cynthia did what she believed was right in her heart, to fight for her son just like any mother would do, but now it was weighing on her. She was never good at fighting, she hated confrontations, and it was taking a toll on her mentally, physically, and even spiritually. She wanted to call the whole thing off and let Alayna win. This was her way of putting her head in the sand and hoping all the fighting would end, but her family encouraged her to not give up. Cynthia was struggling between what her family and friends were telling her, and what Alayna was asking her to do. Cynthia spent night after night on her knees, crying herself to sleep from the confused state of mind she was in. She prayed for the Lord to guide her on what she should do.

The Letter

In August, Sally sent Cynthia a bill for her services. Cynthia was outraged, "I can't believe that she is going to send me a bill, after she betrayed me. I'm supposed to pay for services that she never provided?"

She asked Simona to help her think of something to say, to express her disappointment in her so-called services. Cynthia sent her the payment, but with this letter:

> *It has taken me a long time to express my feelings in a decent manner on your role as guardian ad litum for Matthew Gioia and remain very reluctant to pay this bill.*
>
> *I am still hurt and angered at your betrayal of my confidence at your office on March 2004 and feel you did not do your job in a fair and wise way. In fact, you did the job in a very unethical fashion.*
>
> *First, you did not do my interview with Matthew present so you could see how he feels about being with his family. Yes, he knows Alayna and loves her and therefore is happy around her; but to observe him around his family, you would see how he loves us just as much.*
>
> *Second, in the interview, we trusted that the things we said would stay confidential. Yet, later, we heard our words coming out of Alayna's mouth. She said that you told Ann that I said certain things about her; when it was my daughter who expressed her anger toward Alayna. My daughter loves her brother and therefore felt Alayna should not use Matthew as a pawn nor keep him from his own flesh and blood.*

Third, Ann told Alayna that you were going to try and get the guardian of the estate taken away from me so I wouldn't have anything when it comes to Matthew. Now, I was under the impression that when the Judge picked you, he trusted that you would be unbiased, fair, and looking out for Matthew's best interest for the future. You did not do this.

Matthew is so confused now more than ever when he comes over. He wonders why he has to leave his home after his visit. I feel I have broken my promise to him. He told me all the time how this was his house and that he never wanted to leave. I told him whenever he wanted to get married that this house would be given to him and I would move out. When he comes over, he still states how this is his house.

Since I knew you were totally against me, I withdrew my plea in fear of losing my son altogether. From the beginning, I felt as though I was taken advantage of because I never had anyone explain to me what guardianship consisted of; if I would have known that it meant that I would have no control, no say, or no hand in making choices for my son, I would never have agreed to such a decision. I trusted Alayna and I trusted in you.

I was told by others that I could have had Alayna be power of attorney. When I found out what that consisted of; I assumed that is what I was agreeing to with the guardianship.

I thank God my son did not die that night in May 2002, but having him kept from me every time Alayna doesn't agree with me or is mad at my daughter, I feel I lost him in the worst way yet. It's not as though Matthew has the freedom to come home whenever he wants.

Let me ask you this, what kind of mother would turn her child away? What kind of mother do you think I am?

I grieve every night over my son; not only about him not being able to live here, but about the fact that he has lost his freedom of choice. Do you think that a girl can make all the right decisions for him?

At least at home, we had family meetings on what was right for Matthew. My mother, daughter, sister, Matthew's dad, and I would sit and discuss what was best for Matthew. Even when Alayna lived here; we all would sit at the table and discuss Matthew's best interest. Tell me . . . who is helping Alayna make those decisions? Do you think that just because they have a son together that she knows best?

Next time I go to court, you will not be guardian ad litum. The Judge will know my reason why you are not.

Cynthia also sent a copy to the Judge and the Bar Association, but inside she had a feeling that Sally would do something to hurt her again. Her conscience bothered her and was afraid that they had put too much in the letter.

Sure enough, Sally sent the letter to Alayna and caused Alayna to get upset all over again. Cynthia tried to explain to Alayna that the letter wasn't a slam against *her*, but that it was a mark against Sally; to stop her before she destroyed another family.

"Look what she's done to us, Alayna; we're all stressed. I don't feel I should have to pay someone who was working to take my son away from me. She should have been there for Matthew's best interest."

"Yeah, and Sally said Matthew was best with *me!*" Alayna said confidently. Deep inside Alayna really was afraid of losing Matthew. She loved him and enjoyed his presence in her life. She just didn't know how to express her feelings without sounding so harsh.

Cynthia's heart dropped, "I know you take good care of Matthew, but who has the right to say that Matthew is not best with his own family?"

Both Cynthia and Alayna felt they were in the right to have Matthew live with them. The issue was Cynthia was *willing* to have Alayna still care for Matthew, still have the state pay her to take care of him, but have him home in the evenings when she was off work. Alayna wanted Matthew with her, period. If not only for the money, then to have Jett grow up knowing his dad, then Cynthia wanted that too. Except she would never keep Jett from Matthew like Alayna kept Matthew from her. At this point, Cynthia was just happy that Alayna was at least *voluntarily* letting Matthew and Jett come over; not only the original two days a week, but other little times, too. It was hard for the family to wrap their minds around the fact that Alayna genuinely wanted Matthew with her, regardless of the money she was being paid. Because it was difficult to read what was in Alayna's heart to know her intentions, this had caused such doubt and continuous strain among everyone.

The Wedding

September 17, 2004, finally Tony and Shannan set a date to tie the knot. Tony, the first grandchild to get married, was ready to take Shannan as his wife after dating and living together for seven years. They planned to get married three years earlier, but Tony had cold feet; but now his heart let him know that she was the one he wanted to spend the rest of his life with. Tony was more in love with Shannan this day than any other day before. Shannan wanted to get married in church, the church Tony grew up in, and have his pastor marry them. Before Pastor Steve would accept, he wanted to make sure they were serious about what a real marriage is; he would marry them only if the couple would counsel with him - they agreed.

While planning the wedding, Shannan was having a hard time choosing the right song that represented her and Tony, and asked Simona her advice, "I know you have such a great cd collection of different songs, and I need you to help me find the right one. Our song is not appropriate for a wedding."

Simona suggested Clay Aiken. Right away Shannan was thinking "no way," but when they popped in the cd of Clay singing a song written by Steven Curtis Chapman titled, *I Will Be Here,* Shannan's eyes filled up with tears, "That is so beautiful! Thank you, this is our song!"

This wedding day was also very special, because Matthew was able to be Tony's best man. Tony recollected the night when Matthew lay fighting for his life, just 2 1/2 years before. Remembering the fear of losing his brother, the fear he would never be able to walk or talk, and the fear that all the small things they talked about when growing up might not come to pass. Now miraculously Matthew was walking, talking, and about to be standing beside him. Tony was elated to have Matthew "witness" his vows to be a faithful man to his future wife.

As people were gathering in the church, Simona noticed that some were bewildered that Alayna was present. Those few were aware of the struggles the family had been going through with trying to get Matthew back. Simona knew that she had to let go of the anger she had been holding on to for so long. She dropped those pent up feelings toward Alayna like taking off a heavy coat; she wasn't going to ruin this day for her brother and Shannan. She carried herself along side Alayna as though they never had any problems.

Since Shannan had arrived separately from Tony, the limo driver took the groom, the groomsmen, and the ushers for a drive. This way the bride could get her pictures taken and the couple would not see each other prior to the wedding. But time was moving quickly; the wedding was about to start and everyone was seating themselves, the candles were not lit in the front of the church, and there was no sign of the limo carrying the other half of the wedding party.

Alayna grabbed a lighter and went to the front of the church to light the candles, and Simona escorted her grandma Mandy down the aisle to sit in the front pew. The delivery man forgot a bouquet for one of the bridesmaids and the unity candles. Shannan just figured it was one of those things that happen, no wedding is perfect, and decided to bathe in the happiness of becoming Tony's wife.

Finally, the limo showed up and the ushers got right to work, late, but did manage to do some of their duties. The delivery man showed up the second time, bringing the missing bouquet, but again, forgot the unity candles. Tony walked up and stood beside the pastor. The groomsmen paired up with the bridesmaids, proceeded up the aisle, and split off to stand on their party's side. Jett was the ring bearer and walked in-between two of Shannan's nieces, who were the flower girls. Shannan's oldest niece was her junior bridesmaid. Shannan tried to put the mess behind her, just before she walked down the aisle. She held tightly to her dad's arm as he escorted her, and she breathed in to absorb the day she had been waiting for.

Between vows, Shannan's friend was just about to sing *I Will Be Here,* when suddenly the photographer saw a van pull up under the carport. It was the delivery man, who came back with the unity candles. So the photographer snuck up the side of the small octagon church, hiding behind the pastor, placing the candles in their holders, and lit them. Then he snuck back along the side of the church to grab his camera. When Pastor Steve turned to make way for the couple to light the unity candles, Shannan's face lit up brighter than the flames. She was in awe that the candles were there. As Tony and Shannan took their individual candles to light the unity candle, they smiled, feeling a warm calmness inside that this was their day; the day they became one. All the children, and even Matthew, did a great job standing still for the whole wedding. Everything fell into place and they felt very blessed.

Chapter 19

"And be ye kind . . . tenderhearted, forgiving one another, even as God . . . hath forgiven you." (Ephesians 4:32)

Matthew's Best Interest

January 2005 marked a year since Matthew had been living with Alayna, Jett, and Todd. Alayna and Todd were indeed together, although they denied it up until this point. Now the main concern was if Matthew was happy. The family knew Matthew had come such a long way by the grace of God, and although he still suffered no short-term memory, Matthew was able to answer questions honestly.

Each family member didn't know that they were asking Matthew the same question, "Are you happy living with Alayna?"

Matthew would answer, "Yes."

"Do you want to live back here?"

Matthew would hesitate, " . . . uh, well, I don't know." This was his way of not hurting anyone's feelings.

"Do you want to live with Alayna or here?"

His eyes would drop and he'd have a half smile on his face, "Alayna." There was no more fight to be fought, no one was going to argue or talk him into something that his heart chose.

Simona went the extra step, "Even if she is with Todd and not you?"

Matthew's eyes lowered and he looked sad, "Todd with Alayna?"

"Yes, do you still want to live there when she is with Todd?"

His head nodded, "Yeah, I do." Todd was Matthew's best friend; a familiar person in his life. Todd was deep in Matthews' heart, because he was the *first* and *only* person in his circle of friends that Matthew asked for on his own. Matthew knew he was different now and accepted his best friend and the woman he loved as a couple.

On January 30, Simona and Alayna had a long talk. Prior to their conversation, Jett had been upset and confused, so therefore causing some concerns among the two households. Jett would overhear something that his mom would say, and when he went to Cynthia's, would ask his grandma, "Who's going to take care of me when we move away?"

Cynthia's fear had hit her between the eyes and pierced her heart - move away - would Alayna actually consider moving Matthew away from his family? It took everything that Cynthia had inside her not to call Alayna and ask, or worse, accuse her of taking her son and grandson away. Other little things that Jett would say were being kept under wraps by everyone on Matthew's side of the family.

Jett also mentioned that Todd pulled down his pants to spank him, and that he hated him, because Todd was mean. Again, no one called Alayna because they had to take the source at hand. After all, Jett was only a child. They figured he "heard" or "hated" without fully understanding the situation.

However, when it came to Alayna hearing her son say things, every time there would be a phone call. She would yell at or about what Chuck, Simona, or Cynthia said or did. For example, when Chuck was babysitting his grandson, he was trying to find Jett his favorite cartoon. While going through the guide on the TiVo, a scary movie was playing. Jett barely saw the "monster" before Chuck changed the channel. When Jett went home that night, he didn't want to go to bed. He told his mom that Grandpa made him watch this scary movie, and now he sees monsters when he closes his eyes. Well, needless to say, the phone rang and Alayna gave her usual scolding. This was getting out of hand; the more she was calling, the more Cynthia feared to have her own grandchild over.

Simona told her mom, "You're not doing anything wrong. He's just vying for attention. Look, give me the phone and I'll take care of this."

Simona wanted the anger to go away. It seemed she was the only one who was holding on to it more than anyone else in the family. She began with telling Alayna the things that Jett had been saying to them, Alayna was flabbergasted!

"What? Jett loves Todd and Todd loves Jett. . . . We're not moving . . . If we do go on vacation, we're going to leave Matthew *there,* with you guys . . ." and on and on.

Simona calmly said, "We don't call you every time we hear something come out of his mouth, as much as we wanted to, because Jett *is* only five. He's either confused or just wanting attention."

Alayna totally understood, and even apologized, realizing that she was letting Jett get her upset, "I don't know why I was listening to him . . . even some of the things he said, in my head, I was thinking they wouldn't do that, but I still got mad and called."

Simona wanted to let Alayna know that what happened between them was forgiven, so she brought up Matthew. The main thing the whole family truly worried about was Alayna going on with her life with Todd, and ignoring Matthew in certain degrees. Matthew knew Alayna *was* his girlfriend and needed that extra attention from her. Matthew didn't think about her sexually, since that part of his brain no longer carried that desire, but he did need her to show him that tenderness that he felt during those months he was in the hospital. Simona wanted to bring her point across - because Matthew was content there, the family wasn't going to stand in the way of his happiness. Simona, whose anger had controlled her for the last two years, suddenly faded toward Alayna. She felt free. God let Simona know that she was not any better when it came to her actions.

Then something happened that shook up everyone. February 8th, Matthew rang the doorbell just before 7:00 A.M. at his mom's house. When Chuck went to answer the door, he saw Matthew standing outside in the cold morning air without a coat.

He looked around, thinking that Alayna dropped him off and asked, "How did you get here?"

"I walked. I need to talk to Mom," Matthew said intently. But he had forgotten what he needed to talk to her about. He walked in the house and sat down on the couch trying to search his memory.

Chuck became concerned and wondered just what happened to spark Matthew to walk from Alayna's house, across the five lane highway, to come home so early in the morning. The thought crossed the family's mind that maybe Matthew saw Alayna and Todd sleeping together, because Matthew was clearly upset. For a split second, Chuck thought about not calling Alayna to let her know that Matthew was there; to give her a taste of how easy it is to be human. Alayna had tried to convince everyone that Cynthia couldn't take care of Matthew the way *she* could, and now she was eating those words. Oh, but Chuck's thought passed as quick as it came and he picked up the telephone.

Meanwhile, Alayna was awakened by Jett, who frantically screamed that daddy was gone. She jumped up, and along with Todd and Jett, went in different directions calling for Matthew up and down the streets. Just then her cell phone rang. She was so relieved to hear from Chuck that Matthew was safe, but it opened her eyes to how easily Matthew could have been taken away from her. He could have been hit by a car, suffered a seizure on his way over, or most of all, the possibility of the state finding out. Alayna was shook up. Whatever Matthew felt that day, he made a decision and followed through with it.

Although Matthew's actions brought up the family's interest to fight for him again, but they put it out of their minds for Jett's sake.

In March, Alayna announced that she was pregnant with Todd's baby. She knew that there would be no repercussion; Cynthia had given her word that it was okay that she and Todd were together. They both had come to an agreement - if caring for Matthew became too overwhelming with her finishing up college, caring for Jett, the newborn, and sometimes Todd's three boys, then Matthew could come home. The fight was over between Alayna and Matthew's family; God had done a healing in mending everyone's heart. There was no more judging or putting themselves on their own pedestal. Every one of them was guilty of such selfish behavior.

Alayna knew that Matthew needed the strength to be in church and Jett needed to know about Jesus. (Jett loved Sunday school; he would get up in front of the church and sing with his friends and lift his little hands up in the air to praise the Lord). Alayna envied the closeness the family had with one another and their walk with God. She was not going to deny Matthew and Jett such a wonderful experience. It hurt her to know the family knew she wasn't perfect; that the lies she tried to hide were all too clear, but it comforted her to know that she was forgiven and that they still cared for her. Alayna had been apart of this family for years and the separation between all of them was sorrowful.

The two households were at peace, because everyone gave up their "selves" and let God take over.

In May, Todd had given Alayna a promise ring (since his divorce wasn't final yet). He *promised* to be there for her, their child, Matthew, Jett, and their home. The same month, Alyana graduated with her LPN certificate.

In September, Alayna gave birth to a son. Alayna now had her little family and they *all* took care of each other.

Matthew had proven to be a great help, before and afterwards. He was afraid to hold the baby, but he knew to be careful and gentle.

School really had helped Jett become more balanced; although he still carried quite a bit on his shoulders for a little boy. Jett's teachers loved him and his peers looked up to him.

In October, Alayna was told she would no longer be getting paid to care for Matthew. She became upset, because things had been running so smoothly. While Todd was at work and Jett at school, Alayna spent her days with her baby and Matthew. It was their special time together and Matthew enjoyed feeling like the "man of the house" and helping Alayna with the newborn. Now Alayna faced having to go back to work, putting her baby in daycare, and not having that alone time with Matthew. She feared with working would take her focus off Matthew and even Jett.

Todd offered to work two jobs; that was how much Todd really cared about Matthew. He did whatever he could for Matthew; shaved him and helped him with little things he wasn't quite able to do. Most of all, Todd included Matthew by having him help with things around the house that needed fixing; this helped Matthew feel important and *normal.*

Surprisingly, Simona was more upset by Alayna having to go back to work than anyone else. She knew that Matthew was happy in his routine and now it would be rearranged. She knew Alayna knew how to entertain Matthew and keep him busy for his restlessness.

Over a month later, Alayna got a job. She would drop off Matthew to have Chuck watch him. Chuck changed for the better. He became more thoughtful and kind to Matthew, playing games with him when he came over, which helped Matthew learn to concentrate and follow directions. Even Simona learned to let the past go; she and Chuck had gotten along better. Chuck had stopped drinking; he even stopped smoking cigarettes. The Lord had been really working with him, and Chuck openly responded to God's will.

Christmas shed a new light on Matthew' *best* interest. After church Sunday, Jett went home with his grandma Cynthia. Tony and a very pregnant Shannan came there, too. (Less than two weeks later, she gave birth to their daughter, Kaitlyn).

The family wanted to let Jett open the gifts that his paternal side had given him before heading over to his maternal side for the rest of the day.

As Jett received a baseball, bat, glove, and helmet, Cynthia exclaimed, "Now you can play ball with your dad!"

"Which dad?" Jett asked seriously. The whole room gasped.

Shannan explained, "You only have *one* dad."

"Nuh-uh, Todd is my dad, too."

Simona looked at Matthew and his eyes looked sad as he shook his head back and forth. She rubbed her brother's back and said, "He loves you, Matt."

Later on, the family met at Mandy's for dinner. The incident of "which dad" came up after Cynthia dropped off Jett and Matthew at Alayna's. It was clear that Jett was comfortable with Todd being his "dad" enough to wonder which dad to play ball with. Maybe it was because Jett had a new baby brother that he felt like *they* were a family.

Matthew was no longer Jett's "father", but like a "brother" or "playmate" and even according to Alyana the two fought and argued all the time. Cynthia was beginning to re-think what was best for her son. She and the family wanted (and always have wanted) Matthew, but Cynthia was bound to the courts to have Matthew be in the same home as his son.

Now that Jett saw a "dad" in Todd, it wasn't like a dad would be taken away from him. Matthew could be home with his family and when Jett came to visit his grandma, he would be visiting his dad as well.

Simona asked, "Alyana has her own family now . . . why shouldn't we have ours?"

"What can I do, Simona? It takes money. I need a lawyer, there are court costs, and not to mention, she could get upset enough to keep my grandson away from me," Cynthia stated.

"I can't see us losing again. Back then, Todd was not a proven figure. Now that Alayna has a child by him and the fact they are fighting to get custody of Todd's boys, Matthew's best interest would be back home with us. It's not like Matthew couldn't go there to visit."

Although what the family wanted was out of reach, the family was just thankful Matthew and Jett spent the holiday with them. Yet, inside Cynthia's heart, she ached. She wanted her son back home. Every night she prayed for Matthew to *legally* come back.

As of January 20, 2006, the family's prayers had been answered. Alayna brought Matthew back and all of his things; she told Cynthia she could have complete guardianship. The family is waiting for an appointment with a lawyer to sign the papers.

Epilogue

In the obituaries was the death of Li'Mex's baby. The family didn't know what happened, but Alayna believed it to be justice. Simona couldn't understand the feelings–it was like a bitter-sweet, but more of a bitter taste–she felt awful the child died and how that family must be feeling. Cynthia just stated that maybe God was saving that child from seeing such hate and violence in the world, and maybe at home.

The family heard once Doughboy was released from jail, his enemies still haunted him. When he would come home, the windows would be broken; when he went to leave, his tires would be slashed. They also heard that he was the only one who was truly remorseful, saying he wasn't the one who repeatedly kicked Matthew in the head, but in his heart, he knew he could have stopped it.

As for the others who attacked Matthew, it seemed they never learned their lesson. Darcy was never questioned what she did to Matthew, but she did have run-ins with the law off and on afterwards.

Ronny's name was in the blotter for his arrests about every few months.

Randy spontaneously stopped by Tony and Shannan's, about a year after he was released from corrections, angrily stating, "I don't know what Gioia's [Matthew] been telling you, but I'll tell you the truth . . ."

Shannan responded with, "Matthew can't *tell* us anything, because he doesn't remember!"

It's a shame that they *still* are unaware of what they did to Matthew. They don't know, nor do they care about how extensive they have hurt him. Not one of them has come by to apologize to the family or to Matthew.

Apparently, they didn't learn anything the first time around. Doughboy and both the Bolton boys had together committed another mob action, which Doughboy pulled out a gun. All three were arrested. Unfortunately, Ronny must have made bail, because just before this book was sent out for publication, he was arrested again for home invasion. As he sat in the police car, he kicked out the back window. The family wondered when the court will finally see these boys are a menace to society; regardless of who is related to a police officer.

A Christian isn't perfect, God is always putting them through a trial to test their faith, and yes, they sometimes fail. This family struggled with anger, betrayal, depression, fear, hate, selfishness, and unfairness. With their faith and trust in God, they came through so much, and still learned to forgive and love. Although they came this far, they know that God is not done with them. Does this mean that they have to face each day wondering when another test will befall them? No, but they will have the strength to face it when it does. Joy is that ever-deepening awareness that our lives are hidden in Christ, and that we can be led by the Holy Spirit through anything. The Apostle Paul linked our physical suffering and hardships to the death of Jesus. Our sufferings remind us of the ultimate suffering: Jesus' death on the cross.

Cynthia states, "My life has been a witness to the people I work with everyday. They watch my reactions to my hardships, and their comments let me know they are in awe over the joy I have through my hardship. I never hesitate to give the glory to Jesus."

Peace sounds so simple, but to experience it in all its greatness, you have to trust in God. To have that peace in your heart, your mind, your body, and your soul; you have to trust in the Lord.

The doctors told the family that the type of head injury damaging the frontal lobe could change Matthew's personality. He could go either two ways: be mean, hateful, and even murderous, or keep his own personality. By God's grace, Matthew stayed the same (which by the way outshined by 100 fold) - he is kind, gentle, caring, and helpful. He loves to hug and kiss his family all the time.

Mandy says, "We thank God, for a truly sweet, young man. He could have been mean and violent, but God has touched him, and Matthew is a sweetheart."

Matthew beat the odds–his doctors are amazed. He was in a coma, has a 14 inch scar on the side of his head from three brain surgeries, with five titanium plates and 10 screws in his head. He bares scars from his trachea and feeding tube. He has gone through several procedures and may possibly face more in the future. Matthew's skull bone shrank, causing the muscle to detach and fall to the side of his face, has limited peripheral vision, suffers with seizures, has no short-term memory, and lost most long-term as well. He is teaching himself how to remember by focusing at the task he is asked to do and won't let anything or anyone break his concentration. He is truly a testimony of what God can do. He faithfully takes vitamins, but has been weaned off the many medications, except the one for his obsessive-compulsive disorder.

Meanwhile, Matthew acts like he used to, still has his quick-wit and gentle nature. Sometimes the "old" Matthew comes through and catches everyone off guard (which makes everyone wonder just how much he *really* remembers). The best thing is . . . Matthew doesn't feel hate, the desire to drink, smoke, or do drugs, but he loves, laughs, and helps happily with chores.

I'm so very ordinary - nothing special on my own . . .
When I call on Jesus mountains are gonna fall
'cause He'll move Heaven and Earth to come rescue me when I call.

-Nicole C. Mullen

Miles Across This Tightrope

I've been walking miles across this tightrope – teetering, but ready
To place one foot in front of the other – although my body is unsteady.
My mind is racing in anticipation as the rope grows longer
The fear of falling – they say, will only make me stronger.
God is the only one who is able to give me hope
With what I am going through across this tightrope.
As I focus to keep my balance since the pace is slow
I am miles above the earth and miles to the earth below.

—Simona

Simona holding
Matthew and
Tony in 1982

Tony and
Matthew
grabbed a
hose and some
bubbles to go
"swimming"

Family picture 1983 -
Chuck, Cynthia, Simona,
Tony, and Matthew

Tony and Matthew with their grandparents, Mandy and Sam

Tony and Matthew after a day at Great America in 1993

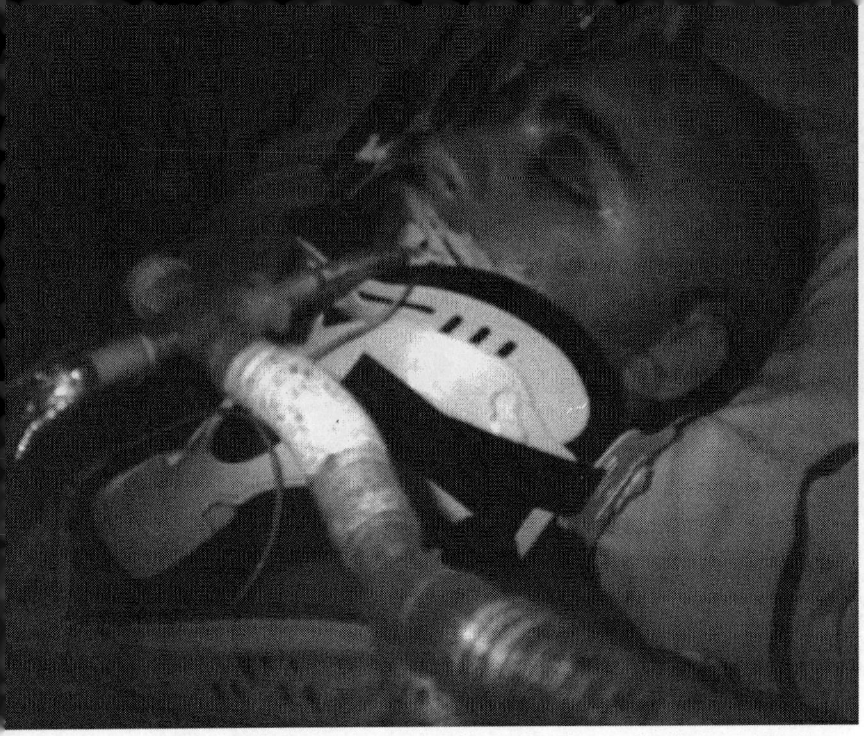

May 11, 2002
- a day after
Matthew's attack

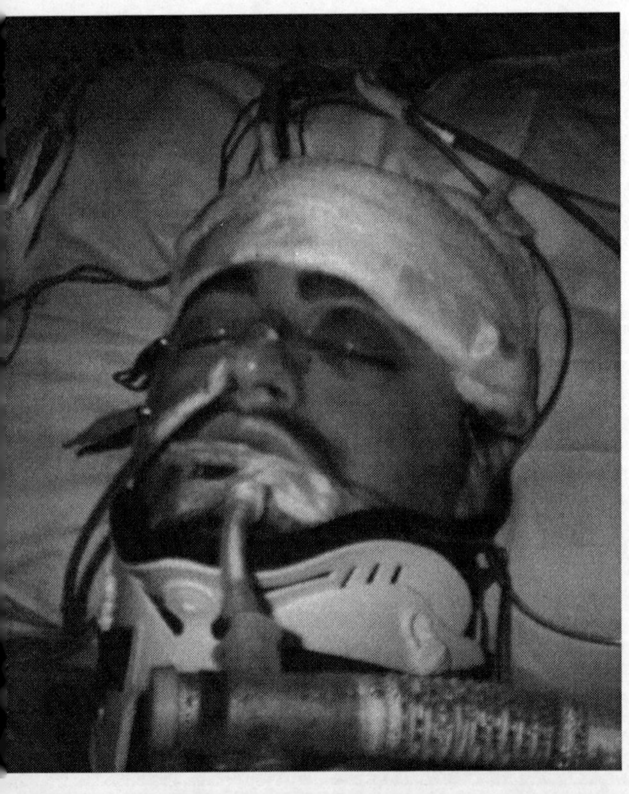

Picture of Matthew
displayed in
businesses for
his fundraiser

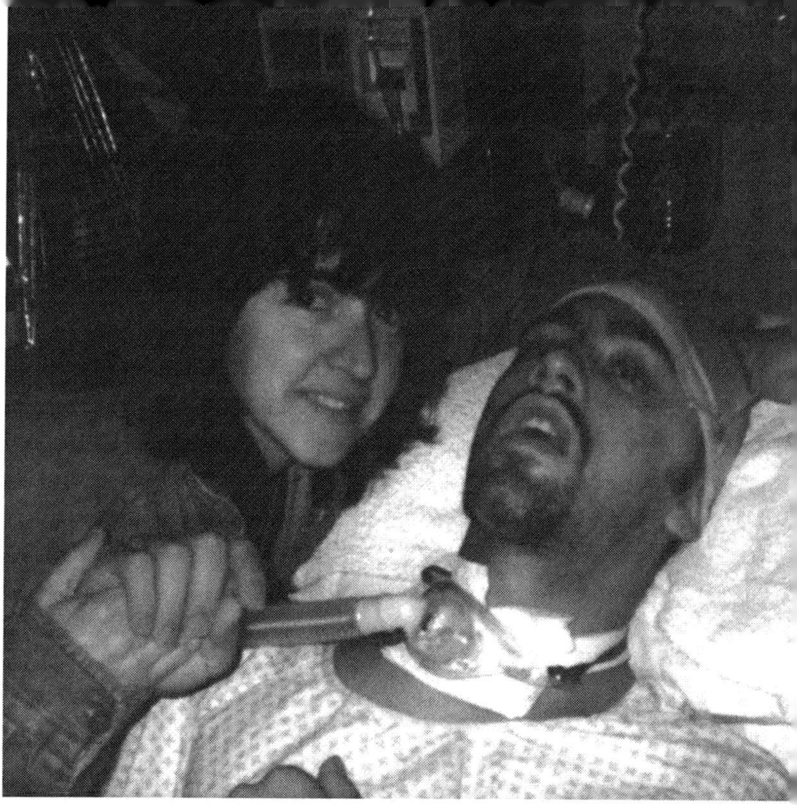

Simona holding Matthew's hand during his first day in the state hospital

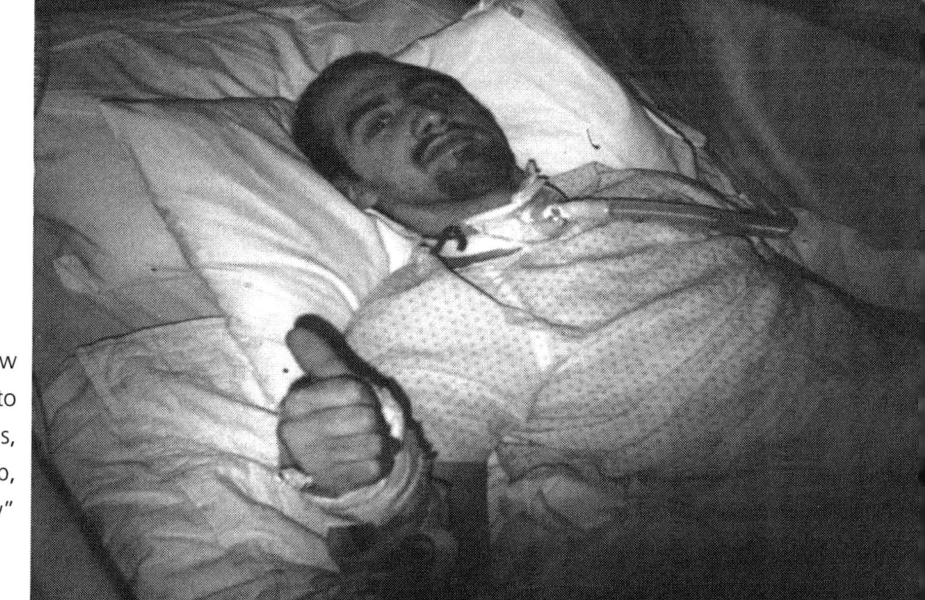

Matthew responding to commands, "Thumbs up, Matthew"

Father and son now getting closer

A recent picture of Cynthia and her children

A picture taken of the family at aunt Julie's on Easter 2004

TATE PUBLISHING, LLC 

Tate Publishing is committed to excellence in the publishing industry. Our staff of highly trained professionals—editors, graphic designers, and marketing personnel—work together to produce the very finest book products available. The company reflects in every aspect the philosophy established by the founders based on Psalms 68:11, "The Lord gave the word and great was the company of those who published it."

If you would like further information, please call
1.888.361.9473
or visit our website at
www.tatepublishing.com

Tate Publishing LLC
127 E. Trade Center Terrace
Mustang, Oklahoma 73064 USA